Network
Architectures for
Distributed Computing

Network Architectures for Distributed Computing

(Arkhitektura vychislitelnykh setei)

Eduard A. Yakubaitis

Institute of Electronics and Computer Science
(Latvian Academy of Sciences)

translated by
Martin Morell

Allerton Press Inc. / New York

Library of Congress Cataloging in Publication Data

ĪAkubaĭtis, Ēduard Aleksandrovich.
    Network architectures for distributed computing.

    Translation of: Arkhitektura vychislitel'nykh
seteĭ.
    Bibliography: p.
    Includes index.
    1. Computer networks.   2. Electronic data
processing—Distributed processing.   I. Title
TK5105.5.I1813 1983   001.64'404   83-70666
ISBN 0-89864-005-9

Printed in the United States of America

TABLE OF CONTENTS

PREFACE

The development of electronic computers and the experience gained with them in economic, scientific, and technical applications have revealed that it is both necessary and efficient to employ remote data input (over data transmission channels) and remote output of the results. This gave rise to the first computer networks, which were initially intended to perform computations.

Over the last decade, there has been vigorous development of processes associated with logical processing of information. Data bases, information retrieval services, and services for processing text and graphic matter have appeared. Control of technological processes and scientific experiments is becoming more and more developed. Electronic mail, remote conferences, and digital telephony and television are becoming part of daily life. Computer networks have become complex information systems, in which computation, although increasing in volume, has ceased to be predominant, giving way to logical information processing.

As a result, the world's major manufacturers have changed over from individual computers to production of hardware for creating a variety of computer networks. The architecture of the SNA and DECNET networks, developed by IBM and DEC, have become well known. Control Data, Hewlett-Packard, Wang, and many other companies and organizations have contributed significantly to the creation of networks.

The Soviet Union manufactures three large groups of computers for network applications. For large users, the Elbrus installations and computers of the Unified System are employed. Minicomputers form another group, called SM computers. Finally, the third group encompasses microcomputers of the Elektronika series.

Present-day computer networks are expanding the types of computers. Not only is the number of terminals rapidly increasing, but entirely new types of devices are appearing and being extensively deployed: copying equipment, speech-recognition and speech-synthesis devices, fascimile equipment, image I/O hardware, and so forth. The number of computers in different computer networks is now to be reckoned in the many tens of thousands, while the number of terminals is approaching ten million.

The appearance of local networks has provided a new impetus to the development of networks. As a result of these networks, a base has been created for efficient automation of information activity at virtually all enterprises and institutions. Accordingly, a new approach to the creation of large global computer networks now presents itself. Such networks will increasingly become systems of large numbers of diverse local networks.

The appearance of information computer networks such as Teletex and Videotex, as well as the extensive assortment of personal computers, open up possibilities for providing network information to society at large.

In many countries, computer networks are becoming a highly productive branch of the economy, in which many millions of different users participate and cooperate with one another. In this respect, present-day computer networks are rapidly becoming bridges for friendship and collaboration linking different countries, through their industry, science, and culture.

Network
Architectures for
Distributed Computing

INTRODUCTION

Electronic computers performing complex mathematical operations have become universal information processing systems. The creation of large and ultralarge memories has led to the appearance of electronic libraries that are rapidly accumulating knowledge gained over the course of many centuries.

Conversion of telephone and telegraph networks into integrated networks for transmission of data, text, graphics, and speech opens up extensive possibilities for information exchange over enormous distances.

Development of methods of interacting with computers and of making most efficient use of their capabilities has led to the appearance of more and more complex multicomputer systems for acquisition, storage, processing, transmission, and delivery of information. The creation of these associations marks a qualitative advance in the development and use of computer technology, electronic libraries, and communications techniques [1–10]. In the near future, multicomputer systems will not only have a major impact on the development of science and of various branches of the national economy, but will also play a key part in processes associated with education, human intercourse, and other social problems of modern society. This book deals with one of the most important classes of multicomputer systems, namely, computer networks. In the near future, computer networks will not only determine the further development of the data-processing industry but will also be of great social significance, furnishing extensive sectors of the population with the ability to obtain information about political events, news, the functioning of transport and domestic services, and so forth. Local computer networks will raise to a qualitatively new level the management of institutions, production combines, and industrial and agricultural enterprises. The use of network architecture will give many users access to the most diverse information and computing resources.

Unfortunately, at present there is as yet no generally accepted terminology for multicomputer associations, and therefore a dictionary of terminology is included at the end of this book. Abbreviations and symbols are also listed; there is also a subject index to aid in using the book for reference purposes.

CHAPTER 1

OPEN SYSTEMS ARCHITECTURE

A basic characteristic of a computer network is its logical description, which enables us to examine and analyze the elements of the network and to determine the functions they perform. This description also includes a consideration of the interaction functions of the elements, the result of which is the computer network.

1.1.
INTRODUCTION TO THE CONCEPT OF ARCHITECTURE

The complexity of automatic control systems is increasing rapidly. Even recently, integrated circuits contained just a few transistors. At present, complex electronic circuitry with tens or even hundreds of thousands of transistors can be created on a semiconductor chip. Many thousands of these integrated circuits interact in a large computer. Hundreds of computers may be combined into a computer network.

There is only one way to analyze and synthesize such complex installations, namely, to separate them into diverse elements and to investigate their set of interaction structures. These problems are reflected in a new line of scientific research, which has come to be known as **architecture of automatic control installations.** Depending on the object of study, it considers the architecture of computer networks, terminal systems, computers, or semiconductor chips (integrated circuits).

Architecture is an extensive concept, which includes three important types of interrelated structures: physical, logical, and software. In addition, in analyzing other aspects of architecture, structures of administrative management, service and repair, data-bank allocation, etc., are frequently considered. Each of these structures is defined by a set of elements and by the manner in which they interact. The mutual relationship of the structures forms the architecture of the installation under consideration.

Physical structure elements are technical objects. Depending on the tasks at hand, these objects may be semiconductor chips, parts of computers and computer hardware, the computers and hardware

4

themselves, or systems made up of the latter. For example, if we are considering the physical structure of a computer, its interrelated elements are generally the processor, channel, I/O devices, printers, disks, and so forth. In addition to these physical-structure elements, there may also be an operator console, display, controller, data transmission device, and so forth.

Investigation of physical structure makes it possible to determine the physical resources of the installation under consideration, to determine the necessary number of computers, hardware, or devices, and to establish what their technical characteristics should be.

Everyone who undertakes an architecture analysis first sees and comprehends the physical structure. However, the creation of any installation begins by investigating another structure, namely, the logical one.

Logical structure elements are functions that determine the basic operations of input, storage, transmission, processing, or delivery of information files. Depending on the object of study and on the depth of the analysis, logical structures may be the operating system of the computer, terminal modules, groups of communications programs, and so forth. Logical structure elements are frequently called logical modules. In addition, the elements of this structure may be more complex entities incorporating several interrelated logical modules.

Analysis of the interaction of logical structure elements makes it possible to consider the operation of the entire installation, to investigate processes associated with processing of information flows, and also to determine the logical resources of the installation.

In most cases, the installation is characterized by extremely complex multipurpose software which performs various types of information tasks. A very important characteristic of the architecture of the installation, therefore, is its software or program structure. This structure is made up of interrelated programs: data processing, access to this process, hardware fault diagnostics, data transmission, channel control, and so forth. Interaction of software-structure elements ensures that the necessary information tasks are executed.

Thus, the architecture of the installation (computer network, terminal system, computer, semiconductor chip) is a concept of the interrelationship of a large number of elements of different types. It is basically characterized by the interlinking of the physical, logical, and software structures of the installation. This interlinking is determined by the arrangement of the logical modules in computers, by the synthesis of these models from sets of interrelated programs, by implementation of the programs in semiconductor chips, controllers, data transmission hardware, and so forth. Investigation of the architecture of a complex reveals its basic characteristics and makes it possible to create an integrated circuit, computer, terminal installation, or computer network that satisfies specified requirements ensuring that the necessary information processes are efficiently executed.

1.2.
GENERAL CONCEPTS

A computer network is a distributed information and computing medium that is implemented by a large number of diverse hardware and software facilities. This medium (Fig. 1.1) can be divided vertically into a number of levels, called **layers.** The logical (N)-layer is made up of the (N)-part of the information and computing medium, which performs one of the fundamental tasks of the network (control of information channels, network control, and so forth). To implement this task, the (N)-layer is divided into logical (N)-entities (entities of the (N)-layer). Each such object is a local set of functions that are interrelated by a common purpose.

The same information and computing medium can be divided horizontally (Fig. 1.2) into local logical parts, called **open systems,** i.e., systems each of which meets the requirements and standards of open systems architecture. Systems that do not meet these requirements are called **closed.** Since we will not consider the latter systems in what follows, we will henceforth refer to open systems simply as **systems.** A computer network has a layered structure (see Fig. 1.1). Therefore, each system divides into the same number of layers (see Fig. 1.2), and all (N)-entities of the network are distributed over the (N)-layers of its systems. There can be one or more (N)-entities on each (N)-layer of the system.

The Reference Model of Open Systems Architecture [11-17] considers **interconnection functions** (Fig. 1.2) that support interaction of all application network processes via physical connection facilities. At the top, interconnection functions engage with application processes (Fig. 1.2) and incorporate the parts of them that deal with data transmission. The principal parts of application processes,

6

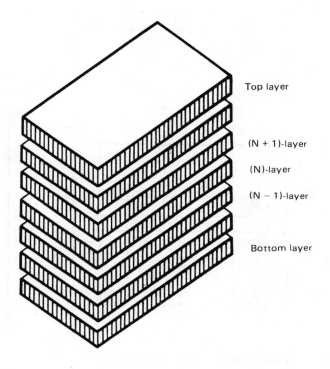

Top layer

(N + 1)-layer

(N)-layer

(N − 1)-layer

Bottom layer

Fig. 1.1. Layered computer-network structure.

which perform data processing and storage, are not considered in the reference model. At the bottom, interconnection functions interact with the **physical connection facilities** over which data is transmitted between systems. The reference model does not deal with the topology, structure of characteristics, or parameters of these connections.

Each layer of the interconnection functions consists of entities, performs a certain task in the network, and provides service for the next higher layer. The set of interaction rules for (N)-entities (Fig. 1.3) is called an **(N)-protocol.** There may be one or more (N)-protocols at the (N)-layer. As for (N)-entities, each of them may employ any number of (N)-protocols.

Connection between an (N)-layer and (N − 1)-layer is described by an interlayer standard, called an **(N − 1)-interface.** The (N)-layer

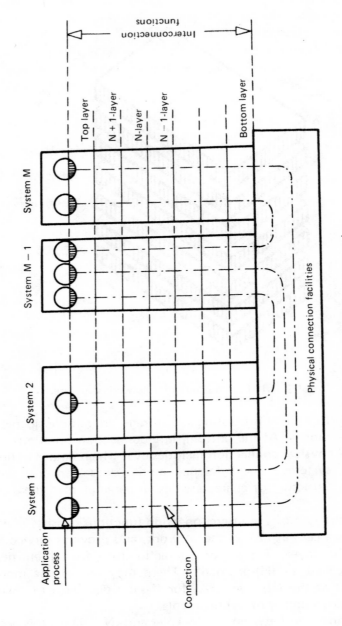

Fig. 1.2. Open systems interconnection.

8

receives **(N − 1)-service** (the service provided by the lower-lying layer) via this interface. The points (see Fig. 1.3) through which the (N)-layer interacts with the (N − 1)-layer are called **(N − 1)-service access points.**

An (N)-entity can interact simultaneously with one or more (N − 1)-service access points in one or more (N − 1)-entities. As a result, an (N)-entity is linked directly to any number of (N − 1)-entities.

Each (N − 1)-layer supports one or more forms of service furnished to (N)-entities. These forms may include the following:
- manipulation and reformatting of data files;
- management of data flows and confirmation of file delivery;
- establishment, maintenance, and termination of communication;
- choice of protocol from the available set of layer protocols;
- data-set addressing;
- opening (activation) of new objects and closing of unnecessary ones;
- routing of information;
- management of system resources, etc.

Entities at the same (N)-layer can interact with one another only via (N − 1)-entities of the lower-lying (N − 1)-layer. A line (dashed line in Fig. 1.3) connecting two (N)-entities via an (N − 1)-entity is called an **(N − 1)-connection.** Three types of connections are employed: one-way, two-way nonsimultaneous, and two-way simultaneous.

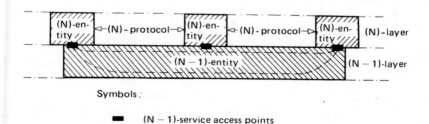

Symbols:

■   (N − 1)-service access points
- - -   (N − 1)-connection

Fig. 1.3. Interaction of (N)-entities.

The first type of connection provides for data transmission in one direction only (from one (N)-entity to another). The remaining two types allow for data transmission in both directions simultaneously or in sequence (in one direction, then in the other).

The functions performed by each layer of a computer network provide for an extensive set of tasks, including the following in particular:

— initialization of interaction of entities;
— data transmission;
— data manipulation (reformatting);
— data multiplexing;
— data switching;
— designation of boundaries between data sets;
— execution of instructions, and so forth.

Information issued by any entity is classified in terms of two types. The first of these includes **user (N)-data,** i.e., information transmitted between an (N)-entity and (N − 1)-entity **or** between (N − 1)-entities, and unrelated to operations of connection of these entities. User (N)-data may be fragmented, blocked, or coded. The second type is made up of **(N − 1)-control information,** i.e., information transmitted between (N − 1)-entities **or** between an (N)-entity and (N − 1)-entity for coordination of the connection procedures for these entities.

Both types of information are transmitted in files called data units. There are three types of such units. The first of them

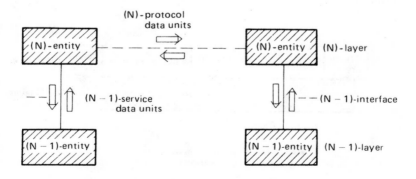

Fig. 1.4. Forms and transmission paths of data units.

10

(Fig. 1.4), or **(N)-protocol data units,** is defined by the (N)-protocol and contains (N)-control information and possibly (N + 1)-user data.

(N − 1)-**service data units** are employed to provide transmission via the (N − 1)-interface between an (N)-entity and (N − 1)-level. The (N)-protocol data unit for transmission may be packed into one or more of these units. In turn, an (N − 1)-service data unit may be placed in one or more (N − 1)-interface data units. Thus, an **(N − 1)-interface data unit** includes part **or** all of the (N)-protocol data unit or the (N − 1)-service data unit. In addition, it is possible to directly pack an (N)-protocol data unit into one or more (N − 1)-interface data units.

The relationship between data units that we have considered stems from the fact that (N)-protocol data units provide exchange of information defined by the (N)-layer protocol. However, exchange of these units is possible only via the adjacent (N − 1)-layer, as a result of the service which the latter furnishes the (N)-layer. Therefore, (N)-protocol data units are directed to the lower-lying (N − 1)-layer, and converted into (N − 1)-service data units. Exchange of information via the (N − 1)-interface between an (N)-layer and (N − 1)-layer is provided by (N − 1)-interface data units. A group consisting of one or more service data units is transmitted in the form of a self-contained element called an **interaction.**

1.3.
APPLICATION PROCESSES

An **application process** is a system element that performs information processing. In an information and computing network, this process is an information source or user. Examples of application processes are as follows:

1. **Man-machine,** in which a human operator works at a terminal console.

2. **Intramachine,** specified by programs that operate with data inside the computer.

3. **Production,** which provides data acquisition and controls a technological process.

On the other hand, in considering control in systems, the International Standards Organization distinguishes three categories of application processes [16]:

a) administrative management;
b) control of information processing;
c) information processing.

Application processes of administrative system management control resources on all levels of the system. The functions of this category of application processes include:

1. Control of **activation** and **deactivation:**
- activation, maintenance in active state, and deactivation of the hardware of a computer installation, including the data links;
- loading of programs;
- establishment, maintenance, and termination of connections;
- change of system parameters.

2. **Monitoring:**
- transmission of messages regarding the status of subsystems;
- acquisition, accumulation, and transmission of statistical data.

3. **Error control:**
- error checking and detection;
- reconfiguration and restart procedures (i.e., repeat start-up after detection of errors and faults).

Application processes of control of information processing include the following typical procedures:
- **initialization** (initial step in executing necessary actions) of the change in parameters of application processes;
- initialization, servicing, and deinitialization of application processes;
- dynamic resource allocation among application processes;
- prevention and detection of erroneous access of two users to the same resource and of appearance of **hang-ups** (stoppage of operation upon appearance of unclear faults);
- management of **data security** (preservation of data from erroneous changes or erasure);
- servicing of procedures for restoring normal operation after appearance of error and faults.

Application information-processing processes are characterized by a high degree of diversity, stemming from the diverse requirements of industry, agriculture, transport, science, and art.

1.4.
SEVEN-LAYER MODEL OF INTERCONNECTION

The problem of determining the boundaries between the layers of the interconnection functions of a computer network, and of choosing the number of layers, is fairly complicated. The basic principles for resolving the problem involve the following:
- creation of a large number of layers provides clear-cut partitioning of the overall information and computing process;
- a large number of layers makes it necessary to create excessive interfaces between them, and makes it difficult to describe the entire information and computing process;
- the boundaries between adjacent layers should be chosen in such a way as to simplify the connection between these layers and to minimize the number of interactions across the boundary;
- each of the layers should implement a group of functions that clearly executes a particular task;
- layering of the information and computing medium should be done in such a way that each of the layers is quasi-independent, so that a particular layer can be modernized and replaced without altering the remaining ones.

On the basis of an analysis conducted by the International Standards Organization, a seven-layer **Model of Open Systems Architecture** (Fig. 1.5) has been proposed [11-17]. The two lowest layers of this model define network channels, while the next two define the transport service. Together the four layers provide for information transmission between processes (or their ports). Processes are subdivided into three layers.

As we indicated, information files transmitted between adjacent layers are called interface data units. Since mutually disjoint units are transmitted between different layers, they are assigned the names of the corresponding layers (see Fig. 1.5).

1.5.
APPLICATION LAYER

The application layer is the principal one in the architecture model. All the remaining layers in this model exist only to support the operation of the application layer. The functions implemented by the computer network on this level are determined by two large groups: **user application processes** and **systems-management application processes.**

The first of these groups is most important, since it determines the basic resources of the computer network. The second group includes application processes of administrative management, which we will call **administration** for brevity. Administration deals with two basic tasks. The first of these involves optimal allocation of system resources and issuance of tasks for controlling these resources. The tasks issued by the administration to the various system levels include the following: requests for diagnostics, submission of operating reports, gathering of statistics, updating of control. Another administrative task involves providing for restarting the system. Restarting can be either complete or partial. In the latter case, the system is restarted from a specified start-up point.

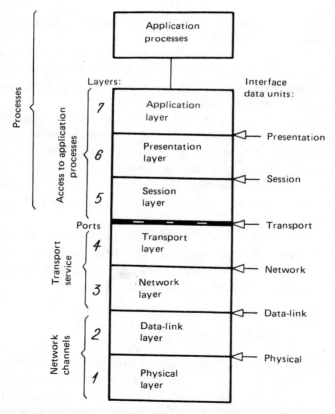

Fig. 1.5. Seven layer model of interconnection functions of computer network.

It should be pointed out that all application processes whose interaction is considered by the Open Systems Architecture are distributed (Fig. 1.2). This means that two **or** more (arbitrary) application processes may combine to handle complex multipurpose tasks. Constant **groups of application processes** may be created in this case. At the same time, when necessary, application processes may also operate independently, exchanging application data units with one another.

The application layer contains functions that ensure that each of these processes is furnished with windows, as it were, through which they can "see" other application processes that exist in the open systems. For this, procedures to access the appropriate services furnished by the presentation layer are executed. These involve the following:

— request for information on application processes that exist in open systems;
— request for connection to one **or** more application processes;
— issuance of statements regarding desired forms of presentation of information to be transmitted;
— control of interaction between application processes.

Procedures for access to the services of the presentation layer utilize two different methods. In one of them, in the **dialog** mode, application processes send out requests for service and receive answers to each of the requests. The second method involves a situation in which an answer to a request that has been sent out can appear (if there is a need) only after an indeterminate time (not synchronously with the request). This method is called a **monolog**.

1.6.
PRESENTATION LAYER

The aim of the **presentation layer** is to provide services that interpret the meaning of the data transmitted between application processes. Also, the presentation layer makes it possible to select, from the available set, the forms of service that are required by application processes in executing the tasks they must handle.

Interaction between application processes also calls for procedures from the presentation layer that are associated with transmission of data and control instructions between these processes. It is necessary that these data and instructions be transmitted and understood independently of the specific characteristics of the interacting systems and transport network.

Various forms of presentation of information are possible. The task of each of them is to provide a standard description of the structure of the data and of the service-controlling instructions. The most frequently encountered forms of presentation of information are as follows: virtual terminal, virtual files, and virtual tasks.

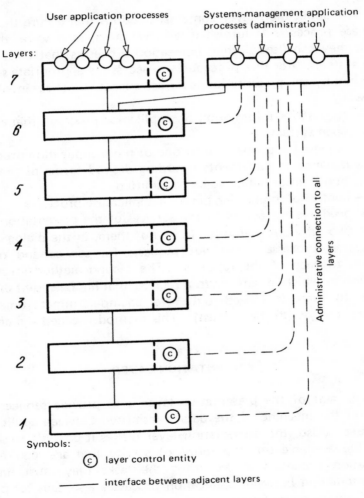

Fig. 1.6. Application processes and their connections to different layers.

16

In addition, there may be complex forms of service, e.g., virtual tasks with virtual files.

The above forms of information presentation furnish application processes with the following services:

- establishment of sessions between application processes which should initiate interaction;
- provision of standard information presentation forms;
- execution of standard presentation of information-exchange procedures;
- control of interaction procedures with distributed transport network via which the application processes interact.

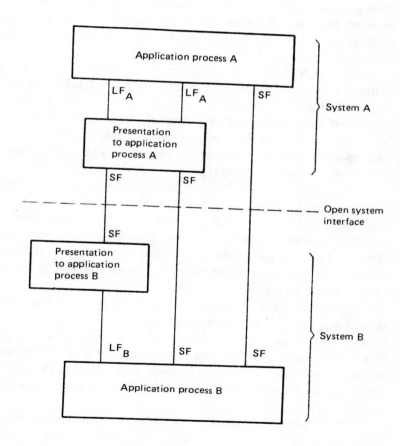

Fig. 1.7. Format conversion structure.

This service includes the following functions:
— conversion of data formats;
— conversion of instructions;
— data compaction/expansion;
— data encrypting/decrypting;
— selection of application processes;
— initialization, maintenance, and termination of interaction sessions for application processes;
— data buffering and flow control.

One of the most important functions here is conversion of data formats (Fig. 1.7). Three cases are possible. The first of these involves conversion of local formats (LF_A) of application process A into standard formats (SF) of open systems, and subsequent conversion of standard formats into local formats (LF_B) of application process B. This case occurs when both processes can operate only with their own local formats.

The second case arises upon interaction of two application processes, one of which (A) operates with local data formats (LF_A), the other (B) with standard formats. In this case the formats are converted only once (when the data are presented to process A).

The third case is observed when both application processes can operate with standard open-system formats. Therefore, there is no need for format conversion.

The operation of the presentation layer is characterized by four successive phases. The **initialization phase** involves procedures associated with preparation of the application processes for the communications session. Then the presentation-control phase occurs. This phase includes the choice of the form of data presentation (display) in a monolog mode (by specifying the form of presentation) or dialog mode.

The presentation-control phase is followed by the **data-transmission phase.** In this phase, the presentation level presents the data and instructions in the chosen form. During this phase the data and instructions are identified and converted, and also the forms of presentation are modified in accordance with changes in the hardware employed **or** improvements in the model of presentation of data and instructions.

The **termination phase** occurs when all transmitted information has been presented to the application processes and the need for execution of presentation-level functions has ended (for the processes under consideration).

The administrative functions of the presentation layer are associated with control of data- and instruction-presentation processes. This deals with the available resources and assures collective access to them for simultaneous presentation of information by several application processes.

1.7.
SESSION LAYER

The purpose of the **session layer** is to establish (via the presentation layer) communications **sessions** between two **or** more application processes (simultaneously). For this, one of the application processes should access the presentation layer with a request for a session and should receive authorization for the session. The presentation layer interacts with the session layer to organize and conduct the session. Sessions providing for interaction of different pairs of application processes can be conducted in parallel; between two processes there may be several simultaneous sessions, during which application processes exchange data units.

The session layer provides for two forms of **session service:**
— connection of application entities so they can interact, and subsequent disconnection of these objects;
— control of data exchange between application entities.

The first type of session service is called administrative, while the second is called data-transmission control.

Administrative session service performs the following:
— establishment of sessions between application processes;
— session identification (isolation of the session in question from the set of other sessions);
— restoration of sessions (after the appearance of errors or trouble);
— termination of sessions (after all necessary sequences of data units have been transmitted).

The **data-transmission control service** provides a set of functions that includes the following:
— data exchange between application processes;
-- determination of boundaries between transmitted data units;
-- dialog control of ordered exchange.

When a session is being set up, procedures for choosing the necessary session protocol (from the available set) are implemented in one of two ways:

— by dialog between two session entities;
— on the basis of previous agreement.

Session objects involved in communications sessions are interconnected via transport connections (logical channels) furnished by the transport layer. Three forms of transmission via these connections are possible: one-way, two-way nonsimultaneous, and two-way simultaneous.

The one-way method involves a situation in which one session object is always a transmitter during a session (entity A in Fig. 1.8), while the other is always a receiver (entity B in Fig. 1.8). The transport connection linking the entities sets up a **data path** and a **control-signal path.** The first path is employed to transmit session service data units containing the primary information. These data units are also transmitted over the second path, but they contain auxiliary information needed to control the session. These units are called **control signals.** When transmitted via a transport connection, control signals have a higher priority than session service data units transmitted via the data path. Therefore, the former are called **expedited** units, while the latter are called **normal.** The one-way data transmission method is employed when it is necessary to transmit a file for local use to some application process.

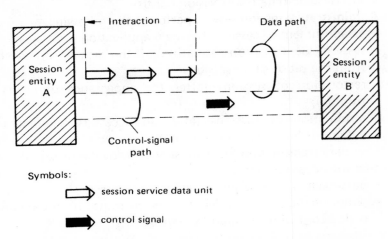

Fig. 1.8. One-way method of interaction of session entities.

In the two-way method, a transport connection provides transmission of information flows in both directions. Two-way nonsimultaneous transmission is most frequently employed when a terminal operator interacts with an application process of the computer. In the case of two-way simultaneous transmission, each session entity, independently of the other, can simultaneously transmit session service data units during a session. This transmission method is the most universal and efficient.

Information is transmitted between session entities by **interactions,** each of which contains one **or** more session service data units. Regardless of the method employed, dialog session control is performed during transmission. This control ensures execution of interaction transmission procedures and ensures receipt of confirmation of correctly received data units.

1.8
TRANSPORT LAYER

The purpose of the **transport layer** is to transmit information between session-layer entities. The latter are called **transport users.** To these users the transport layer furnishes **transport connections,** whose endpoints are ports of the computer network. One **or** more transport connections may be established between a pair of transport users. The transport service is supported by transmission of both **normal** and **expedited** (high-priority) **transport service data units.**

Operation of the transport layer is governed by its protocols, these being **"end-to-end" protocols.** This definition stresses the fact that transport-layer protocols specify information transmission over the entire transport network from one port (see Fig. 1.5) to another.

In confirmity with the protocols, the transport layer provides the following:
— establishment and termination of transport connections;
— conversion of transport connections into network ones;
— control of information flows on the entire path from port to port;
— error detection on this path;
— recovery of transmission after the appearance of faults and errors;

21

— checking of the sequence of transmission of data files over the entire path from one port to another.

The types of service furnished by the transport layer are chosen by the users upon establishing transport connections. When necessary, the type of service can be altered.

The operation of the transport layer is governed by parameters of service quality, which include the following:

— undetected error rate;
— readiness for service;
— delay in data transmission;
— delay in establishment of connection;
— transmission capacity;
— guaranteed delivery of data units.

The transport layer may segment or combine data units transmitted through the entire transport network from one port to another. If there are sufficient resources, these procedures may be combined with functions for error correction and for assuring error-free data transmission. When necessary, confirmations are sent to the sender indicating that the data have been transmitted and contain no errors.

Transport (or transport-layer) functions may utilize somewhat different communications resources, thus making it possible to create integrated (combined) communications networks that perform packet switching and that furnish application processes with direct channels.

1.9.
NETWORK LAYER

The purpose of the **network layer** is to execute functions associated with exchange of network service data units between transport entities. A connection linking two **or** more such objects is called a **network** connection. It is possible to use more than one network connection between a pair of transport entities.

Network connection between two transport entities may be permanent **or** temporary. It may be a "point-to-point" **or** "multipoint" connection. In the first case, two transport entities interact with one another. In the second case, an entity is linked to several other entities via a network connection.

The network layer performs **routing**, which provides switching of data flows. This layer may also perform multiplexing, so that several network connections can be linked to one channel connection.

Network service data units are exchanged via network connections. The size of a network data unit may be restricted, but it may also be of arbitrary length. When necessary, network-level functions perform segmentation or blocking of data units, upon conversion of network service data units into channel service data units and vice versa. These functions also include procedures for error correction in the data-unit formats. The quality of service of the network layer is governed by the same criteria as in the case of the preceding layer.

1.10.
DATA-LINK LAYER

The purpose of the **data-link layer** is to execute functions of establishment, maintenance, and termination of channel connections linking network entities. These connections are also called **information** or **data channels.**

The quality of data-link layer service may vary for different channels and directions of transmission. It is chosen at the time a channel connection is established. The parameters of service quality are virtually the same as for the transport layer.

Data-link layer functions are related to control of data-link connections, and they include the following:

— requests for physical connections, directed to physical layer;
— control of the use of physical connections;
— linkage between data-link and physical connections;
— provision of necessary transmission sequence for data-link service data units;
— detection of errors in transmitted units;
— correction of detected errors and notification of uncorrected ones.

Like a number of other layers, the data-link layer provides for control of the flow of information transmitted by it.

1.11.
PHYSICAL LAYER

The purpose of the **physical layer** is to establish the physical (electrical, electromagnetic, optical, acoustic), mechanical (couplers), functional, and procedural characteristics of the activation, maintenance, and deactivation of **physical connections.** The latter (Fig. 1.9) connect **data-link entities** to one another.

The physical layer provides the service of transmitting bit streams via physical connections. The latter may be permanent or switchable, while transmission over them may be full-duplex, half-duplex, or simplex. When switchable connections are employed, physical-layer functions accept calls and execute the activation and deactivation procedures for these connections.

The physical connections in question are activated (see Fig. 1.9) on the basis of a point-to-point **or** multipoint arrangement. They can provide either serial (bit-by-bit) or parallel (k bits at a time, k > 1) data transmission. In the former case, the **physical service data unit** contains only one bit, while in the latter it contains k bits.

Physical service units are transmitted synchronously **or** asynchronously. In both cases, bits are received at the end of the physical connection in the same order in which they were transmitted at the

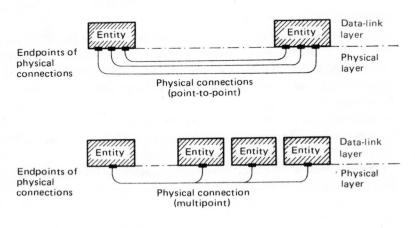

Fig. 1.9. Types of physical connections.

origin. The service-quality parameters are chosen by the data-link entities upon activation of the physical connection. The parameter list is roughly the same as for the transport layer.

1.12.
PROTOCOLS

Open systems methodology makes it possible to develop standard **subsystems,** which are becoming widely disseminated. These subsystems describe functions executed by application entities, and incorporate a hierarchy of service that is required at all levels of the seven-layer architecture model under consideration. Subsystems are governed by protocols, which may be either **unbalanced** or **balanced** in relation to interacting application processes. An example of an unbalanced protocol is provided by the standards that govern access of terminals to application processes. Balanced protocols are protocols that describe interaction of several application processes. Each system may incorporate one or more of the subsystems in question. In the future, the list of subsystems may be very large; in what follows we will consider the most widespread ones.

Virtual terminal. One of the most important problems of open systems is the exchange of interactions between a human operator of a terminal system and various application processes in the host system. Figure 1.10 shows a subsystem that performs this interaction.

In the subsystem under consideration, the interacting partners (human operator and application program) are above the application layer and their communication is governed by a special protocol. It is supported by the requisite presentation service, provided by a virtual terminal — a logical model that represents in standard fashion in the computer network a real terminal at the application level. A **virtual terminal protocol** is a set of rules and agreements that govern exchange of interactions between a human operator and an application process.

After a decision has been made to employ a virtual terminal, it is initialized (i.e., all programs representing it are activated). During initialization, in the first place, one of the classes of virtual terminals (scroll, page, word-by-word, graphic) is chosen. Then the chosen class is started.

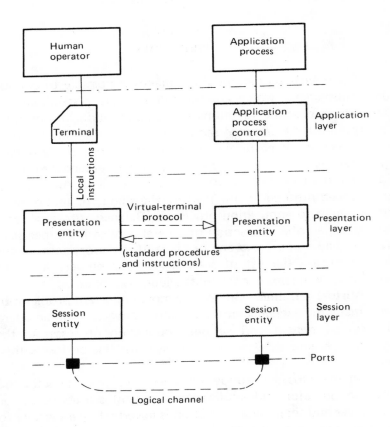

Fig. 1.10. Structure of virtual terminal.

After the initialization procedures have been performed, the phase of data exchange begins. Each class of virtual terminals employs a certain set of instructions for this. For example, for the stream class the set includes the following: enter data into memory; reproduce on display screen; read text; begin data transmission; interrupt data transmission; and so forth. In addition, manipulations are performed so as to represent the actual available type of terminal in the form of the virtual terminal of the chosen class. The instructions and modes of data description and allocation are transformed in this case.

Virtual files. This subsystem provides interaction between application processes and virtual files. These files are a logical form of representation of actual file storage that utilizes standard names, formats, and directories of files.

Virtual files provide a set of types of service furnished to application processes. They include the following in particular:
— description of types of file control;
— a procedure for file layout in different storage devices;
— description of data allocation in file storage.

The presentation functions for virtual file storage can be divided into two groups. The first group describes the internal structure and characteristics of the file contents, while the second specifies the principles for representing the file as a closed container of data, and contains the external tags of the file.

File control functions are related to changes in the external characteristics of files. The list of these functions may include the following: analysis of file tags; alteration of tag characteristics; opening (introduction) of new forms of access to files; closing (erasing) of unnecessary forms of access. Operation with files is effected by using sets of instructions that perform the following operations: open file (write it in storage); combine files; transmit file; close (erase) file; read file; modify (alter) file. The subsystem under consideration offers the possibility of controlling the set of file storages, located in one or more than one system. Local and remote methods of access to files are correspondingly defined.

Virtual jobs. There are two ways of creating subsystems intended for remote job input. The first of these involves a situation in which a user desiring to transmit a job to a subsystem via the communications network is required to set it up in the job control language of the subsystem under consideration. This method is simple but it requires execution of as many types of jobs as there are different types of remote job input subsystems in the network.

Recently, therefore, a virtual-job model with a job control language that is unified for the entire network, into which all available real languages are converted, has been gaining greater currency. In this subsystem, application job-execution processes that realize a remote job input protocol are placed in the application layer (Fig. 1.11), while job presentation service functions are placed in the presentation layer. The protocol may provide for execution of the following instructions: transmit job; provide information on job

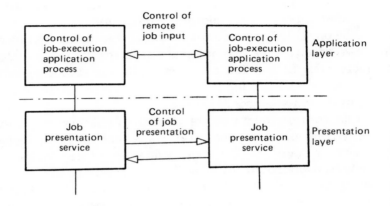

Fig. 1.11. Remote job input.

execution status; cancel transmitted job; transmit user file; connect two human operators; transmit system message.

As for the service functions of the presentation layer, they employ the following forms of presentation:

— representation of data in transmission phase;
— representation of external devices (punchcard readers, printers, punched-tape output, and so forth);
— representation of access (activation of instruction) of virtual job;
— representation of application processes.

In the subsystem under consideration, moreover, the requisite file control functions that maintain the remote job input protocol are executed on the session level.

Implementation of virtual subsystems. Each open system may employ one **or** more virtual subsystems from the outset. Moreover, various virtual subsystems can be used to create combinations that supplement one another and expand the capabilities of open systems.

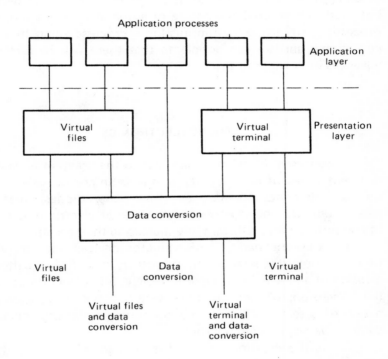

Fig. 1.12. Set of presentation functions.

An example of a system that incorporates virtual files, a virtual terminal, and a data converter is shown in Fig. 1.12. Here the application processes are supported by service of three types, enabling them to operate in five modes: virtual files; virtual files with data conversion; virtual terminal; virtual terminal with data conversion; data conversion. The **data-conversion model** recodes and reformats the data, and encrypts, decrypts, and compacts information.

CHAPTER 2

DEVELOPMENT TENDENCIES IN INFORMATION AND COMPUTING TECHNOLOGY

The rapid development of many lines of scientific research, and the gradual blurring of the distinction between science and industry, have led to significant advances over the last decade that have radically altered the nature of automatic installations for data processing, storage, and transmission. Progress along these lines is continuing, and we can anticipate that there will be further major advances in the near future.

2.1.
MICROELECTRONICS

Advances in electronics have led to the creation of layers with different types of conductivity in the same crystal. This has given rise to semiconductor devices (transistors, diodes) that greatly reduce the size and power consumption of electronic components of computers, while substantially increasing their reliability.

On the one hand, semiconductor devices have truly revolutionized computer science; on the other, they have resulted in the creation of a new field of science, namely, microelectronics. Whereas the dimensions of vacuum tubes were reckoned in centimeters, the region of a semiconductor chip containing a transitor or diode has come to be reckoned in microns.

Since the creation of the first integrated circuits, there has been a natural tendency to "pack" as many functional elements as possible into one semiconductor chip. Thus, a new field of electronics, known as **chip architecture,** has arisen.

The importance of research in chip architecture stems from the fact that, by increasing chip complexity, it is possible to reduce the number of components of computers. This entails a reduction in size and cost and increase in operating reliability.

As we know, any computer can perform only four types of operations: three logical operations (disjunction, conjunction, and negation) and storage. Execution of complex mathematical calculations and information functions reduces to implementation of sequences of a large set of the above four operations. Initially, therefore, efforts were aimed at getting integrated circuits to perform one of the logical operations or elementary combinations of them, e.g., negation of a disjunction or negation of a conjunction.

The successes achieved in this area made it possible to speed up developments and to begin to manufacture integrated circuits performing complex logical transformations on one chip. The number of circuit elements in chips, which originally amounted to a handful, increased to tens and hundreds; at present the number runs to many tens of thousands. Hence, **integrated circuits** came to be known as large-scale integration, and then as very large-scale integration.

Integrated circuits are created on the surface or in the interior of a single monolithic semiconductor crystal, different areas of which function as electronic elements (transistors, diodes, resistors, and so forth) after appropriate technological treatment.

In accordance with the theory of discrete semiconductor devices, the smaller an element is, the better: the higher its operating speed, the lower the power dissipation, and the greater the number of elements that can be placed on the chip. Therefore, reduction in size of integrated circuit elements is an important part of current research. By creating different combinations of elements on chips, and by combining them into the necessary circuitry, extremely diverse computer components can be obtained. For example, on one semiconductor chip it has been possible to create a storage device that has come to be known as a **solid-state memory.** At present, storage devices called **main memories** are being mass-produced on a large scale. In this type of memory, data is entered and read out at high speed. A standard main storage chip now has a capacity of 64 kbits.* The capacity of memory that can be placed on one chip is increasing rapidly [7]. Figure 2.1 shows the predicted development [20]; it follows that in the near future we can expect to see semiconductor chips containing up to 262 kbits or more of main storage.

Storage devices called **read-only memories** (ROM's) have appeared and have gained widespread currency. Information is stored

---

*Here and henceforth, $k = 2^{10} = 1024$.

31

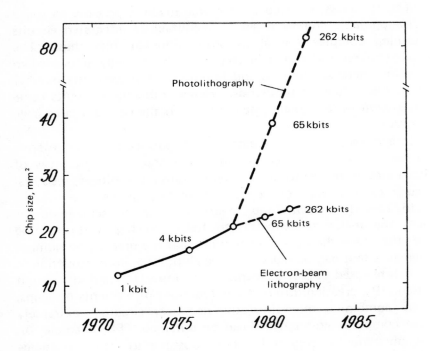

Fig. 2.1. Development of technology of single-chip main memories.

in these memories during manufacture (by placement of masks on the chip) or prior to use (by burn-out of jumpers, electrical reconfiguration, and so forth). For this reason, information is entered into read-only memory either once or more than once, but at a very low rate. In all cases, information is read out at the same high speed as for main storage. Read-only memory is cheaper than main storage. Therefore, it is extensively used when there is no need for rapid modification or replacement of data: for implementing modules of computer operating systems, systems programs, translators, emulators, and so forth. It should be borne in mind that, when the supply voltage is cut off, the information written in a main storage crystal disappears (i.e., it is erased). With read-only memory, the information in it can be preserved even when there is no supply voltage.

Recently there has been an intensive search for a **chip architecture** which would allow for even greater reduction in the size of memory elements. An idea that has appeared involves the input and output of data to and from a semiconductor crystal by means of an electron beam. This procedure is capable of yielding higher-capacity memories. For example, a 32-Mbit memory* has been created on a silicon chip [18], for which the access time is 30 μsec. A memory module with a capacity of 600 Mbits has been created on the basis of these chips. It is anticipated that the capacity can be increased by a factor of 30. Experiments have shown that it is possible to access single-chip memories with capacities to 1600 Mbits.

Storage devices were initially constructed in the form of arrays of interconnected transistors. Then the idea arose [19] of creating transistorless memories. In such devices, a unit of information (or bit) is stored in a specially created "potential well." As a result, the size of the memory element is reduced by a factor of 5 (as compared to a single-transistor memory element).

Intensive development of large-capacity solid-state storage devices led to the creation of so-called **magnetic bubble memory.** A device of this type is a garnet crystal with a magnetic film deposited on it. Permalloy control structures, which determine the paths of magnetic domains under the action of a rotating magnetic field, are deposited on the film. The field is created by a coil that surrounds the crystal. An important feature of these memories is their ability to retain their contents even after the supply voltage is switched off. A shortcoming of magnetic bubble memory is the necessity of bitwise, i.e., serial, entry and readout of information (rather than parallel entry and readout, as in other solid-state memory devices). This severely reduces the operating speed. This shortcoming can be moderated by creating several memory paths in the device. As a result, it has been possible to achieve operating speeds for bubble memories on an order of magnitude higher than for magnetic disks. In addition, bubble memories are more reliable than disk storages.

---

*Here and henceforth, $M = k^2 = 1024 \cdot 1024$.

33

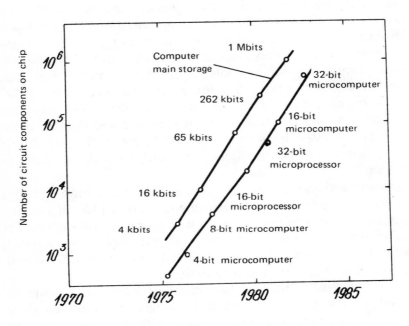

Fig. 2.2. Increase in integrated-circuit complexity.

Advances in technology have led to the appearance of new type of computer component, called a **microprocessor.** This is a real central processing unit, but it is implemented on a single semiconductor chip. By combining microprocessors with read-only or main storage, it is possible to create **microcomputers,** i.e., computers based on one or more chips.

The progress to date and development prospects for single-chip integrated circuits are illustrated by Fig. 2.2 [20], from which it follows that the first to be created on one chip was a 4-bit microcomputer. This machine consisted of a processor and a modest main and read-only memory. It was employed effectively for controlling simple technological hardware, in calculators, and in data conversion equipment. Its cost was considerably less than that of a conventional telephone set.

This was followed by 8-bit and then 16-bit microcomputers with a fairly complicated architecture [21-22], which are now

34

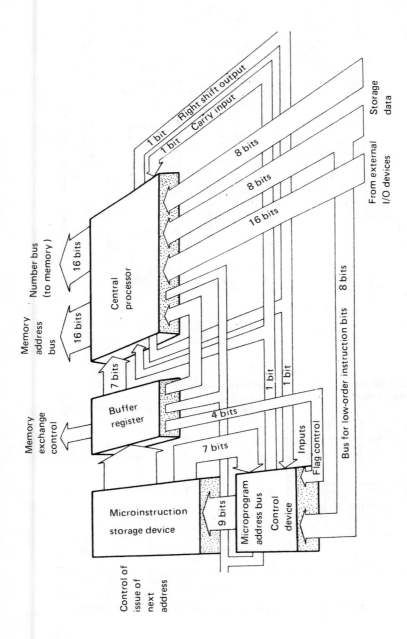

Fig. 2.3. Structure of 16-bit single-chip microprocessor.

35

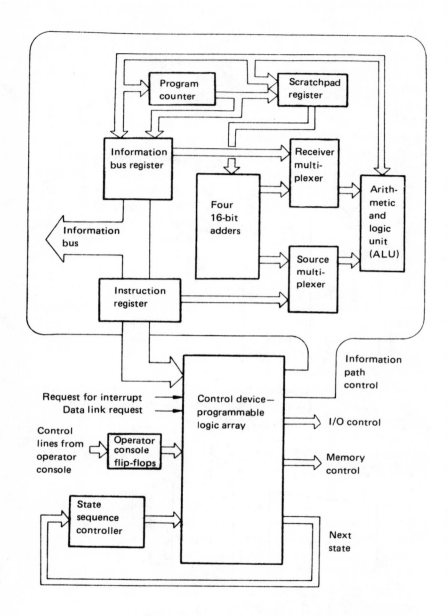

Fig. 2.4. Structure of 16-bit single-chip miniprocessor.

mass-produced in large quantities. Such computers contain a central processor, an electrically programmable read-only memory with a capacity of 8 kbits, scratchpad and main memories, data I/O, a timer, and a clock generator. Finally, it has proved possible to create 16-bit and then 32-bit single-chip microprocessors. The logical structure of a 16-bit chip is shown in Fig. 2.3; the complexity of a circuit created on one semiconductor chip is clearly evident. It incorporates a central processor, buffer register, microinstruction storage device, control device, and a set of busses that connect these blocks.

A substantial increase in the list of executable instructions has made it possible to create a single-chip miniprocessor [23-24]. It replaces the standard miniprocessor board containing around 100 medium-scale integrated circuits. The miniprocessor structure (Fig. 2.4) is characterized by a large number of interconnected components that perform data processing. This processor can control up to 63 peripherals. Its operation requires a main memory whose structure is shown in Fig. 2.5. Currently manufactured integrated circuits provide the miniprocessor with a main memory of up to 64 kbytes.

Ordinary photolithography, which is extensively employed in manufacturing integrated circuitry, has now reached the limits of its capabilities [25]. Therefore, electron-beam technology is becoming more widespread (Fig. 2.6); the number of elements on a crystal can be increased to 10 million in this fashion. Attempts to obtain still larger numbers of elements on one crystal have led to exploration of the possibility of using X-ray lithography in the manufacture of very-large-scale integrated circuitry.

Together with general-purpose mini- and microprocessors, microprocessors intended for creation of multiprocessor systems have begun to be manufactured. For example, Fig. 2.7 shows the architecture of a single-crystal microcomputer that is a universal programmable 8-bit peripheral controller for linking (interfacing) the primary information-processing processor with peripherals.

Single chip peripheral components that provide effective interfacing of computers have appeared. They contain up to 22,000 transistors on a chip and replace circuit boards with discrete components. They include, e.g., the following [26]:
— controllers for physical links;
— programmable controllers for magnetic disks;
— programmable controllers for displays.

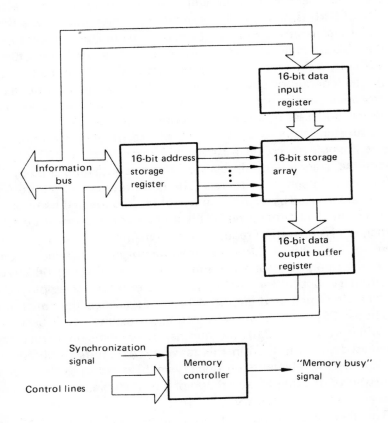

Fig. 2.5. Structure of 16-bit single-chip main storage device.

Attempts to increase the complexity of the data manipulations have led to the creation of a multichip integrated circuit contained in one package. For example, a microcomputer integrated circuit has been created [27] that contains a 16-bit processor chip, data I/O chips, four interface buffers, and a 16-kbit read-only memory.

Recently a new type of integrated circuit, known as the **programmable logical array**, has appeared. Figure 2.8 shows the architecture of a four-input two-output array. The rectangles denote logical elements that perform operations of negation (NOT), conjunction (AND), and disjunction (OR). When the array is set (programmed), the necessary connections are made at the requisite

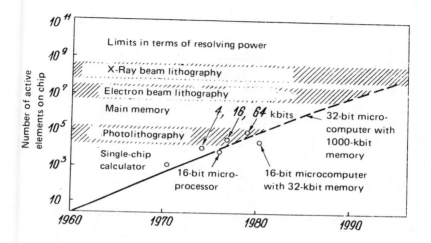

Fig. 2.6. Prediction of the development of VSLI manufacturing technology.

points of intersection of the busses (circles). As a result, the programmable logic array under consideration can execute logical functions of four signals $A_1 - A_4$. Arrays containing up to 20 inputs and 24 outputs are currently being manufactured [28,29]. Each of them can realize 2^{20} functions.

Logical arrays may be programmed in three ways. The first way involves the use of masks in manufacture of the array; the second, which is less expensive, involves burning out of bridges connecting different busses (performed by the user). Finally, the third and most expensive way allows users themselves to repeatedly reconfigure arrays by electrical means.

An important advantage of programmable logic arrays, and one which distinguishes them from processors, is the possibility of executing any complex logical manipulations over just one cycle. Their use makes it possible to develop new types of relatively simple and inexpensive high-speed data converters.

Creation of integrated circuitry offered an immediate solution to several important problems related to the development of computer engineering. These include, in particular, low cost, high reliability, long operating lifetime, small size, and diversity of tasks performed.

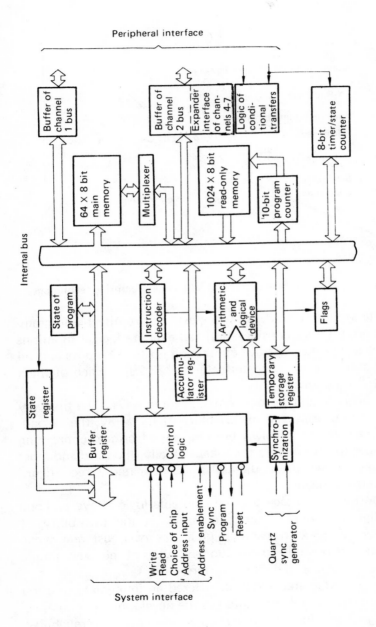

Fig. 2.7. Single-chip programmable peripheral controller.

40

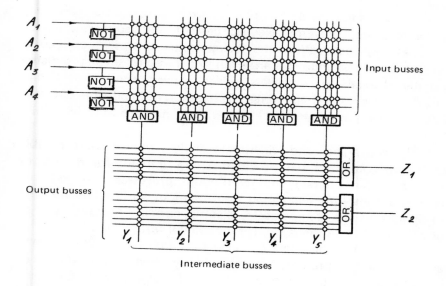

Fig. 2.8. Structure of programmable logic array.

The cost of integrated circuitry is steadily dropping, and will decrease by an additional factor of 10 over the next five years [30]. Therefore, further developments in microelectronics will promote the improvement of computer methods and hardware to an even greater degree.

2.2.
COMPUTERS

About 40 years have passed since the first electronic computers appeared. There have been several successive generations of computers. Computers transformed rapidly from devices performing mathematical calculations into complex general-purpose data processing facilities.

Digitalization of computer techniques. For a long time, two types of machines, namely, analog (modelling) machines and digital machines (computers), were developed in parallel.

In contrast to analog machines, the operation of computers is based on mathematical logic. This opened up extensive areas of application for them in the most diverse types of data processing systems.

Even in areas involving processing of continuous signals, such as temperature, pressure, electric current, and so forth, analog machines have receded into the background. At present, computers interact with continuous signals on the basis of **analog-to-digital** and **digital-to-analog converters,** which convert continuous signals into discrete ones and vice versa. It has even been possible to create a data acquisition system [31] in a 62-lead package only 58 × 36 × 6 mm in size.

The appearance and widespread deployment of cheap reliable **single-chip converters** has provided a new impetus for the use of computers that interact with continuous processes. In addition, there is a constantly increasing assortment of sensors that measure continuous values (temperature, electric current, pressure, and so forth) but that yield signals directly in digital form.

As a result, the use of analog machines has rapidly become restricted, and at present they are employed only in a number of a special cases. Attempts to create hybrid machines in which analog machines and computers interact in an organic fashion have not led to an increase in the demand for analog techniques.

A similar process, but with a considerable shift in time, is observed with memory devices. Both analog memory devices (ordinary tape recorders, video recorders, phonographs) and digital devices (disks, tapes, cards, and drums) are widely used at present. However, attempts to create unified data banks in which retrieval is performed by computers have led to extensive efforts to introduce digital methods into tape and phonograph recording processes.

Units that provide digital recording of color video signals on magnetic tape have now appeared [32]. An information (and image) storage system has been developed [33] in which a laser beam, by burning microscopic holes onto a rotating disk, can record data in digital form. The disk rotates at 25 rps, and a complete television frame can be recorded on it during each revolution. A disk 32 cm in diameter can store around 10,000 Mbits of data.

As a result, (digital) computers have come to be used in almost all areas of human activity, and have even started to become a part of daily life. At present, they have become multipurpose systems in which the volume of information activity (acquisition, storage, retrieval, processing, transmission, and output of data) exceeds the volume of computation. Computers are particularly important in newer branches of the national economy. In the United States, for example, the expenses of the Apollo space program for computers and computer science amounted to 9 billion dollars, or one-seventh the cost of the entire program.

Computer architecture. There have been several successive generations of computers, and their architecture, characteristics, and parameters have changed significantly. The rapid development of computer software has caused a corresponding increase in its importance. As a result (Fig. 2.9), the cost of software has come to exceed the cost of hardware severalfold [35]. In the world at present, the creation of new programs (taking account of user programs), consumes around 90% of all the labor involved in creating new computer facilities [36].

Widespread use of cheap integrated circuitry, in particular read-only memories and programmable logic arrays, has resulted in a situation in which it is more expedient to implement programs (in particular, frequently used ones) using integrated circuits, rather than to store them on disks or tapes. Such programs have come to be called **firmware.** For example, the IBM 5100 series computers provide for program implementation in the form of cassettes with programmed read-only memory [37]. On the other hand, computer

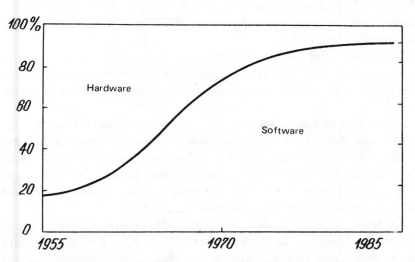

Fig. 2.9. Relative increase in cost of computer software.

structures employ highly diverse equipment for data input, storage, transmission, and output. To emphasize the flexibility of this structure, it has come to be known as a **"soft"** architecture.

Because of progress in microelectronics and advances in computer architecture, the cost of data processing has been dropping by an order of magnitude every three to five years [38], and this tendency is continuing. New types of computing facilities, known as minicomputers, have appeared. These were followed by microcomputers, which have gained exceptionally wide currency as a result of their simplicity and low cost.

An example of a large computer is the two-processor IBM-370/168—3. Each of its processors operates at a rate of around 3 million operations per second [36].

An important development trend in present-day large and small computers is the constantly expanding use of large-scale integration. For example, one currently manufactured computer that is an analog of the IBM-370/168 is only one-third as large and expensive [39].

With each passing year, computers containing large numbers of microprocessors become more serious competitors of "ordinary" large computers. Studies have shown [40] that a computer containing 10—20 microprocessors that interact with a minicomputer can handle complex tasks tens of times more rapidly than the IBM-370/168. The cost will inevitably be lower. The possibility of creating computers containing around 10,000 microprocessors is also under consideration [40].

Progress in the use of microprocessors in computer engineering has become so significant that a computer conference in the United States [41] even raised the question, "Are large computers necessary?".

Class of small computers. The tendency toward decentralization of data processing has provided a powerful impetus for the development of minicomputers. Therefore, the increase in their number is running substantially ahead of the increase of large computers. It is assumed that minicomputers will amount to around 80% of the computer pool in the near future [39].

In terms of their characteristics, minicomputers have become much more similar to large machines. They have a high operating speed (access cycle to main storage less than 1 microsecond). Main storage of minicomputers has begun to exceed 1 Mbyte [42]. An expanded instruction list (200 or even more) allows them to effectively perform data processing. Minicomputers have a variety of I/O devices, large-capacity disks and tapes, and an exceptionally wide assortment of peripherals. They have started to employ LSI read-only memories containing 48 kbits per chip [43].

Even IBM, which manufactured primarily large computers until recently, has gone into production of minicomputers. Their Series/1 minicomputer [44] has an access time to main memory of only 660 nsec, is inexpensive, and has a large assortment of peripherals.

Data General Corporation, which has developed the MicroNova minicomputer, has taken a similar path. In this case as well, the basic element of the computer is a microprocessor. However, it employs a multiprogrammed operating system, performs tasks in real time, operates with high-level algorithmic languages (FORTRAN 4, expanded BASIC), and is inexpensive.

The field of **microcomputers** is developing at an exceptional rate. For example, in Western Europe alone, around 2.5 million microcomputers are sold each year [34]. In terms of cost, they have virtually become comparable to telephone sets.

An example of a current microcomputer is the LSI—11, manufactured by Digital Equipment Corporation. The computer fits onto one 216 x 254 mm. board [46]. The LSI—11 has been followed by the LSI—11/2 microcomputer [47], which is half the size and offers expanded capabilities and greater economy.

Microprocessors have become widely employed in controlling technological processes and in data acquisition and conversion hardware. A new field of application for them is in office work. By equipping typewriters with one or more microprocessors, it has become possible to convert them into universal control facilities. As a result, more than 350,000 typewriters with automatic text processing are currently in use in the United States [48].

Personal computers. The rapid drop in cost of microprocessors has led to the appearance of a new type of computer intended for use in daily life. In some cases (to reduce the cost), mini- or microcomputers are connected to ordinary household devices such as television sets, tape recorders, telephones, and so on; in other cases special external devices are employed.

For example, the MicroMind computer has a microprocessor with a modest main and read-only memory [49]. If desired, the main memory can be expanded to 32 kbytes. The computer employs a television set as a display, and a standard cassette tape recorder for external storage. A set of programs is supplied, including an editor routine, expanded BASIC, game programs, and so forth.

Commodore Business Machines Corporation has developed a personal computer [50] with a 8-bit microprocessor, a 0.5—4 kbyte main storage, a display with a 23-cm (diagonal) screen, and 73-key keyboard. The computer uses BASIC, and its cost is roughly comparable to that of a large black-and-white television set.

A **professional personal system** is manufactured by IBM [51, 52]. Personal Computer consists of a 16-bit high-speed processor with a 16-256 kbyte main memory, two 160-kbyte floppy disks, and 83-key keyboard, a display, and a printer. The system has an adapter for connection to a 9600-bit/sec telephone channel. The display produces symbols, diagrams, and graphics in 16 colors on an eight-color background.

Like all other computers, personal computers were initially intended for scientific, business, or domestic calculations. Recently, however, these computers have begun to be extensively employed for information purposes and for a wide range of games.

The use of personal computers is in the initial phase of development. As they become more widespread, however, new computer applications, related to the work and leisure activities of millions of people, will appear.

Hierarchy of memory devices. Because of the increasing complexity of the calculations to be performed, and also the rapid expansion of the amount of information-related tasks, it has become necessary to increase the capacity and operating speed for memory devices. Advances in microelectronics have abruptly lowered the cost of memory components. As a result, the specific cost of main storage (per bit) has decreased by a factor of almost 25 over the last decade (Fig. 2.10).

The cost of other types of memory is also dropping rapidly. At the same time, the cost of information on paper media has tripled worldwide over the last five years [54], and this tendency is continuing. In turn, this means that with each passing year the amount of information that can be feasibly placed in computer storage is increasing. At present, up to 70—90% of the physical size and cost of present-day computers is attributable to auxiliary storage devices [55].

Different types of memory (Fig. 2.11) are characterized by their capacity and the access time to it [41].

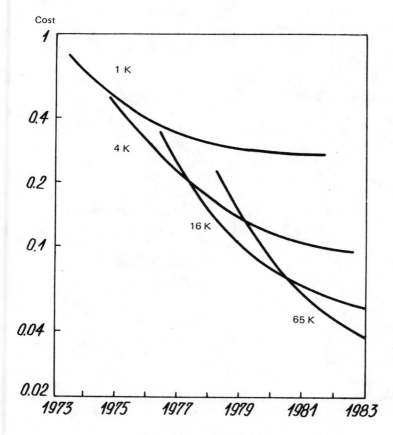

Fig. 2.10. Specific cost of main storage devices.

Main storages are currently based on LSI and VLSI circuitry. The size of disk storage is rapidly increasing. For example, disks with a capacity of 635 Mbytes per disk drive are currently being manufactured [56]. The rate of data exchange with these disks runs as high as 1.2 Mbytes/sec.

Improvements in **optical memories** are appearing with each passing year. The use of coherent laser light and precision optics yields an information recording density of up to 100 Mbits/cm².

An example of an optical memory system is provided by a device manufactured by IBM [57]. In the 1360 device, 5 Mbits

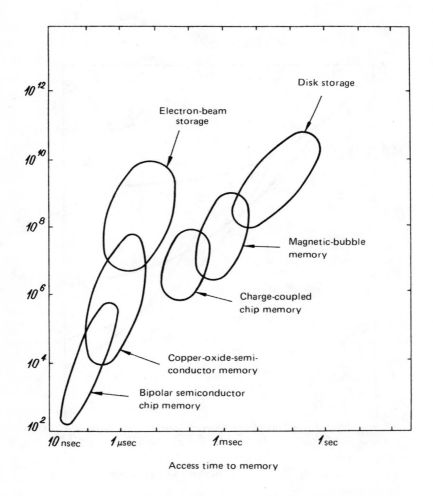

Fig. 2.11. Capacity and speed of various memory devices.

of data are recorded on photographic film. Each cell of the device has 32 films, and 7000 cells make up a memory with a capacity of 100,000 Mbytes. A pneumatic transport arrangement provides access to any film within 100 sec.

Automatic libraries, which give computers access to very large memories, have also appeared [58,59]. For example, the IBM–3850 library contains cassettes with a total memory of 472,000 Mbytes. The required cassette is selected from its storage compartment, moved to the read/write device, and returned to its place in 15 sec on average.

Terminal devices. Every year more and more attention is paid to methods that provide human beings with convenient modes of communication with computers. Therefore, both the assortment and numbers of **terminals** are increasing rapidly. The display has become virtually an obligatory feature. This stems from the fact that human users think in images, and thus, a screen that can display text and graphic information is extremely convenient. In most displays, the computer-produced image is projected onto the screen of a television tube. At the same time, flat plasma screens that do not require continuous image regeneration and that allow for extremely compact displays, are now being manufactured [60]. High-speed printers have been created [61] in which the active element is a laser beam that makes drawings and writes out text.

Intensive studies are currently under way in the area of inputting images (text, drawings, photographs, or any real objects) into computers. Creation of such devices will allow computers to perceive their surroundings and to accept exceptionally large amounts of information inputted at high speeds.

Devices that enable spoken man/machine dialog have appeared. One system for information input [62] allows a restricted number of users (whom the machine is trained to comprehend) to conduct a dialog regarding a data base containing information on ship movement. Voice data input devices are improving rapidly, and computers are now capable of recognizing up to 1000 words. Output devices, that convert digital computer signals into natural-language speech, are also being produced. In this case words are synthesized by selecting the corresponding morphemes recorded on magnetic tape.* This enables the computer to pronounce any necessary number of words [63,64].

The more convenient terminals become, the more rapidly their production will increase. In Western Europe, the number of terminals in use is currently reckoned in the hundreds of thousands [65,66], while in the United States it is in the millions. The predicted growth in the number of terminals in the United States and in Western Europe is shown in Fig. 2.12 [67].

---

*A morpheme is a part of a word (root, suffix, prefix, and so forth) that has a self-contained meaning.

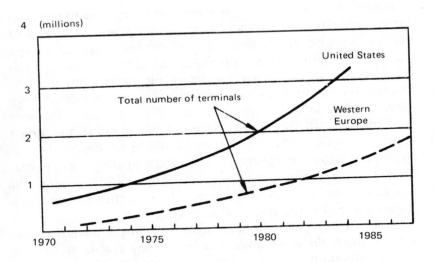

Fig. 2.12. Prediction of increase in number of terminals.

TABLE 2.1.

Name of method	Prediction, %		
	1975	1980	1985
Punched paper media	73	53	32
Terminal keyboards	6	16	28
Tapes and cassettes	16	19	21
Other	5	12	19

The expansion of terminal production and the use of data preparation devices based on magnetic tape will entail major changes in modes of inputting information into computers. These changes are shown in Table 2.1 [68]. They testify that terminals are starting to be preferred to punched paper tape.

2.3.
DATA TRANSMISSION TECHNIQUES

Rapid increase in the amounts of transmitted data, as well as economic considerations, have led to extensive research related to the creation of forms of data transmission providing inexpensive transmission of huge information flows. Figure 2.13 shows the cost of data transmission (referred to one channel for three types of data transmission channels). It should be pointed out, however, that the cost of data transmission is declining at a slower rate than the cost of data processing.

Satellite communications are steadily gaining more widespread currency. In the first place, this stems from the fact that the power of satellite transmitters is increasing rapidly, with the result that the size and cost of ground-based communications stations are decreasing sharply. For example, it has become possible to receive satellite data using an antenna 11 m in diameter [69], or even less. In the second place, satellites can span enormous areas. Satellites with a synchronous orbit, maintaining fixed positions at points of the Earth's equator, are becoming particularly popular. Such satellites provide continuous communication and do not require search and tracking by ground-based stations. Figure 2.14 shows the reception/transmission zone for one such satellite over the Atlantic Ocean [38].

A satellite communications structure is shown in Fig. 2.15. Here the satellite combines three terrestrial networks (A, B, and C), located in different parts of the world, into a single whole. Satellite communications can transmit large information flows, but involve a delay time of up to 0.25 sec because of the large distances.

The importance of satellite communications will increase substantially in the next few years. For example, a digital communications network employing three satellites is now nearing completion [70]. The network is intended primarily to service the territory of the United States. It is planned to establish 500 unattended terrestrial stations with antennas 5 and 7 m in diameter at user sites. Computer information, television, and speech will be transmitted via this network.

The sphere of application of computers in communications engineering has begun to expand rapidly. Figure 2.16 shows the structure of one of the largest electronic switching systems [71]. The system contains six 32-bit computers and is intended for tele-

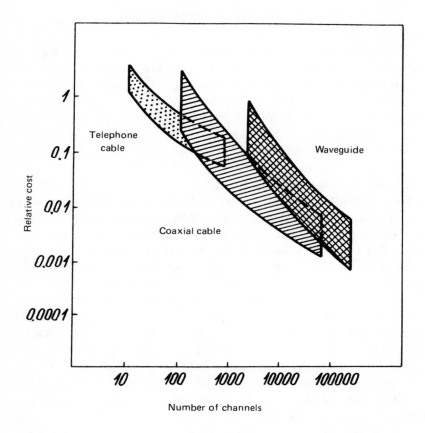

Fig. 2.13. Cost of communications channels.

phone, telegraph, and information switching centers. It can switch up to 32,000 input and 32,000 output communications channels.

Communications engineering, like computer engineering, operates with information in both analog and digital form. The first means of communications was the telegraph, whose operating principle is based on discrete information. However, representation of data in the form of dots and dashes was extremely inconvenient, and the transmission rates were too low. The development of telephony and television, which provide rapid transmission of information in forms to which human beings are accustomed, led to extensive development of audio and video communications networks. Accordingly,

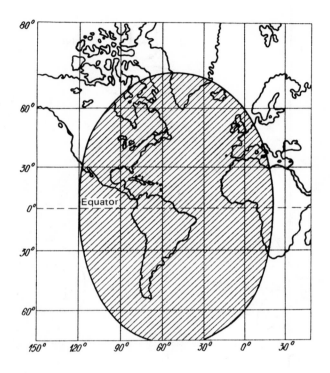

Fig. 2.14. Area of Earth's surface spanned by communications satellite in synchronous orbit.

analog communications assumed a leading role, leaving only secondary functions to the telegraph.

It would seem that the explosive development and widespread dissemination of telephony and television would have definitively established analog communications methods and techniques. With the appearance of computers and the subsequent development of terminals, however, a new problem arose, namely, that of data exchange between devices of different types involved in processing digital information.

Before feeding output to an analog (telephone) network, digital computers were compelled to convert data to a form convenient for this network. As long as the amount of data transmitted between

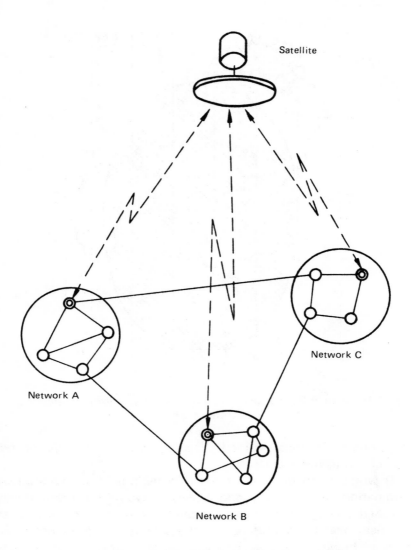

Fig. 2.15. Structure of satellite communications.

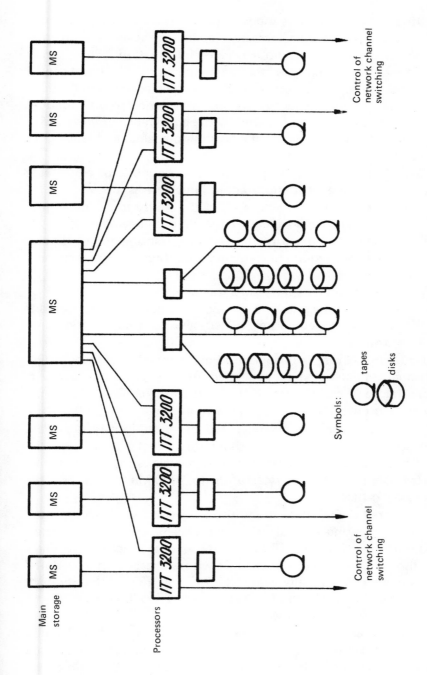

Fig. 2.16. Physical structure of multicomputer switchable system.

55

computers of terminals was modest, this method was an acceptable one. The volume of data increased rapidly, however, and now exceeds the dimensions of audio and video information. Thus, rather than connecting computers to analog networks, it has become economical to construct special high-speed digital communications networks and to adapt audio and video information to their requirements. This has also been fostered by the appearance of inexpensive and highly reliable single-crystal digital-to-analog and analog-to-digital converters.

Digital communications channels have a number of advantages over analog ones, the most important of which are as follows:

— high noise stability, as a result of the ability to regenerate the received signal and to remove the noise it has acquired;
— economy, as a result of the fact that transmission of 0's and 1's does not require high-quality amplifiers and other channel elements;
— simple-to-implement data compression;
— flexibility, which allows for combination of signals of different types (computer, video, audio, etc.) in the same hardware.

Naturally, before a telephone signal is transmitted over a digital channel, it must first be converted into digital form. However, this can be done rapidly, efficiently, and with the necessary degree of accuracy on the basis of existing hardware.

Digital channels are characterized by exceptionally high data transmission rates. Studies have shown [72] that a paper-insulated twisted-pair cable can transmit digital signals at rates up to 10 Mbits/sec. Transmission at rates of up to 1000 Mbits/sec is possible over coaxial cables.

The first digital data transmission system was implemented in Japan [73] using coaxial cable, and became commercially operational in 1970. Rates of 100 Mbits/sec were attained. Four years later, also in Japan, a coaxial channel with a capacity of 400 Mbits/sec was made commercially available [74]. In 1975, intercity high-speed digital channels operating at speeds of 274 Mbits/sec appeared in the United States and Canada [75,76].

Still greater transmission rates are provided by digital channels based on optical-fiber cables. A cable 7.3 km long has been used for experimental signal transmission at a rate of 800 Mbits/sec.

A **digital data transmission network** called DATAROUTE became operational in Canada in 1973 [78]. Figure 2.17 shows the structure of a network element. Operating at a rate of 1544 Mbits/sec, the network can accomodate a wide range of hardware. As early as 1975, the network linked 26 cities. The operation of the communications facilities of the network is controlled by minicomputers. The error probability for the network on the 600-km Montreal-Toronto link is only 0.017%. The transmission time with errors is around 15 sec per day on average. Unavailability of the network as a result of malfunctioning has amounted to 11 sec per day.

The Ministry of Communications of the Federal Republic of Germany has decided [79] to create a nationwide digital data transmission network with channels having a capacity of 2 Mbits/sec. The first link, between Mannheim and Frankfurt, became operational in 1977.

The advantages yielded by digital techniques are so substantial that widespread efforts have begun to introduce them into radar systems [80] and television [32]. Development of **digital television** will greatly increase the fidelity of transmitted information and has opened up new possibilities associated with image processing: insertion of captions and titles, frame splitting, fade-outs, zooming, and other special effects.

Even now, microprocessor hardware for a studio television installation has been created [32] that demonstrates the basic elements of digital video signal processing. In this installation, the analog signal of the image is converted into digital form and is placed in computer storage. An intercity digital channel for color pictures has commenced operation [81]. Simultaneously with digital video signals, this channel handles, in compressed form, the accompanying sound track and signals of 60 telephone lines. The rate of digital data transmission is 43 Mbits/sec.

Work to date demonstrates that television will be digital in the future. It is assumed that television centers will largely convert to digital signal processing in the mid-1980's.

Digitalization of telephone communications is proceeding at a rapid rate. The possibility of enhancing the reliability and noise stability and of reducing the cost calls for expanded research in this area. Manufacture of fully **digital telephone exchanges** has already begun. One such station employs five microprocessors [82]. Two of them perform call-processing functions, while a third provides

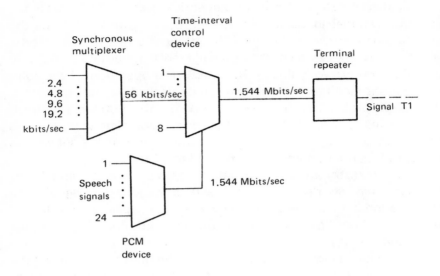

Fig. 2.17. Structure of DATAROUTE digital communications point.

the customary technical servicing of the station and administrative functions. The fourth and fifth are preprocessors that interact with the customers. Digital automatic telephone stations are now being manufactured [80], each of which can switch up to 107,000 communications channels, with a capacity of around 100 calls per second.

Thus, although analog methods and facilities are still dominant in communications, the problem of digitalization has already been resolved. The changeover to digital data transmission networks will be slow, however, since reconstruction of extremely expensive analog networks requires substantial amounts of money and time.

CHAPTER 3

TERMINAL INSTALLATIONS

With the development of computer architecture and the expansion of the sphere of computer use, an acute need has been created for methods and facilities that provide dynamic interaction with computers. The result has been the appearance of an extensive assortment of **terminals,** including displays.

As before, however, users whose work sites were at a distance from the computer were unable to communicate with it directly. Hence, **terminal installations** were created, i.e., sets of hardware and software facilities allowing users to interact with computers via telephone and telegraph networks (chiefly the former).

Despite the fact that digitization of communications methods and facilities has only just begun, the merging of computers and of communications techniques into unified installations has already been effected. Terminal installations are employed for data acquisition and transmission, reference services, and remote data processing.

3.1.
LOGICAL STRUCTURE OF REMOTE PROCESSING

Terminal installations (Fig. 3.1) consist of multiplexers, modems (M), communications channels, and terminals. One **or** more terminal installations may be connected to one computer; the number is determined by the size of the machine. Each terminal installation has a tree structure. The base of each such "tree" is a multiplexer. The branches of the tree are formed by communications channels, with terminals at its "nodes." Sequences of communications channels that connect the multiplexer to the terminals form **physical links.** For example, a physical link between the multiplexer and terminal No. 6 is created by channels a, b, and c.

In addition to terminals, terminal installations may include computers that are **emulated** by terminals. Such computers are satellite machines and are controlled by the computer at the base of the tree of the terminal installation. This computer (shown in the upper part of Fig. 3.1) is called **central** (or **main**). The **multiplexer** performs functions of interfacing the computer channel to the communications channels.

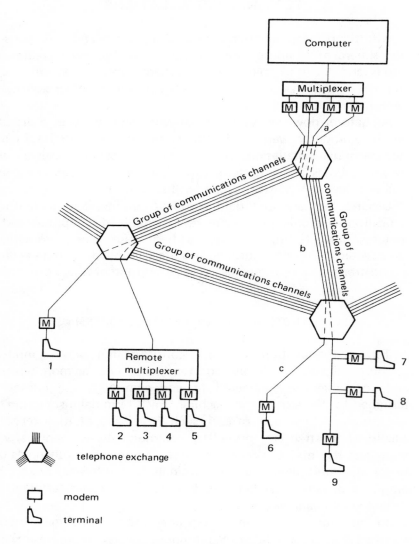

Fig. 3.1. Physical structure of terminal installation.

60

In addition to a multiplexer connected directly to the computer, terminal installations frequently employ **remote multiplexers.** They are intended for compression of information transmitted from a group of terminals (2–5) over one communications channel. Multiplexers and terminals interact with a telephone network via special converters called **modems.** These devices provide transmission of digital data over analog communications networks.

In terms of the way in which they interact with terminals, physical links can be divided into two types. The most widespread type is the **point-to-point link.** It connects only one terminal to the multiplexer. An example is provided by the physical link (Fig. 3.1) that connects terminal No. 1 to the multiplexer.

A physical point-to-point link may be **nonswitched or switched.** A nonswitched link is one that is permanently connected between the objects in question (computer, multiplexer, terminal). In contrast, a switched link is a physical link that is created between objects (by dialing up the telephone or telegraph apparatus) only during the time that data is transmitted between them. For the rest of the time, the constitutent communications channels are used for telephone conversations or telegrams, or to create other physical links between computers, multiplexers, and terminals.

Nonswitched physical links offer enhanced reliability and are never allotted to other users. However, they are much more expensive than switched ones. In turn, switched physical links are cheaper and permit one terminal (if it is so equipped) to operate with computers connected to different terminal installations.

A second type of physical link is the **multipoint link.** An example is provided by the link (Fig. 3.1) connecting the multiplexer to terminals 7–9. This type is employed in cases in which it is necessary to maximally reduce the cost of physical links.

In Unified System computers, terminals are called **user stations,** thus stressing the fact that they pertain to users. Most terminals have a block design, and each includes one or more data I/O devices, a memory device, and a control device. The most widespread **I/O devices** are typewriters, teletypes, displays, punched-tape and punch-card hardware, and printers. **External storage devices** are most frequently provided by tapes (both large and minitapes) and disks (hard and floppy).

The appearance of new methodologies for interacting with computers has made it possible to create new forms of data processing, involving the creation of electronic libraries (data and program banks) and information services.

The circle of computer users has expanded considerably. This stems from the fact that the drastic reductions in machine access times has made it feasible and economical for computers to handle the following:

— jobs requiring immediate execution (data retrieval, issuance of information, priority calculations, and so forth);
— "layered" problems, in which stages of information retrieval or computation alternate with phases in which creative involvement and decision-making of a specialist are required;
— straightforward computations which could not be feasibly handled formerly by computer centers.

The savings and convenience provided by remote data processing have been so substantial that the number of terminals that interact with computers has begun to increase rapidly.

3.2.
COMMUNICATIONS CHANNELS

Both telephone and telegraph channels are used to transmit data between computers and terminals. Telegraph channels are discrete, and therefore, they conform better to the characteristics of computer signals. Telephone channels, however, have much higher data transmission rates, running as high as **9600** bits/sec. Terminal "intelligence" increases with each passing year, and therefore, higher and higher speeds of interaction with computers are required of them. In the last few years, therefore, the use of telephone channels has become predominant, and telegraph channels now are used only for interaction with the simplest low-speed terminals.

Depending on the nature of transmission over them, physical channels are divided into three types: **simplex, half-duplex,** and **full-duplex.** Simplex channels are used in those rare instances in which data is to be transmitted only in one direction, from computer to terminal or the reverse. The most frequent type is the half-duplex channel, which provides transmission in either direction, although not simultaneously. When large amounts of data are transmitted, full-duplex channels are employed; they provide simultaneous transmission in both directions. However, they are more expensive than half-duplex channels [83], and their interfacing with computers and terminals is much more complicated.

There are two ways of transmitting data over physical channels, **synchronously** and **asynchronously**. In asynchronous transmission, data is fed to the channel one symbol at a time, each symbol containing 5—9 bits. Transmission of each symbol begins with a Start signal and ends with a Stop signal. Therefore, asynchronous transmission is frequently called **start-stop** transmission. The asynchronous method is the simplest, and is used primarily for transmission from keyboard devices that do not have storage buffers to accumulate data. However, asynchronous transmission is slow, and a considerable part of the time is spent in transmitting Start and Stop signals. Therefore, its utilization of communications channels is very inefficient.

Synchronous transmission is free of these shortcomings. However, it requires more expensive and complicated data-transmission hardware. In synchronous transmission, data are accumulated in a buffer storage, and then fed to the physical channel at a high rate in the form of a data file of specified size. To distinguish one file from another, special synchronization symbols are transmitted in between.

After reception from a physical channel, a data block is checked. If even one error is detected, the block is discarded and transmitted over the channel anew. Therefore, although in the synchronous method a data file containing an arbitrary number of bits may be transmitted in one session, its size is still limited. Assume, for example, that statistically one erroneous bit will be received every 10^9 bits. If the files contain 10^9 or more bits each, then there will be an error in each of them, and thus, transmission becomes impossible. Therefore, the maximum number of bits in a file must necessarily be limited. The more noise in the channel, the more stringent the limitation. Usually, a data file contains no more than 10,000 bits; frequently, however, the number is reduced to 1000—2000.

In accordance with the above, the asynchronous method is employed in telephone channels at low data transmission rates (up to 300 bits/sec). The synchronous method is employed for transmission at high rates.

Most terminal installations employ both transmission methods. Therefore, the multiplexers they employ have adapters that provide for both synchronous and asynchronous transmission.

3.3.

SOFTWARE STRUCTURE OF REMOTE PROCESSING

The software for terminal installations consists of two inter-related parts: **message control programs,** which provide various methods of remote access to processes executed by the computer, and **message processing programs,** which perform the necessary information and computing tasks.

The basic functions of message control programs are transmission of data between user programs in the computer and terminal operators. Among the most widespread access methods in the Unified System computers are the BTAM (Basic Telecommunications Access Method) and GTAM (General Telecommunications Access Method).

The **Basic Telecommunications Access Method** is a set of programs that provide data exchange between computers and terminals connected to them via half-duplex synchronous and asynchronous physical channels. For this the method performs the following functions:

- polling of terminals: the macro READ initiates scanning (polling) of terminals, and if any terminal wishes to transmit a message, it is accepted;
- calling of terminals: when the macro READ appears in a user program, address accessing of the necessary terminal is performed, and a message is received from it;
- transmission of messages to terminals: when the macro WRITE appears in a user program, a message is transmitted to the necessary terminal;
- error processing: error-detecting codes may be employed in transmission;
- organization of buffer storage: memory required for recording messages is allocated dynamically during operation;
- code conversion: a special subroutine performs the necessary code conversion;
- testing: diagnostics for all terminals connected to the terminal installation;

— statistics: assembly of statistical data regarding errors detected in transmission;
— initiation of transmission: the macro OPEN, which forms part of the access method, activates the physical channels; the macro CLOSE terminates a communications session.

The advantage of the Basic Telecommunications Access Method over other methods lies in its simplicity and flexibility. It requires modest amounts of main and external storage and is therefore employed in relatively small computers.

The **General Telecommunications Access Method** is a more complex set of programs and requires a great deal of computer memory. However, it can simplify the programs which the user must write in interacting with the computer.

This method executes all functions that are realized by the Basic Method. Because it employs a special language and extensive set of additional programs, however, the method also provides for the following:
— simultaneous processing of large numbers of messages;
— organization of message queues;
— message editing;
— control of the priority policy of data processing;
— when necessary, return of messages;
— alteration of the list of terminals that interact with the computer.

The message-processing programs perform an extensive set of tasks. These include, in particular, computation, data banks, information-retrieval and reference services, and so forth. The Unified System computers employ a large set of message-processing programs. Three of them are considered below.

The **TSS (Time Sharing System) program** is a complex entity that enables users to execute seven classes of functions. For this the TSS controls the following:
— data,
— user programs,
— job input,
— operating sessions,
— time sharing,
— instruction procedures,
— development of user programs.

This resource performs time sharing of the computer among a large number of users. In the background mode (with lower priority), the TSS executes user jobs. For operation, each user obtains, in a dialog mode, time slices during which he utilizes the resources of the computer. The size of a slice is chosen in such a way that, over the allotted interval, the user is able to perform a substantial part of the data processing he requires.

In addition to executing their jobs, users of the TSS program can create, translate, edit, and debug new programs in a dialog mode. The TSS aids in this process by prompting when procedural lapses occur and by detecting logical errors in programs being prepared. For this purpose, the user can operate with a large set of instructions.

In the TSS, jobs are executed and new programs are prepared using high-level algorithmic languages such as BASIC, FORTRAN, and PL/1. The modularity of the TSS and the interaction rules between modules make the program flexible and simple to adapt to particular applications.

The **KROS program** performs automatic buffering of input and output data and plans computation on the basis of specified priorities. This system provides the following:
- Increased computer performance. This is achieved through job control in the OS operating system of the Unified System, and also through the presence of special access methods for operating with input flows of jobs and output flows of results.
- Automation of operator functions. KROS automatically performs part of the actions customarily executed by operators. In particular, KROS plans and runs systems input, systems output, and initiator programs.
- Expansion of computer capabilities. KROS provides the computer with some new features, the most important of which are the following:
a) dynamic ordering of tasks on the basis of allowance for the utilization of the central processor and of the I/O devices;
b) automatic incorporation of all jobs into the input flow;
c) transmission of part of the input job flow corresponding to the program being processed, bypassing the planner of the OS of the Unified System.
- Reduction of resource requirements. As a result of dynamic allocation of external storage, less storage for buffering input

and output data sets and for setting up job queues is required when KROS is used.
- Capability of remote job input. As a result, users at great distances from KROS-equipped computers can utilize the capabilities of these computers and of the KROS system.
- Transparency. In the general case, KROS is transparent for both the OS of the Unified System and for user programs. In relation to the OS of the Unified System, this property manifests itself in the fact that the use of KROS does not entail any modifications in the computer's operating system. In relation to user programs, transparency means that most jobs prepared for execution under the control of the OS of the Unified System can be executed without any modifications. Therefore, KROS can be implemented without altering the majority of existing user programs.

It is important to note that KROS is independent of the version of the OS US. Therefore, KROS can provide the basis for developing new capabilities that do not affect the OS US and already-written user programs.

The **KAMA program** is a package intended for processing information messages transmitted by terminals, that provide remote communication between users and the data base and library of applied programs written in PL/1, COBOL, and ASSEMBLER. It performs message switching and data I/O control. KAMA furnishes users with the following:
- a single data base for all user programs;
- controlled remote access to the data base;
- priority utilization of data processing facilities;
- service facilities necessary for setting up information systems.

KAMA is based on a modular principle, is open-ended, and consists of a number of libraries. KAMA performs information retrieval against user requests and issues information. In addition, it provides the user with the capability of scanning information in cases in which the characteristics of the desired object are not precisely known. In addition, the KAMA program can perform computations.

This system is used to carry out an extensive set of operations associated with input of information into computers. It is also possible to edit the inputted information and to gather data from a large number of terminals. Special components distribute messages among all the terminals connected to the computer. The distribution algorithm is specified by a user-written program.

3.4.
THE NASDAQ TERMINAL INSTALLATION

Conversion from isolated computers to terminal installations with remote-processing hardware and software has yielded substantial savings and has made it possible to create dynamic data transmission and processing systems. It has become possible to transmit a data-processing job directly from the user site, and to reduce the information retrieval time to a few seconds. All this has entailed a rapid increase in the number and size of terminal installations. In what follows, we will consider one of the largest such installations.

The terminal installation of NASDAQ (National Association of Securities Dealers Automatic Quotation) was set up on the basis of the Univac 1108 large computer and is intended for collecting and transmitting messages regarding prices of securities [84—86]. Its structure is shown in Fig. 3.2.

The terminal installation employs a three-level hierarchy for linking terminals to the computer. The first level is made up of 1700 terminals located in different cities in the United States (not shown in Fig. 3.2). These terminals are relatively simple, and each one has a keyboard and a display.

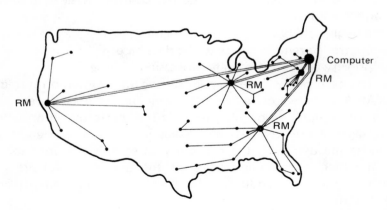

Fig. 3.2. Structure of NASDAQ terminal installation.

The second level contains the system control components (points in Fig. 3.2), each of which can accomodate up to 24 terminals. However, most securities offices have more than one terminal. The systems control components are linked to the terminals by physical channels that transmit data at 1600 bits/sec. These components perform most of the work associated with remote message control (message buffering, adjustment to a certain format, message addressing, and so forth).

The third level comprises regional remote multiplexers (RM in Fig. 3.2), located in New York, Chicago, San Francisco, and Atlanta. Each of them is based on a DDP-516 minicomputer, with a 16k main memory. A remote multiplexer combines up to 48 channels operating at 7200 bits/sec. The systems control components are connected to them. The remote multiplexers are paired and share all message flows in normal operation. When one of them malfunctions, message flows are processed by the other. Switching to the other remote multiplexer can be effected in a few minutes. The remote multiplexers poll the systems control components, store messages, control their flows, perform multiplexing functions, and handle a number of other communications tasks.

A Univac 1108 computer (Fig. 3.2), located in Trumbull, Connecticut, is connected to each remote-multiplexer site by two leased full-duplex physical links that operate at 50,000 bits/sec. In the event one link breaks down, the other is capable of handling all the necessary information. For reliability, the links are even separated geographically. The central computer is a large data bank. It receives requests from terminals, retrieves and updates information, and provides answers.

CHAPTER 4

STRUCTURE OF COMPUTER NETWORKS

Remote data processing offers such convenient ways of interacting with computers that data exchange has been increasing rapidly; at present it is rising at an annual rate of 18% [87]. It is anticipated [88] that the demand for data transmission hardware (reckoned in terms of cost) will continue to increase by 30% per year. As for production, in quantitative terms, it will increase to an even greater extent as a result of reductions in cost.

4.1.
MULTICOMPUTER SYSTEMS

The use of advanced computer technology has made it possible to handle extremely large volumes of information, both already available (books, reports, business documents, patents, articles, and so forth) and that obtained in the process of research and of operation of sectors of the national economy. Current production processes require high rates of data processing, convenient forms of storage and transmission, dynamic modes of access, data retrieval, mathematical calculations, and logical manipulations.

The increasingly complex management of the national economy makes necessary the participation of large teams located in different institutions, cities, or even countries. Such activity requires rapid and convenient information exchange and close interaction in the management process.

Moreover, analysis of the work performed reveals that the complexity of the tasks to be solved is inversely proportional to their number. Therefore, most tasks can be handled by small computers. In acquiring computers, however, users frequently choose ones capable of handling virtually all the tasks at hand, including complex ones. As a result, the computers are not heavily loaded and are frequently idle. Using large computers to handle simple tasks is inefficient. The ideal solution of this problem involves furnishing users with the capability of dynamically handling simple tasks on small computers and complex tasks on large ones.

It is not possible to create all necessary information, reference, and retrieval services using one computer. Nor is it possible to have large numbers of necessary algorithmic languages, mathematical models, and programs. To overcome these difficulties, several computers should be available, each specialized for certain tasks: information and reference services, computation, user dialog, and so forth.

The dynamic nature of the national economy and the appearance of information and dialog remote-processing installations require a high degree of reliability of data processing. It is not possible to ensure such reliability with only one computer, since even a short-term malfunction halts the entire process. Therefore, it is necessary to have the capability of executing jobs on more than one computer.

In view of the above, it is necessary to convert from using individual computers to data processing with **multicomputer systems** distributed over extensive territories. In turn, the appearance of a broad spectrum of diverse macro-, mini-, and microcomputers, the creation of diverse storage devices, and the development of data transmission networks are making it possible to create these systems, and to ensure that they meet the necessary requirements of economy, dynamicity, and reliability of data processing. This processing may involve large number of computers at great distances from one another, interconnected by means of a variety of data links.

The use of multicomputer systems for data acquisition, storage, transmission, processing, and output marks a qualitative advance in the development of computer science, one that is having a marked impact on the development of science and of various sectors of the national economy.

There are three types of multicomputer systems:
— terminal installations;
— computer installations;
— computer networks.

In **terminal installations**, satellite computers emulate the terminals of a central (main) computer. Therefore, terminal installations can only provisionally be referred to as "multicomputer". Even this manner of combining computers, however, has made it possible to resolve a number of important problems associated with remote data processing.

In a **computer installation,** terminal emulation is no longer required for machines to communicate. However, the installation incorporates only a group of side-by-side computers that jointly execute a unified information and computing process. Computer installations, therefore, are essentially large computers.

Computer networks, a new form of multicomputer system, satisfy all the requirements of distributed data processing involving large numbers of interconnected computers located as needed anywhere throughout the world.

A basic component of a computer network is a **system** capable of performing data processing and of executing functions described by protocols. A system consists of one or more computers, their software, peripherals, (possibly) terminals, and also human operators. Systems are divided into user and communications systems. **User** (or **host**) **systems** are the principal ones, since they furnish or use information and computing resources. **Communications systems** are auxiliary, since they are intended for switching and routing of information transmitted between user systems.

A **computer network** is an association of user systems that interact via a communications network. Figure 4.1 shows an example of a computer network with six user systems (1—6). The task of the **communications network** is to transmit data between all user systems. The points of connection of user systems to this network are customarily called **interface points of the communications network.**

There are many types of communications systems; Fig. 4.2 shows three basic ones. The arrangement in Fig. 4.2a characterizes a **cellular communications network.** It consists of d communications systems connected by data trunk (or "backbone") channels. For $d = 1$, the network degenerates into a **star-shaped** network. User systems are connected to the interface points of the communications network (Fig. 4.1). When the number of communications systems is large, cellular networks are employed to create large computer networks. For $d = 1-3$, a cellular network can be used as a basis for a modest network intended for an institution or small enterprise.

A **ring-shaped communications network** (Fig. 4.2b) consists of simple **nodes** combined into a ring by backbone channels. As a rule, one user system is connected to each node. Therefore, the address of the node is the address of this system. Ring-shaped communications networks are employed in small computer networks.

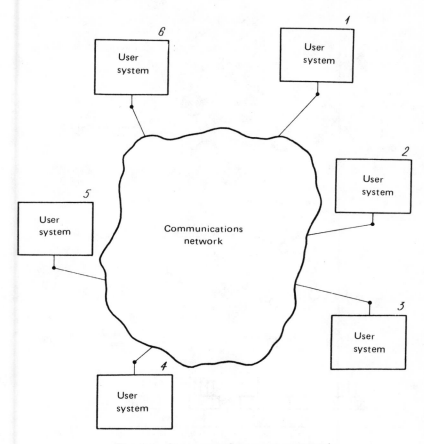

Fig. 4.1. Structure of computer network.

Figure 4.2c shows the structure of a **broadcast-channel com-munications network.** Here special devices, called **access units,** ensure connection of user systems to a common trunk, called a **broadcast channel.** When a radio channel is employed, a broadcast-channel network can link user systems distributed over a large area. When wire communications are employed, the length of the channel rarely exceeds 2 km.

A **computer network** differs from a terminal installation both quantitatively and qualitatively, since it is determined by the fol-lowing basic characteristics:

— large number of interacting computers that perform functions of data acquisition, storage, transmission, processing, and output;

73

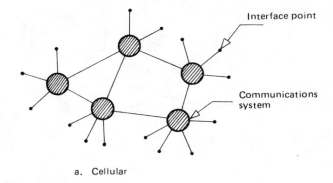

a. Cellular

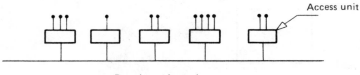

b. Ring-shaped

c. Broadcast-channel

Fig. 4.2. Types of communications networks.

— exceptionally large computational capacity;
— distributed data processing;
— reliable and flexible communication between user and computational capabilities;
— symmetrical interface of data exchange between computers;
— quasi-independent control levels;
— ease of expansion to any desired power and geographical extension.

In terms of mode of operation, computer networks can be subdivided into three classes: circuit, message, and packet switching networks. Because of their simplicity, **circuit switching networks** were the first to appear. We will illustrate the specific features of circuit switching networks using the example shown in Fig. 4.3. To transmit data between user systems II and VI, it is necessary to form a direct connection incorporating backbone channels of one of the following four groups: (1, 2, 4, 6), (1, 2, 5, 7), (3, 4, 6), or (3, 5, 7). The connection formed by these channels should remain unaltered at least over the entire interaction time of the user systems.

The ideas embodied in circuit switching networks are fairly simple and corresponded to the manner of operation of telephone networks. Therefore, they were rapidly implemented. However, an important negative feature of the circuit switching method soon became apparent: it is necessary to simultaneously employ a large number of backbone channels between interacting systems. For example, to transmit data from Moscow to Vladivostok, it is necessary to wait while the circuits between these cities are successively connected. As a result, the time required to establish connection between user systems is relatively large, while the channel utilization efficiency is low.

As the territory of network increases, these difficulties are rapidly exacerbated and become a hindrance for efficient interaction of systems. This led to a search for new solutions, with the subsequent development of **message switching networks** [89].

We will illustrate the message switching method using the same example shown in Fig. 4.3. Here information is transmitted between user systems in large batches (units), called **messages.** Therefore, to transmit data from user system II (Fig. 4.3) to user system VI, there is no longer a need to establish a direct connection between them (i.e., simultaneous use of all backbone channels of one of the groups (1, 2, 4, 6), (1, 2, 5, 7), (3, 4, 6), or (3, 5, 7)). Data transmission can begin immediately after one of the first channels (1 or 3) is available. Then the data will be transmitted through the network as other channels are successively freed up, and thus the data moves closer to system VI. Transmission is completed once one of the last channels (6 or 7) is freed up. The message switching method has greatly increased the operating efficiency of communications networks and has opened up prospects for creating large computer networks.

As already noted, because of channel noise, data units of modest size are transmitted over them. When the message switching method is employed, therefore, each (user or communications) source system breaks down the message into small batches, called

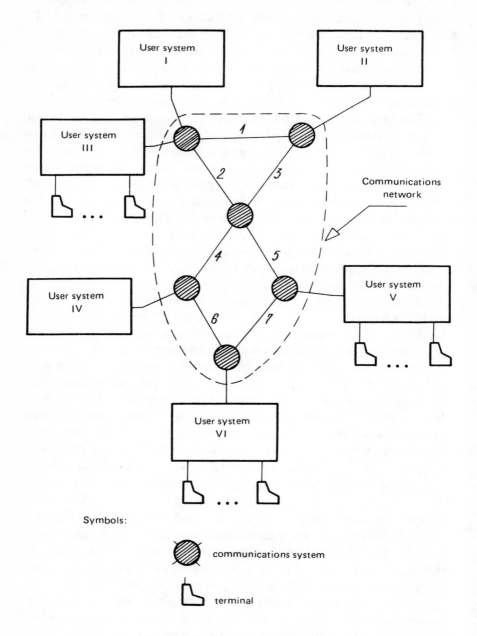

Fig. 4.3. Cellular computer network.

frames, prior to transmission. Frames are transmitted over the channel to an adjacent (user or communications) addressee system, and the transmitted message is assembled (reconstructed) from the frames.

Message switching required the creation of communications computers capable of storing and processing considerable numbers of messages. Therefore, it proved desirable to organize for users, in the same computers, capabilities for prolonged message storage, preparation of copies, and dissemination of the copies to the requisite addresses. As a result, communications computers increased considerably in size, and began to acquire large memories; they came to be known as **message switching centers.**

Operation of message switching networks revealed more than their advantages as compared to circuit switching networks. A major shortcoming quickly became apparent, namely, their low data tranmission rate, which rendered dialog between user systems impossible. This was due to the need for assembly and disassembly of all messages in each communications system. Attempts to find ways of eliminating this shortcoming led to the appearance of communications networks of a new type, whose operation is based on rapid tranmission of packets in the communications network. These networks have become known as **packet switching networks.**

In message switching networks, messages may be arbitrarily long. For message tranmission, therefore, communications computers employed large and, hence, slow-acting memories. In packet switching networks, in contrast, long messages are broken down into short packets, which are reassembled into messages only at their destinations.

The so-called hot-potato method is employed in packet transmission; a packet arriving at a communications system via a backbone channel is switched as rapidly as possible to another channel of the network. This method can greatly curtail the amount of storage required in communications systems. External storage devices became unnecessary, and the data transmission rate increased substantially. It was then necessary to avoid prolonged storage or copying of messages in communications systems. As a result of conversion to packet switching, communications systems became much smaller in size and the use of modest highly reliable mini- and microcomputers became feasible.

Packet switching networks possess a number of major advantages, some of which are listed below.

Rapid connection. In a circuit switching network, long waits for connection are necessary. Packet switching networks accept data immediately.

Low error level. In a circuit switching network, an error appears every 10 million bits on average. In packet switching networks, as a result of special information-checking methods, an error appears roughly every 1000 billion bits [90].

Reliability. In circuit switching networks, the down time amounts to 1–2% of the operating time [90]; the time required to recover the network exceeds 1 hr in half the cases. In a packet switching network there are always at least two routes over different trunks between two user systems, so that the network is highly reliable. In addition, in most packet switching networks there are back-ups for the communications computers. As a result, malfunctioning of two computers in a communications system should occur no more frequently than once per 100 years [90].

Efficient network utilization. The cost of computer facilities is dropping more rapidly than that of communications channels. For example, in the United States, the annual figures are 36 and 11%, respectively [90]. Data transmission in networks is characterized by large numbers of short data bursts, between which there are considerable pauses. As a result, a circuit switching network is usually only 1–10% loaded [90]. Packet switching networks, in contrast, may have a high load figure and may respond to short-term bursts by reducing the packet transmission rate.

In addition, the fact that the circuit switching method provides two user systems with a direct link yields a number of advantages that are of particular importance for telemetry and remote control of various technological processes. When such a link exists, the network is said to be transparent in time (it does not distort the time dependence of the measured parameters and control signals); moreover, it reliably ensures the frequency passband of the data. Speech transmission also becomes simpler.

Direct linkage furnished to two user systems is more efficient, the more intensive the load during communications sessions. Therefore, when the amount of data to be transmitted over a session is small, the use of direct connection becomes inefficient.

Recently, as a result of the development of a large assortment of integrated circuitry (including analog-to-digital and digital-to-analog converters) and the development of data transmission techniques, various forms of information (computer data, speech, television) have begun to be transmitted in the same digital form. As a result, it has become possible to create comprehensive communications networks that perform both packet and circuit switching. Such networks have come to be known as **integrated** networks.

Integrated communications networks employ high-speed backbone channels, each of which provides transportation of both packets and data transmitted via direct connections. To support these functions, the necessary set of subchannels is allotted in each backbone channel. This can be done in two ways. **Frequency multiplexing** makes it possible to isolate q frequency ranges (bands) in the channel, and thus to create q subchannels. Similarly, in **time multiplexing,** real time is divided into q small successive segments. When q users are successively furnished with one segment each, it is also possible to set up q subchannels.

Frequency multiplexing requires allocation of guard bands between the frequency ranges of the channel; distortion caused by nonlinearity of expensive filters may appear. In integrated networks, therefore, time multiplexing of channels is more frequent than frequency multiplexing. Moreover, with time multiplexing in communications systems it is possible to convert the transmission rates of data supplied by computers and synchronous or asynchronous terminals.

Integrated networks ensure simultaneous execution of both packet switching and circuit switching. It should be pointed out, however, that circuit switching as performed in this network differs substantially from the circuit switching that was described above. In this case the creation of a direct connection does not involve allocation of a real circuit connecting two user systems, but in furnishing these systems with communications facilities that permit interaction such that the data transmission time between them is always constant and independent of the load of the communications network. In contrast, in the case of packet switching the information transit time between two interacting user systems depends on the loading intensity of the communications systems.

The nature of operation of direct connections in integrated networks is also unusual. Let us consider, for example, speech transmission in this case. As we know, speech is characterized by large numbers of pauses between individual words and sentences. Although speech is transmitted over a direct link, the pauses it contains can be used for packet transmission. For this, the direct connection is eliminated during pauses and is restored only when the next work appears. As a result, a conversation takes place over a direct link that consists of sequences of different subchannels at different points in time. Naturally, to ensure this mode of operation, direct links have priority in obtaining subchannels. The remaining free subchannels are provided for packet switching.

In integrated networks, therefore, the packet and circuit switching modes are implemented through a complex priority policy of allocation of subchannels, and, from the user's standpoint, these modes differ chiefly in terms of whether or not the transmission time from one user system to another system is constant. The primary information flow is transmitted in the form of packets; when necessary, pairs of user systems are furnished with direct links.

Integrated communications networks provide efficient utilization of all communications facilities. However, methods of rational design and operation of these networks are still in the research stage.

Although they appeared only very recently, packet switching networks have already become widespread. They are used to transmit documents and telegrams, as well as computer data. Speech transmission is also being initiated [91]. The advantages offered by packet switching are so great that new networks are being built on this basis. In the forthcoming chapters, therefore, we will consider only packet switching networks.

To achieve efficient dynamic utilization of computer hardware and software, computer networks must meet a large number of requirements. The principal ones are as follows:
— flexible connections between processes (user programs) performed by different user systems;
— access to peripheral devices of any user systems;
— interaction with data stored in any user systems;
— use of various types of data transmission channels connecting user systems to the communications network (synchronous or asynchronous serial channels, and also parallel ones);
— possibility of incorporation of user systems of various types and sizes, employing different operating systems.

Present-day computer networks are based on already existing terminal installations and self-contained computers. When they are combined into networks, therefore, it is necessary to reduce the resultant redundancy of the extant simulation, computing, and information systems through specialization of computers. This makes possible substantial increases in computer operating efficiency.

The creation of computer networks is of exceptional economic importance, since it makes possible the integration of the data processing industry. Conversion to the use of computer networks yields many major advantages, in particular the following:

- high degree of reliability of data processing;
- shared use of computer facilities and software;
- achievement of computer powers that cannot be realized in individual computers;
- high efficiency of computer utilization;
- increased computer efficiency as a result of structural and software specialization;
- efficient utilization of relatively expensive memory;
- ease of providing a broad spectrum of information activity (computation, information retrieval, dialog, remote processing, and so forth);
- ease of development and modification of data processing technology;
- creation of distributed data banks;
- reduction in the cost of data processing.

Computer networks can provide users with an extensive set of services, including the following in particular:

a. Information systems:
- data and program banks,
- reference services,
- retrieval installations,
- file exchange;

b. Dialog systems:
- debugging of programs,
- services for developing new technology,
- instruction services,
- processing of graphic information;

c. Logical and computing systems:
- mathematical calculations,
- interaction with models,
- logical data manipulations;

d. **Electronic mail, telephone, and telegraph:**
— exchange of documents, drawings, graphic matter,
— digital speech transmission,
— remote conferences and meetings,
— collaborative efforts by teams at great distances from one another,
— mass information services (transmission of newspaper and journal pages), news, political and economic surveys, and so forth,
— financial and commercial operations.

A feature that is gaining particular importance in computer networks is information systems that allow users at terminals to gain access to knowledge and data accumulated by large teams in different cities or even in different countries.

An example can be provided by a system containing information on power engineering: reference data in the field; results of research conducted over many years by various scientific organizations; applied technical developments on energy processes, new machines, and equipment; patents in the field of power engineering; product inventories for plants that manufacture power-engineering equipment, and descriptions of this equipment; characteristics of existing power plants and energy systems; geography of fuel and its characteristics.

An example of a network intended for serving the public is the Viewdata network, created in England by the Post Office Corporation [92, 93]. In this case a terminal is a group of equipment including a television set, telephone, alphanumeric keyboard, and network interfacing device. The terminal can be used to access any page of the London Information Bureau and can solve mathematical problems. Requests to the network are entered via the keyboard, while answers are displayed on the television screen. The first phase of the network employs 500 terminals, but it is planned to increase the number to 300,000. The information bureau provides information on the educational system, job opportunities, sightseeing routes, and so forth. In terms of cost, output of 20 pages of text is equivalent to a one-minute telephone conversation.

Classification of computer networks in terms of geographical extension is widespread. This criterion can be employed to distinguish three types of networks. A **local network** is one whose user systems are at short distances from one another. Usually local networks cover one or a few adjacent buildings.

A **wide-area network** is one that encompasses systems at considerable distances from one another. The systems may be spread out over a city, region, or entire country.

The third type is a **global network,** which unites user systems in different countries or on different continents. Global networks are generally implemented in the form of **satellite** networks. The advantage of this is that satellites "see" enormous areas. If a receiver/transmitter is installed on the satellite, large numbers of systems may be connected via a single radio channel.

Combination of global, wide-area, and local networks makes it possible to create **multinetwork systems** that offer economically feasible processing of huge data sets. Local networks are the base elements of these systems.

A very important feature of any type of computer network is the possibility of distributed data processing, performed by different user systems. This ensures the possibility of obtaining virtually limitless information resources, as well as highly reliable multipurpose data processing.

To gain a more thorough understanding of the essential features of computer networks, it is necessary to analyze their logical, physical, and software structures. The interrelationship of these structures determines the **computer network architecture.** We will examine the architecture using the example of a computer network based on a cellular communications network. The analysis and resultant conclusions can readily be transferred to ring-shaped or broadcast-channel computer networks.

4.2.
LOGICAL STRUCTURE OF COMPUTER NETWORK

Analysis of data transmission and handling processes performed by a computer network requires that these processes be divided into specific groups and that the interrelations and interactions of these groups be considered. The result is the **logical structure of the computer network,** whose elements are groups of functions that perform certain tasks associated with the operation of the network.

In Chapter 1 we considered general characteristics pertaining to all systems comprising any computer network. For the purpose of ensuring efficient network operation, however, it is best to specialize the component subsystems for execution of certain tasks.

Depending on the tasks they perform, user systems are customarily divided into four basic groups:
- host;
- terminal;
- administrative;
- interface.

Host systems furnish network resources, while **terminal systems** use them. As for **administrative, interface, and communications systems,** they perform functions that support the operation of the host and terminal systems. Table 4.1 shows the tasks implemented by the types of systems we have considered. The number of terminals in a terminal system is determined by the size and number of the computers in the system. A terminal system, therefore, may have from one terminal to many hundreds of them.

As a result of systems specialization, the logical structure of a computer network assumes the form shown in Fig. 4.4. The

TABLE 4.1.

No.	Name of system	Tasks performed by system
1.	Host	Provision of information resources: storage of data files; information retrieval; computation; simulation of processes, phenomena, and entities; software development.
2.	Terminal	Consumption of information resources: control of terminal operation, job setup, interfacing with technological processes for measurement and control.
3.	Administrative	Administrative management of information and computing network (assembly of statistics, logout, reports, fault diagnostics, information on network operation, and so forth), or part of network.
4.	Communications	Routing, switching, and control of flows of information transmitted between host, terminal, or administrative systems.
5.	Interface	Interfacing of networks and host and terminal systems of different types.

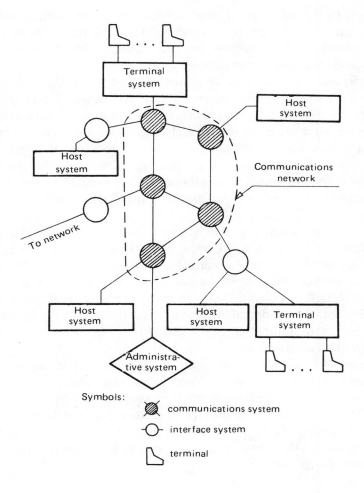

Fig. 4.4. Logical structure of computer network.

number of subsystems of different types is determined by the tasks and size of the network. As for administrative subsystems, there may be more than one of them in a computer network. In this case their duties are split (e.g., control of different regions of the network), and one of the administrative subsystems is designated as the principal one.

4.3.
PHYSICAL STRUCTURE OF COMPUTER NETWORK

Each of the subsystems of a computer network is implemented in computers or in special hardware. The optimal allocation of logical functions of the system in these technical devices determines the **physical structure of the network.**

The nature of the physical structure depends on the task to be handled. For example, in some cases a computer is one of the elements of this structure. In other cases, the same computer is represented by a set of elements such as a processor, main memory device, channel, printer, and so forth. Then problems of interaction of systems in the network are considered. Therefore, the physical structure considers computers, physical links, and, when necessary, data-transmission hardware (adapters, controllers, modems, and so forth).

In principle, a subsystem may be implemented in one computer. Most frequently, however, in order to increase the efficiency, the system is placed in several computers that are specialized for execution of certain functions. For example, it is advisable to place transport functions (layers 1—4) in one computer of modest size. Execution of the principal information and computing functions (layers 5—7 and application processes) is best entrusted to another, more powerful machine.

Figure 4.5 shows an example of the physical structure of a computer network. Here every communications subsystem is represented by a shaded circle with small rectangles next to this circuit. It consists of five microcomputers (a central one and four channel microcomputers). Each of the user systems 1—4 is implemented in two computers. User system 5 incorporates four computers, while user system 6 has six.

4.4.
SOFTWARE STRUCTURE OF COMPUTER NETWORK

Analysis of the software structure makes it possible to consider the hierarchy of **network software.** The interrelated elements of this structure are the programs implemented in the computers or hardware (modems, adapters, controllers).

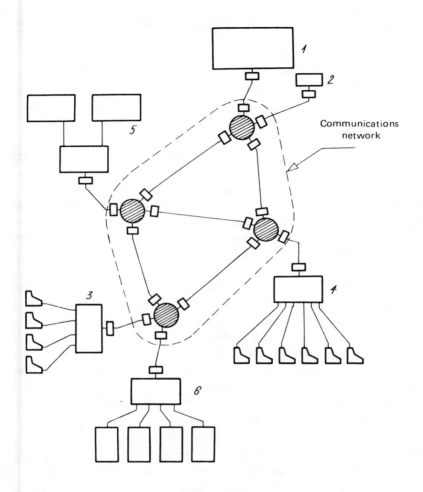

Communications network

Fig. 4.5. Physical structure of computer network

The basic elements in the network software structure are those that perform information and computing tasks for users (computations, implementation of data banks, dialog information systems, and so forth). These elements are applied processes (user programs) and the interrelated application-process, presentation, and session control programs. The ensemble of these elements is customarily called a **process.** The basic task of the computer network is to create interacting processes implemented by different user systems. Interaction of these processes is effected by transmission of data arrays (or units) to one another.

Fig. 4.6 shows the interaction of two directly linked processes. When it becomes necessary to transmit data, application process A (user program) issues a data unit. The application-process, presentation, and session control modules add a header to this unit, forming a **message**. Information is entered into the message header so that messages can be distinguished and the necessary addresses specified.

Messages are of arbitrary length. For this reason, prior to transmission they are customarily divided into parts, or **blocks**, whose maximum size is restricted to a certain value. As a result, each message yields K, $K \geqslant 1$, blocks. These blocks are transmitted (see Fig. 4.6) to process E. Here the session, presentation, and application-process control modules assemble the message from the K blocks, analyze it, and then discard the header. The resultant data unit is transmitted to process E (user program).

This (direct) interaction of processes is possible only in those rare instances in which the processes are in the same system. Usually processes in a network are in different systems and interact via data transmission hardware and channels, and frequently communications and interface systems as well.

In this case, a new element of the software structure of the network must be added to each process (Fig. 4.7), namely, a **transmission control program** for managing data transmission from one process to another. A point located between a process and transmission control program is usually called a **port**.

In the case under consideration, the structure of the transmitted data unit is more complicated, and the file, called a **fragment**, has two headers (see Fig. 4.6): a process header and a transmission header. The body of the block and its header (process header) are the same as in Fig. 4.6. The second header (fragment or transmission header) contains control data that describe the transmission: type of data unit transmitted from one process to another, addresses of initial and final processes (more precisely, addresses of ports), and identifier (name) of the unit.

In this case, information is transmitted from process A to process E as follows. When it becomes necessary for an application process (user program) to transmit data, process A issues a block (see Fig. 4.7) which is transmitted to the transmission control program. This program adds a transmission header to it, and the resultant fragment is directed to the transmission control program.

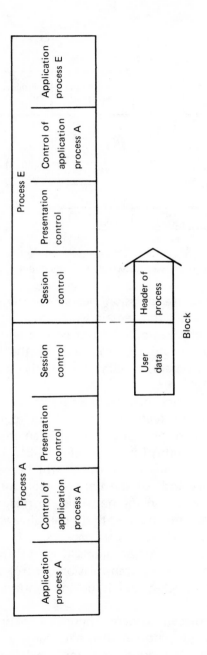

Fig. 4.6. Interaction of two processes.

89

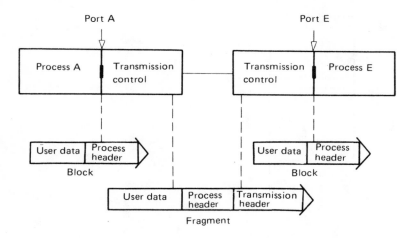

Fig. 4.7. Linkage of processes in two different systems.

This program picks off the transmission header in the fragment and reads it, and then transfers the remainder of the data unit to process E. Here messages are assembled from blocks and the user data they contain are transmitted (see Fig. 4.6) to the addressed application process (user program). Data is similarly transmitted from process E to process A.

In a computer network, one process may be linked to several processes executed in different systems. In addition to the transmission control program, therefore, yet another element is introduced, namely, the **network control** program (Fig. 4.8). Lines that connect network control programs in networks will be called **network channels**. The primary task of the network control program is to organize routing of packets in the network. Correspondingly, a packet header is added to the fragment. It contains all control information needed to switch and route packets. The resultant packet is transferred to the group of programs (Fig. 4.9) associated with process E. Here the network and transmission control programs, by using the corresponding packet and fragment headers, transfer the received block to process E.

Between any pair of adjacent systems there is a channel whose operation is controlled by yet another element, namely, the **data link control** program. The corresponding channel will be called a

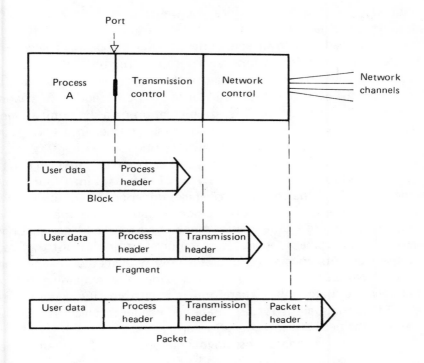

Fig. 4.8. Packet make-up procedure.

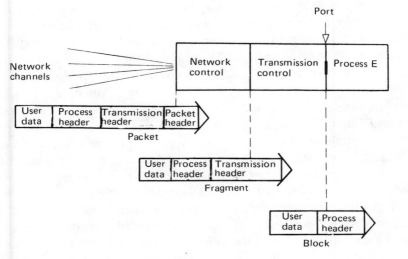

Fig. 4.9. Packet reception procedure.

data link (or channel). Before transmission of a packet over the data link, the data link control program "frames" it (Fig. 4.10) with a channel header in front and a channel trailer in back. The channel header contains information needed to control the data link. The channel trailer includes information for checking the packet after transmission over the data link. The result of adding a channel header and trailer to a packet is the creation of a data unit called a **frame.** Frames in a data link follow one another in a continuous stream. They are separated by control symbols called **flags.**

The process of setting up a frame can be illustrated (Fig. 4.11) by a procedure of successive stuffing of user data into four "envelopes." Each of the four control stages under consideration involves stuffing of the user data or envelope obtained from the preceding program structure element into a new envelope and designating a new address (header) on it. It is important to point out that each of the elements considered operates only with its own header (and trailer), without considering (or analyzing) the remaining part of the received data unit. Therefore, it is customarily said that this element is transparent for user data and header received from higher levels of the network software structure.

The reverse operations, involving opening of the envelopes, are performed at the receiving end. Each of the software structure elements reads the header (and trailer) on the envelope, opens it, and transmits the contents upward to the next element.

The above analysis of software structure does not take account of the need for connecting each pair of systems by a physical link, for maintaining this connection during sessions, and for eliminating the connection after each session. These operations are performed by the element known as the **physical link control** program.

Thus, we have a layered software structure of the network, consisting of elements on seven layers. Table 4.2 shows the principal tasks and functions that are executed by these layers. Layers 1 and 2 define functions that support transmission between two systems connected by a data link. Software layers 3 and 4 effect transmission from a port at one user system to a port at another user system. Layers 5—7 describe interaction of user-system processes.

The eight interconnected software structure elements of the network that we have considered are shown in Fig. 4.12. In the general case, there are several application processes at the uppermost

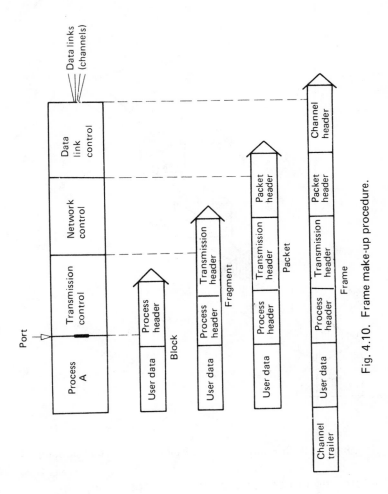

Fig. 4.10. Frame make-up procedure.

level, rather than just one (as considered above). Moreover, a process may have more than one port. Ports are interconnected by a logical arrangement called a **transport network.**

It should be pointed out that a computer network also includes a special application process (administrative process) that manages the network. Its functions include the following:

— correction of programs that provide routing procedures;
— acquisition of data on network operation;

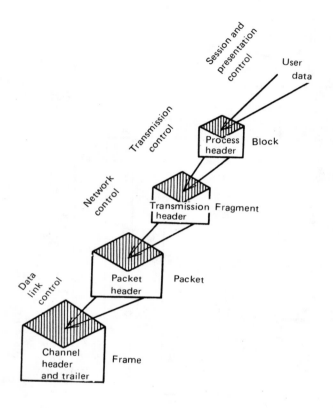

Fig. 4.11. Structure of four-envelope information packing.

— provision of statistics on network operation;
— diagnostics of network faults;
— management of network resources.

Routing programs are modified when a data link malfunctions or when the configuration of the transport network is altered (creation of new links or elimination of old ones).

The standards and characteristics of computer networks and systems may differ substantially from one another. In such cases, programs that convert standards and characteristics (change of addresses, formats, control symbols, and so forth) are used to provide

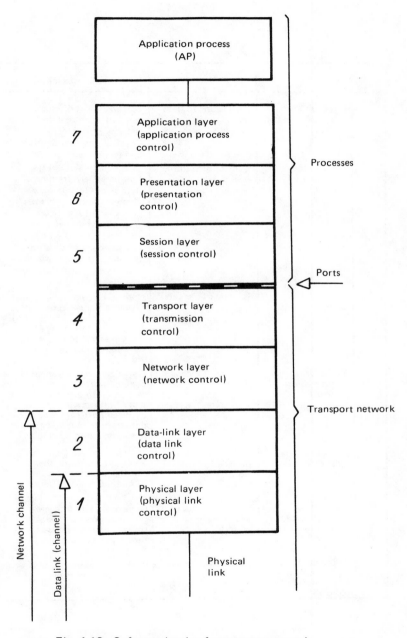

Fig. 4.12. Software levels of computer network.

TABLE 4.2.

Layer	Name	Primary task	Functions executed
1	Physical layer (physical link control)	Interfacing to data link	Establishment of connection with physical link; maintenance of connection with physical link; termination of connection with physical link
2	Data-link layer (data link control)	Control of transmission over data link channel	Checking of state of data link (channel); framing of data arrays by auxiliary channel control symbols; checking of data to be transmitted over data link channel; assurance of transparency of data link channel; control of frame transmission over data link channel
3	Network layer (network control)	Routing of packets	Control of communications resources; organization of packet routing (if necessary); framing of data units by auxiliary transmission symbols over communications network
4	Transport layer (transmission control)	Control of logical channel	Organization of permanent or temporary logical channels between processes; control of information flows between ports; framing of data units by auxiliary request or response symbols
5	Session layer (session control)	Support of communications sessions	Interfacing with transport layer; organization, maintenance, and termination of communications sessions
6	Presentation layer (presentation control)	Representation of data in necessary form	Generation and interpretation of process interaction commands; presentation of data to user program
7	Application layer (application process control)	User program control	Control of computation, information-retrieval, or reference services

interaction between networks, or between a network and a user system. Such programs are called **translators.**

The layered nature of the network software structure ensures that programs are relatively independent of one another. Therefore, the establishment of clear-cut interfacing rules for adjacent programs makes it possible to alter (i.e., improve) one of the software layers without affecting the remaining ones.

The greater the number of layers into which the network software is divided, the easier it is to improve it by replacing only one of the layers. As the number of layers increases, however, the entire software becomes more complicated, since problems of standardizing the interfaces to adjacent layers must be resolved each time a separate layer is created. Therefore, it is necessary to choose an optimal number of layers that provides both reasonable simplicity of the software and a substantial number of independent layers.

By placing programs in computers and data communication hardware, it is possible to consider the interrelationship of the software and hardware structure elements of the network. Figure 4.13 shows an example of this analysis. Here the software structure layers have the same numbering as in Fig. 4.12. For simplicity, all the systems are single-machine systems. The host, terminal, and administrative systems include all the function layers shown in Fig. 4.12. In contrast, the communications system contains only the three lowest layers that implement communications functions.

Finally, the interface system has the most complex software structure, supporting communication between different kinds of networks or machines. In effect, it consists of two sets of software modules with a common special process. Figure 4.13 shows its structure for the case in which systems are inserted between network. The software of the interface system between the host and communications systems has a similar structure (Fig. 4.14).

It should be pointed out that in Figs. 4.13 and 4.14, as in actual computer networks, physical link control is implemented not in the computers but in the data communication hardware connected to them. Data link control programs are more and more frequently implemented in this hardware as well. In Figs. 4.13 and 4.14, however, they are implemented by computers.

As already noted, there are ports between transmission control levels and processes. A line between ports of different host or terminal systems is customarily called a **logical session channel.** For

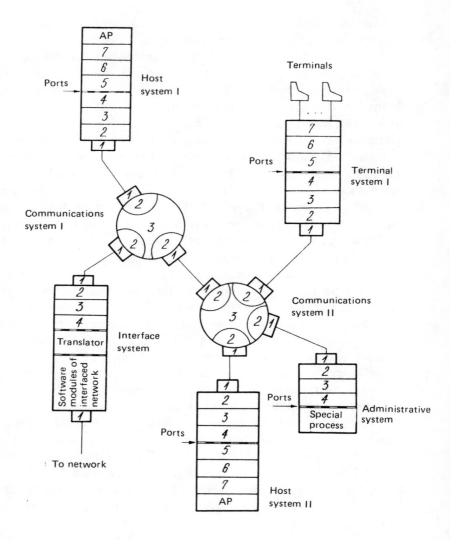

Fig. 4.13. Allocation of programs in network hardware.

instance, Fig. 4.15 shows a logical session channel that connects process H in host system I with process E in host system II. This channel runs from a port in host system I through communications systems and data links to a port in host system II. It should be borne in mind that during data transmission, depending on the load and state of the transport network, a logical channel may follow not only

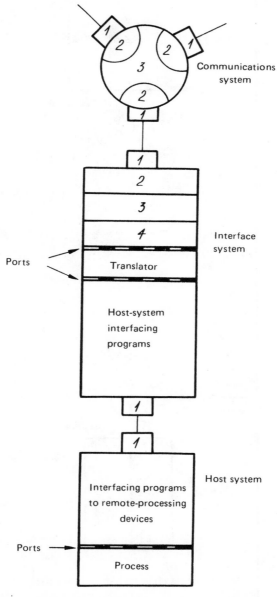

Fig. 4.14. Software structure of interface system connecting host and communications systems.

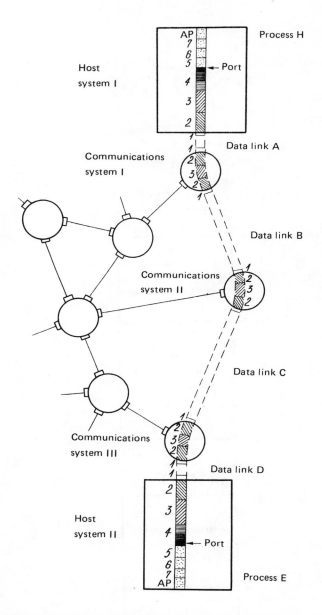

Fig. 4.15. Session logical channel between processes H and E.

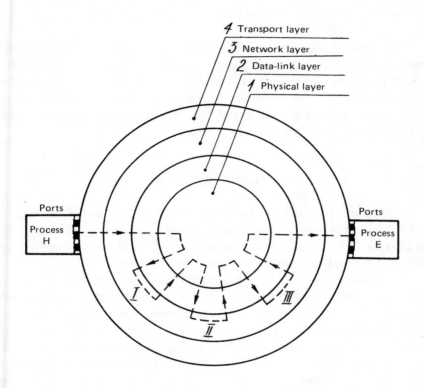

Fig. 4.16. Information passage through layers of software structure upon transit over session logical channel.

the route shown in Fig. 4.15, but also other routes that are possible in the network.

Data transmission from one port (process) to another involves multiple passage through different levels of the software structure of the network. For example, when information is transmitted over a logical session channel from process H to process E, the layers are traversed as shown in Fig. 4.16. Initially, information from process H passes through the software structure layers of host system I (dashed line). Then in each of the three communications systems

(I, II, and III), it is transmitted through three layers, first in one direction, then in the other. Finally, after passing through the layers in host system II, the information reaches process E. Information in the network is similarly transmitted over any other logical channel.

A network may simultaneously contain (either permanently or temporarily) large numbers of different logical channels. A temporary logical channel is set up between a pair of processes for the duration of the time required to exchange data. After the communications session is completed (i.e., the necessary data are transmitted), the logical channel is eliminated.

4.5.
NETWORK PROTOCOLS

Computer networks embody two types of data transmission control. The first is related to ensuring interaction of processes executed by user systems (data banks, retrieval or computing services, and so forth). This form of control will be called **primary.**

The second form of control is intended for gathering information on the state of the network and its elements, as well as on incorporation or elimination of new systems and physical connections, for diagnostics, assembly of statistics, reports on network operation, and so forth. This type of control will be called **administrative.**

In accordance with the seven layers of the Reference Model of Open Systems Interconnection, a seven-layer hierarchy of network protocols is introduced. In the case of primary control, the interaction of user systems is governed by the scheme shown in Fig. 4.17. Primary control is related to transmission of data between application processes of user systems. The upper layers of the communications systems (4—7) are not involved in this control, and therefore they are not shown in Fig. 4.17.

It is easy to see that protocols are divided into two groups. The first group is made up of the protocols of the physical, data-link, and network layers. They govern the interaction of pairs of any types of adjacent systems with physical connections. There are two such pairs in Fig. 4.17, namely, user system A/communications system and communications system/user system B.

The second group is made up of the protocols of the transport, session, presentation, and application levels. They govern interac-

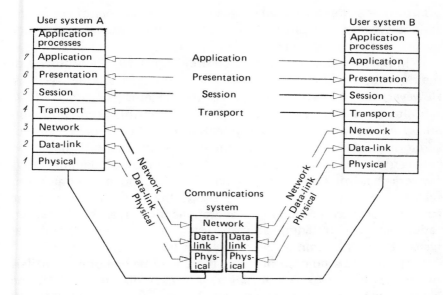

Fig. 4.17. Host-computer interaction protocols with primary control.

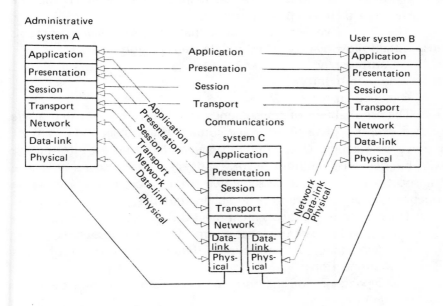

Fig. 4.18. Administrative management protocols.

tion of user systems that are connected via any number of communications systems and physical connections (for simplicity, only one communications system is shown in Fig. 4.17).

In the case of administrative control (Fig. 4.18) the protocols of the three lower layers also govern the interaction of adjacent systems. However, the points of application of the higher-level protocols (4-7) are altered in this case. With primary control, these protocols linked arbitrary pairs of user systems (Fig. 4.17). For the case of administrative control, however, these protocols support interaction between a user system specialized for purposes of administrative network control and all the remaining user and communications systems. For example, Fig. 4.18 shows that the protocols of the transport, session, presentation, and application layers support interaction between the administrative system (user system A) and user system B and the communications system (system C).

It should be pointed out that there may be one or more different protocols on one network layer. For example, in Fig. 4.18, the interaction between systems A and C in the physical and data-link layers may be described by one pair of protocols. However, the interaction between systems C and B in these same layers may be governed by a different pair of protocols.

The Reference Model requires that the lower-level protocols ensure the following properties in data transmission:
— transparency;
— noise immunity;
— independence.

The requirement of transparency stems from the fact that users wish to transmit data of arbitrary content that is encoded by any of the available codes. Noise immunity guarantees that the information will be delivered without error. Independence means that the transport service should be separated from processes and should be independent of their structure and characteristics.

The high-level protocols must meet different requirements:
— independence of the location of information resources;
— independence of the nature of data transmission and of types of connections;
— independence of the form of synchronization and transmission rate;
— independence of the structure of the software and hardware that implement the protocols;

104

— independence of the structure and form of the lower-level protocols.

Each network protocol is determined by three characteristics: syntax, semantics, and synchronization. The **syntax** determines the structure of the instructions and answers and of the transmitted texts encoded in rows or fields. The **semantics** characterize the meanings of the requests, actions, and answers implemented by both sides involved in data transmission and processing. Finally, **synchronization** standardizes processes of execution of procedures and the associated events.

Depending on the relationship between the interacting systems, protocols are divided into unbalanced and balanced protocols. An **unbalanced** protocol is one that describes interaction of unequal partners, e.g., the sender (initiator) and addressee. For instance, interaction between a terminal and an applied process is unbalanced. If, however, the protocol specifies the interaction of equal partners (in the logical sense), it is called **balanced.** Balanced protocols include, e.g., interaction protocols for two user programs or two human operators at terminals.

The protocols of the seven levels are customarily divided into three classes:
— network-dependent;
— transport;
— network-independent.

Network-dependent protocols include all protocols of the network, data link, and physical layers. Their characteristics are determined directly by the architecture of the communications created for system interaction. **Transport** protocols are in the transport layer and execute intermediate functions associated with data transmission between interacting user systems via all the communications systems and physical connections that are between them. **Network-independent** protocols are found in the application, presentation, and session layers. Their characteristics and structure are independent of the communications set up and employed in the network. They are determined only by the tasks which they must perform.

Protocols of all layers must be quasi-independent. This is necessary so that alteration of a protocol in one layer will not require modification of protocols in other. In addition, it is necessary that the protocols of each layer be **transparent** for protocols of higher layers, i.e., that they not introduce distortion into their operation.

4.6.
INTERNATIONAL STANDARDS

International standards for computer networks are specified by the International Standards Organization (ISO) and by the Series X recommendations established by the International Consultative Committee on Telegraphy and Telephony (CCITT). The ISO developed the Reference Model of Open System Architecture. In addition, it has proposed the HDLC data link control protocol [94].

The Series X recommendations of the CCITT describe standards for "public data networks" [95]. For circuit switching networks the principal recommendation is Recommendation X.21, which specifies the interface characteristics to digital data transmission channels. The principal characteristics of packet switching networks are specified by Recommendations X.25 and X.75. They describe the protocols of the physical, data-link, and network layers.

Recommendation X.21 [95] defines a universal physical interface for synchronous operation of two systems connected by a data link. Recommendation X.21 assumes that only digital physical channels are employed. At present, however, analog telephone channels are still widely used. Therefore, the CCITT has also published **Recommendation X.21bis.** This recommendation describes a combined physical interface that is suitable both for the digital channels specified by Recommendation X.21 and for analog telephone channels with modems that perform digital-to-analog conversion functions.

The second (channel) level is specified by the international **HDLC protocol.** It characterizes control of a **data link** formed by a physical link and interface facilities for two systems. On this level, systems exchange control and information **frames** with one another. Each control frame contains an instruction or answer. In addition, it may contain data transmitted by the information processes of both systems. Information frames must necessarily contain data. A particular case of HDLC is the **LAP B protocol**, which characterizes the second layer of Recommendation X.25 [95]. Unlike other versions of HDLC, data are transmitted only in information frames in the LAP B protocol.

The international protocols of the physical, data-link, and network layers that are specified by **Recommendation X.25** have gained widespread acceptance. This recommendation has undergone a brief but intensive development, and its latest version was approved by the

Seventh General Assembly of the CCITT, held in Geneva in November 1980. This version defines three forms of transmission in packet switching networks:
- (permanent) virtual channel;
- (temporary) virtual call;
- datagrams.

As already stated, a **virtual channel** is a form of data transmission via a communications network such that user systems that interact via this network are under the impression that a direct data link exists between them. Packet sequences are transmitted over the virtual channel furnished by the network. Within each sequence, the network guarantees that the packets will be delivered in the same order in which they were received for transmission. As a result, the user-systems procedures assembling packet sequences into messages after transmission are simplified. An important part of the transmission is receipt of confirmation that a packet sequence has been received by the addressee and that there are no errors in it.

A permanent virtual channel, called a **virtual circuit**, is established between a pair of interacting user systems over a prolonged period of time. There may be a very large number of interacting pairs of user systems in a computer network. If each pair is furnished with a permanent virtual channel, therefore, the number of such channels in the network will be excessive. This leads to unjustifiably complicated data transmission procedures.

Analysis of network operation reveals that most pairs of user systems do not interact very frequently with one another. There is no need to constantly maintain virtual channels for them. Hence, temporary virtual channels, called **virtual calls,** are allotted to them for each communications session. When virtual call is provided for, the functions performed by the virtual circuit include procedures for establishing a virtual call prior to a communications session and for disconnecting the call after the session is completed.

A **datagram** is a packet transmitted over a data network not as part of a sequence (via a logical channel), but independently. This simplifies the procedures associated with its transmission. In datagram transmission, however, situations may arise that involve loss or duplication of datagrams. Additional functions should be executed in the user systems, therefore, to ensure reliable data transmission.

In the CCITT recommendations [95], any source or consumer of information is referred to as **data terminal equipment** and denoted

TABLE 4.3.

No.	Symbol	Name
1.		Data terminal equipment
2.		Data switching exchange
3.	DCE	Data circuit-terminating equipment
4.		Multiplexer
5.		Transit data switching exchange
6.		Communications satellite

DTE. Since in a computer network the data sources and consumers are user systems, they are frequently designated in this way. In diagrams of public data transmission networks, Recommendation X.92 of the CCITT (Table 4.3) proposes that data terminal equipment be denoted by triangles, with the letters DTE written inside or adjacent to the symbol.

The CCITT recommendations introduce the concept of **data switching exchange** (DSE), denoted by a shaded circle (Table 4.3). In a computer network, this element corresponds to a communications system that provides packet switching.

In communications networks, a **communications channel** is understood to mean the physical medium and hardware required to service it. **Data circuit-terminating equipment** (DCE), whose symbol is shown in Table 4.3, is separately distinguished. This equipment includes modems, signal conversion devices, error-protection devices, automatic calling devices for users of telephone networks, and so forth.

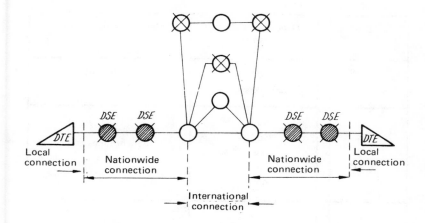

Fig. 4.19. Connections of public communications network.

For efficient loading of communications channels, the CCITT recommendations provide for extensive use of **multiplexers** (see Table 4.3). These devices provide data compression in high-speed communications channels, as well as interfacing of hardware (primarily terminals).

Transit data-exchange switching devices are provided for linking different types of public communications networks (see Table 4.3). In computer networks, the analogs of these devices are **interface systems,** which convert the protocols of one network into those of another or of a user system.

A special symbol (Table 4.3) is included for satellites, thus emphasizing the constantly increasing importance of this mode of communication.

Recommendation X.92 of the CCITT specifies three classes of connections for public communications networks (Fig. 4.19): local, national, and international. **Local** connection is understood to mean connection of data terminal equipment to a national (transit) data-exchange switching device. All data-exchange switching devices and the channels they connect that are located in one country make up a **national** connection.

National connections are combined by means of **international** connections.

TABLE 4.4.

Class	Data transmission rate, bits/sec	Mode of transmission
1	300	Asynchronous (start-stop)
2	50-200	
3	600	Synchronous
4	2400	
5	4800	
6	9600	
7	48000	
8	2400	Packet
9	4800	
10	9600	
11	48000	

Depending on their extent, all connections are divided into five types:
 — connections of moderate legth (1000 km);
 — long connections (10,000 km);
 — longest terrestrial connections (25,000 km);
 — trunk connection via satellite (80,000 km);
 — international trunk connection via two satellites (160,000 km).

Recommendation X.1 defines 11 classes of users of public communications networks, combined into three groups that represent DTE with asynchronous, synchronous, and packet transmission (Table 4.4). To perform the necessary conversions on the symbol flows employed in asynchronous and synchronous transmissions, the concept of PAD **(logical packet assembler/disassembler module)** is introduced into Recommendation X.92.

Recommendations X.3, X.28, and X.29 are devoted to standards associated with interaction between asynchronous (start-stop) DTE and public communications networks. For example, Recommendation X.3 describes the characteristics of a PAD module, its basic functions and parameters. Recommendation X.28 considers the interface between DTE and DSE for an asynchronous DTE connected to a public network via a PAD module. Finally, Recommendation X.29 describes procedures for exchange of control and user information between DTE's that operate in the packet mode and a PAD module.

CHAPTER 5

NETWORK CHANNELS

Data transmission in computer networks requires the solution of a number of complex problems. Prominent among these is the interconnection of two or more systems linked by a data link. In a computer network, this is done by a logical arrangement called a network channel. This arrangement, which is determined by the data link and physical link control protocols, is the topic of the present chapter.

5.1.
TYPES OF DATA LINKS

A **physical link** is what we will call a physical medium, hardware, and (possibly) software intended for data transmission between two or more systems. A **physical medium** is the space or material whose physical properties provide signal transmission (twisted pair, coaxial cable, waveguide, the ether, light conductors, and so forth).

We will divide data links into three groups:
— point-to-point;
— multipoint;
— point-to-multipoint.

A point-to-point link (Fig. 5.1a) is intended for connecting two adjacent systems. Henceforth we will also call it a **physical link.** A multipoint link (Fig. 5.1b) is used to link more than two systems. We will call it a **broadcast channel.** A point-to-multipoint link (Fig. 5.1c) is primarily employed to connect a group of terminals or satellite systems to a central system. This type of link is rarely used in computer networks, and therefore, it will not be considered in what follows.

5.2.
PHYSICAL LINK

When two systems are relatively close to one another, a physical link between them can employ direct connection (twisted pair, coaxial cable, light conductor, and so forth). When the distances

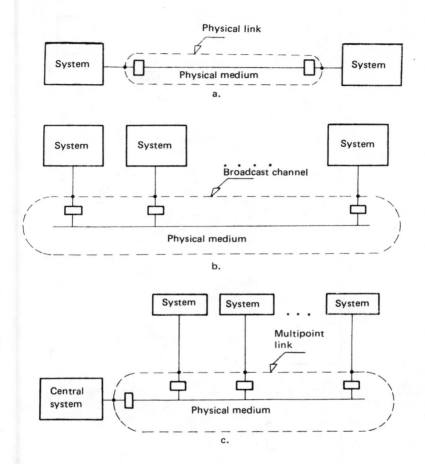

Fig. 5.1. Types of data links.

between adjacent systems are considerable, the physical link is set up on the basis of a sequence of telephone or digital communications channels.

Figure 5.2 shows an example of a physical link that is set up using telephone channels. Here the physical link between adjacent systems A and B is created by a sequence of three communications channels (1, 2, 3) switched by two telephone stations. This physical link also includes two sets of **data circuit-terminating equipment**. A point located between the data transmission equipment

113

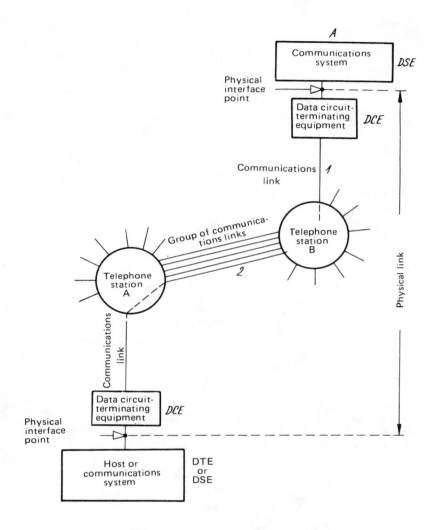

Fig. 5.2. Structure of physical link created in telephone network.

and the system is called a **physical interface point.** Therefore, the physical link is a medium that includes everything between the two points of physical interface (inputs/outputs) of the systems.

The number of communications channels and switching stations making up a physical link determines its reliability, size, and noise immunity. However, the data transmission functions performed by a physical link are independent of the number of con-

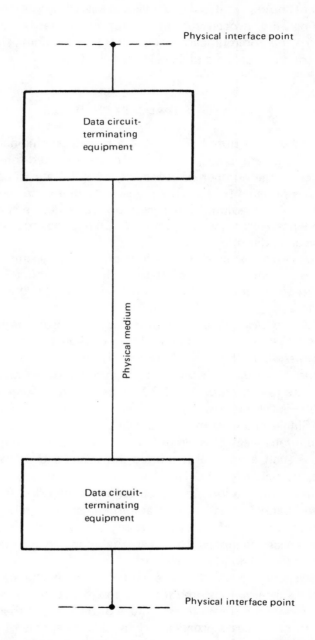

Fig. 5.3. Structure of physical link.

stituent communications channels and switching stations. In considering the operating procedures, therefore, all the hardware and software (if any) of the communications channels and switching stations is replaced by a solid line called a physical link (Fig. 5.3).

5.3.

BROADCAST CHANNELS

As already noted (Fig. 5.1b) a **broadcast channel** is a physical medium, hardware, and (possibly) software intended for data transmission between large number of user systems. A broadcast channel consists of two components (Fig. 5.4): a physical medium and access units (AU) to the physical medium. An **access unit** is a device that supports interaction between a user system connected to an interface point and the physical medium.

A broadcast channel provides **broadcast transmission** of data: if the data is directed to one of the interface points (e.g., point A), then it will reach all the remaining interface points (in this case points B, C, D, and E).

A broadcast channel is intended for shared use by a large number of user systems. This is possible only when the channel provides data transmission at fairly high rates. Therefore, any type of broadcast channel is set up with a view to high-speed data transmission. In most cases the rate is around 1–20 Mbits/sec, but it frequently runs as high as 300–500 Mbits/sec.

Single channels may be active or passive. A **passive channel** does not contain electronic amplifiers; therefore, it is highly reliable. The size of such a channel is limited, however, and its capabilities are not large, particularly when light signals are employed. Therefore, monorouting information and computing networks frequently employ **active channels** that contain amplifiers or repeaters for signal regeneration. The use of repeaters greatly increases the size and capabilities of broadcast channels. However, the appearance of repeaters naturally reduces the reliability somewhat.

Depending on the size and nature of the network, broadcast channels generally assume three forms: trunk, tree-shaped, and star-shaped. Figure 5.5 shows the structure of **backbone broadcast channel.**

In many cases broadcast channels are capable of data transmission in both directions, e.g., when the physical medium is a coaxial cable without repeaters or amplifiers. In these cases a backbone broadcast

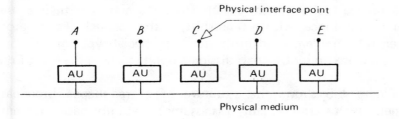

Fig. 5.4. Structure of broadcast channel.

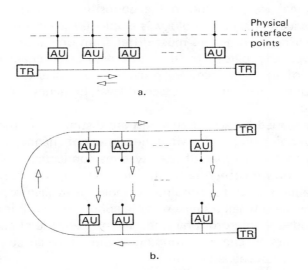

Fig. 5.5. Backbone broadcast channel.

channel assumes the form shown in Fig. 5.5a. It frequently happens, however, that broadcast channels can transmit data in only one direction. This is always the case when an element contains uni-directional repeaters. In these cases the structure of a backbone broadcast channel becomes much more complicated; it assumes the form shown in Fig. 5.5b. Here every user system connected to the channel at points 1,2,. . .,n has two access units. Each of these units transmits in only one direction.

117

At high data transmission rates, signals may be reflected from the endpoints of a backbone line. Therefore, simple devices called **terminators** (TR) are placed at the ends of the line. They are intended to prevent reflection of signals from the end, and their subsequent reappearance, with a time shift, in the channel. Terminators are generally implemented in the form of special types of resistors. When they are present, signals dissipate upon reaching the end of the line.

Figure 5.6 shows the structure of a **tree-shaped broadcast channel.** In this arrangement, it is assumed that information is transmitted in both directions in the channel. If, however, information is transmitted in one direction, then the channel contains two identical trees, connected to one another at the base of the trunk. Then information is sent from the base of the trunk to the ends of the branches via one tree, and in the opposite direction via the other. This broadcast-channel topology is employed when the transmission rates in different branches must differ from one another; the trunk of the tree is provided by the most high-speed coaxial cable, the branches of the first level are provided by cables with a moderate transmission rate, while the second-level branches are cables with a low rate.

Star-shaped broadcast channels are distinctive in that they have one nodal point (Fig. 5.7), while the number of channel elements corresponds to the number of user systems connected to the channel. In comparison with other forms, star-shaped broadcast channels require considerable outlays for running extended links. However, they are very convenient when a single-node telephone network is reorganized into a nodeless monorouting one. In this case the already-installed data transmission channels running to the node can be readily converted into a star-shaped channel.

5.4.

PHYSICAL LINK CONTROL

The physical link (or circuit) control protocol characterizes the first, lowest level of the program structure hierarchy of the network (see Fig. 4.12). This protocol determines the type and characteristics of physical links set up on the basis of the following communications channels:

— physical pair;

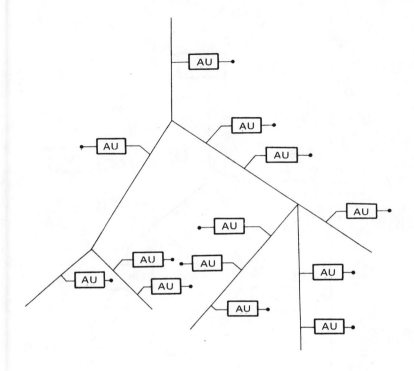

Fig. 5.6. Tree-shaped broadcast channel.

— analog telephone channel;
— telegraph channel;
— digital coaxial channel;
— radio channel;
— satellite communications channel, and so forth.

Depending on the nature of data transmission, physical links are subdivided into **serial** and **parallel** links. In the former, data is transmitted in streams of successive bits. In the latter, data is transmitted simultaneously in parallel over f physical circuits, f bits at a time. The most frequent case is $f = 8$.

In conformity with Recommendation X.25 of the CCITT [95], the first-layer protocol describes "the physical, electrical, and procedural characteristics of establishment, maintenance, and disconnection of a physical link at a point between terminal data equipment (system) and data transmission hardware."

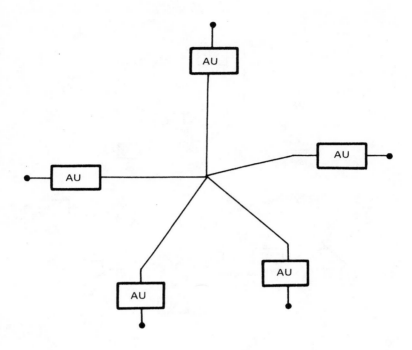

Fig. 5.7. Star-shaped broadcast channel.

Since at first only analog telephone channels were employed in computer networks, the CCITT earlier developed and established standards pertaining only to such networks. Thus, Table 5.1 gives standards [96] that specify the characteristics of **modems,** namely, data transmission hardware that allows systems to interact with analog telephone channels. These modems provide data transmission at rates of from 200 to 40,000 bits/sec. Of particular importance here is Recommendation V.24, which specifies the characteristics and access procedures for a system to an analog telephone channel. It contains the information and time characteristics, and also control procedures used for data transmission.

Recently, there has been intensive conversion to **digital communications channels,** which are in turn employed in backbone channels of communications networks. Accordingly, the CCITT has approved the first standards aimed at defining the characteristics of

TABLE 5.1.

CCITT recommendation number	Name of recommendation
V.21	200-bit modem intended for switched telephone networks
V.23	600/1200-bit modem intended for switched telephone networks
V.24	Characteristics of exchange circuits between data terminal equipment (DTE) and data circuit equipment (DCE)
V.26	2400-bit modem intended for four-wire leased telephone channels
V.26bis	2400/1200-bit modem intended for switched telephone networks
V.27	4800-bit modem intended for leased telephone channels
V.27bis	4800-bit modem with automatic stabilization, for use with leased telephone channels
V.27ter	4800/2400-bit modem intended for switched telephone networks
V.29	9600-bit modem intended for leased telephone channels
V.35	Data transmission at 48 kbits/sec, using group of 60-108 kHz channels
V.36	Modem for synchronous data transmission employing group of 60-108 kHz channels

high-speed digital communications channels. These standards (Table 5.2) create five stages of digital channels, that transmit data at rates of from 1.5 to 400 million bits/sec [97].

The first hierarchical level of the standards for the North American zone of digital communications channels specifies data transmission over symmetrical cables for distances up to 80 km [97]. The second level is used for intercity channels up to 800 km in extent. The third level is intended for transmission of signals with frequency multiplexing and of television signals with reduced redundancy. The fourth level characterizes the most rapid transmission of data via coaxial cables or radio relay systems.

5.5.
PHYSICAL LINK CONTROL PROTOCOLS

Protocol X.21. Physical link control in a public communications network is characterized by Recommendation X.21 of the CCITT,

TABLE 5.2.

Hierarchical level	Transmission rate, Mbits/sec		
	European zone	North American zone	Japan
First	2,048	1,544	1,544
Second	8,448	6,312	6,312
Third	34,368	44,736	32,064
Fourth	139,264	274,176	97,728
Fifth	—	—	307,200

which specifies standards for "universal interfaces of synchronous operation in public communications networks" [95]. A physical interface point is located between a user system (DTE) or communications system (DSE) and the data circuit-terminating equipment (DCE). Recommendation X.21 describes the following:

— use of exchange circuit;

— the signal arrangement at the interface point;

— the method of synchronizing symbols between system and circuit.

The interface considered by Recommendation X.21 employs eight circuits (Fig. 5.8) which define data exchange between the system (DTE or DSE) and the data circuit equipment (DCE). Interaction is effected in three successive phases or stages: establishment of connection, data transmission, and disconnection. Data are generated by the system and can be represented in the form of any bit sequence.

The byte timing circuit (Fig. 5.8) is optional, since two methods of synchronizing symbols transmitted between the system and data transmission equipment are possible at the interface point under consideration. In the first case, there is no byte timing circuit. Therefore, two or more synchronization symbols SYN are transmitted before all sequences of control symbols transmitted to the communications channel or received from the channel. In the second case, the available timing circuit is employed. Eight-bit sequences ensuring synchronization are transmitted via this circuit.

Protocol X.21bis. In view of the fact that most systems are still connected to analog telephone channels by means of modems, the CCITT developed and approved Recommendation X.21bis [95], which is compatible with Recommendation V.24 [96].

For low-speed operation (20 kbits/sec or less), Recomendation X.21bis employs a subset of exchange circuits defined by Recommendation V.24 (Fig. 5.9). Its use makes it possible to connect systems via standard modems (see Table 5.1) to analog telephone channels. In addition, Recommendation X.21bis makes it possible to operate with the digital communications channels defined by Recommendation X.21. As a result, the X.21bis interface is universal and provides for system connection to both analog and digital communications channels.

RPI protocol. When the distance between systems is small (up to 2 km), it is efficient to employ a **high-speed physical link** specified by the RPI protocol [98]. A similar standard (No. 4421) has been accepted in England [2]. The RPI protocol is used for high-speed transmission of large data flows, e.g., data from scientific experiments.

The Radial Parallel Interface (RPI) characterizes the following:
— the set of physical-link signals;

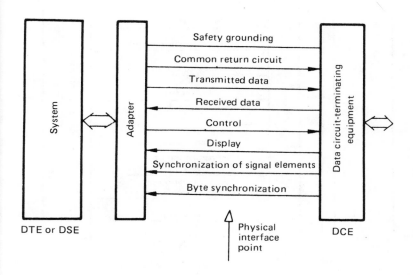

Fig. 5.8. Exchange circuits in X.21 protocol.

— the requirements on functional characteristics of signals;

— the data exchange procedure.

Figure 5.10 shows the set of signals employed by the RPI protocol. It includes up to 40 circuits. Circuits indicated by asterisks in Fig. 5.10 are optional. The protocol specifies data transmission in one direction (from source to receiver). If two-way transmission is required, two sets of circuits should be employed, as shown in Fig. 5.10.

A circuit in the RPI protocol, called Screen, protects control signals and data (from interference). This circuit is coupled to the metal chassis of the device in which the protocol is implemented. The Zero circuit is connected to the point taken as the zero point in the device in question.

The appearance of a 1 in the Ready circuit of the source (receiver) means that the source (receiver) is operational and ready to transmit information. Absence of a 1 (i.e., a 0) is a message that the source (receiver) is not ready to operate.

A 1 in the Gate circuit of the source indicates that the data to be transmitted are valid, but there must be a 1 in the Request circuit

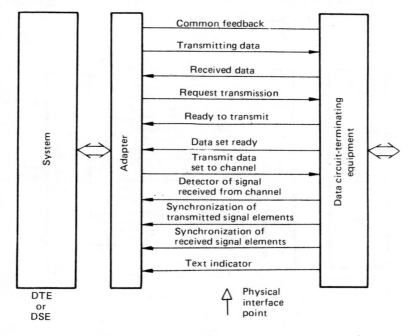

Fig. 5.9. Exchange circuits in X.21bis protocol.

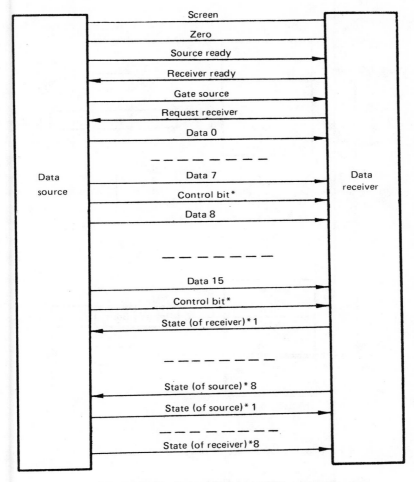

Fig. 5.10. Exchange circuits in RPI protocol.

of the receiver, which governs the receiver's request for information from the source.

Data, transmitted via the Data circuits, may be arbitrarily coded. Figure 5.10 shows 16 Data circuits. When necessary, however, their number may be reduced. The symbol (0 or 1) in the Control Bit circuit is set in such a way that the sum of 1's in the corresponding nine circuits (Data and Control Bits) is odd. This provides a check on the data transmitted via the Data circuit.

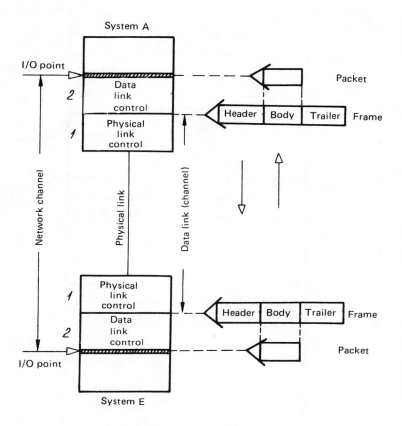

Fig. 5.11. Structure of physical link control.

The maximum number of State circuits, characterizing the data source, is eight (Fig. 5.10). They may be used to transmit command signals, control signals, and so forth. The state of the receiver may also be characterized by not more than eight circuits, via which error signals (after a parity check), signals indicating completion of service operations, and others are transmitted.

Data is exchanged in a "request/response" mode, implemented by signals transmitted over the Request circuits of the receiver and the Gate circuits of the source. The latter is an enablement for data transmission requested by the receiver.

The English standard No. 4421 specifies the same set of circuits as the RPI protocol. However, it establishes only three State circuits transmitting control data: reception error, source transmission ended, error present. The number of Data circuits is always specified to be eight; the Control Bit circuit is added to them. Thus, the total number of circuits in the 4421 standard is 18.

5.6.

DATA LINK CONTROL

A **data link** is an installation (Fig. 5.11) consisting of two logical modules for physical link control, interconnected by a physical link. The **data link control protocol** (Fig. 4.12) is at the second level of the overall hierarchy of protocols. This protocol specifies a large number of data link control functions, including the following in particular:

— control of link initialization and deinitialization procedures (establishment and termination of connection);
— packing of data into frames prior to transmission and unpacking after transmission via a physical link;
— generation and reading of control frames;
— transparency of data link (procedures for introducing and removing special symbols before and after transmission);
— transmission and receipt of confirmations regarding frame reception;
— generation of check symbols and checking of frame contents after transmission over physical links;
— repeat transmission of frames that were lost or in which errors were detected;
— control of frame flows in both directions of physical link.

Data link control makes it possible to create **network channels** (Fig. 5.11), these being logical facilities consisting of two logical modules connected by a physical link, each of which provides **data link control** and **physical link control.** Network channels are the basis of **transport networks,** which transmit data from processes in one user system to processes in another.

The task of any network channel (see Fig. 5.11) is to transmit packets from an I/O point of this channel in one system to a similar point in another. Data are transmitted in frames, which are a transport facility that transmits **packets.** For this, each packet arriving at an I/O point of a network channel in one system is subjected to the necessary processing, is packed into a **frame**, and is transmitted via a physical link to another system in the form of a stream of bytes or bits. In the second system, the packet is extracted from the frame and, after being checked, it is transferred to a second I/O point of the network channel.

An important factor determining network channel operation is the reliability of data transmission. To reduce the number of errors, appropriate measures are taken at the data link and physical link levels. However, this proves to be insufficient. Therefore, as will be shown below, special measures are taken to ensure reliable data transmission at the network-channel level, i.e., by the control program for the data link. For this purpose, the network channel checks each frame; frames in which errors are detected are discarded and transmitted again. As a result, it is possible to reduce the number of errors by factors of hundreds or even thousands. For example, Table 5.3 gives statistics on errors observed in communications channels (points 1–3) and network channels (points 4 and 5) [90]. It can readily be seen that the numbers differ markedly.

There are several ways of implementing network channels. The most efficient of these is to employ a special microprocessor controller which implements both network channel programs outside of the

TABLE 5.3.

No.	Type of channel	Number of errors per billion bits
1	Telephone channel, 200 bits/sec	50 000
2	Telephone channel, 600-2400 bits/sec	200 000
3	Bell System digital channel (USA)	200
4	SITA network channel	100
5	ARPANET channel	0.001

computer. Frequently, however, in order to simplify the hardware the problem is handled in a combined manner in which data link control is performed partly by the computer, while the remaining part of the control procedures and physical link controls are provided by the controller.

As was shown, physical links employ two different methods of data transmission. The first involves parallel transmission over f channel circuits of f-bit symbols (words). These channels generally employ simultaneous transmission of one byte (eight bits). Parallel channels are used when very high transmission rates are required.

The second method is serial (bit-by-bit) data transmission over the same physical-link circuit. To transmit a byte in this fashion, it is necessary to stipulate the order in which the eight constituent bits are transmitted. Then the transmitting end feeds each byte into the channel a bit at a time, while the receiving end assembles the bytes from the received bits.

The nature of control of packet transmission over a data link depends on the type of procedure employed. Two types of procedures, **byte-oriented** and **bit-oriented,** are most widespread in present-day networks. Byte-oriented channel control protocols involve byte-by-byte (symbol-by-symbol) data transmission. In bit-oriented protocols, streams of bits not divided into bytes are transmitted.

A widespread byte-oriented data link control procedure is the BSC protocol, developed by IBM. This protocol is employed in a large number of computer networks and is essentially an international standard.

Byte-oriented protocols are quite compatible with the characteristics of computers, but they utilize telephone networks rather inefficiently because of the large number of control symbols that are transmitted. In recent years, therefore, much attention has been paid to bit-oriented control procedures.

As already noted, each data link control protocol specifies standards and procedures for transmitting data over the channel (see Fig. 5.11). Data is exchanged over the channel by synchronous transmission of frames. In this case, "synchronous" means that the data-receiving system recognizes symbols marking the beginning and end of each transmitted frame. Depending on their relationship to the current frame (in time), systems are called transmitting and receiving systems, respectively. Data link control protocols ensure transparency of the channel and thus make it possible to encode the transmitted data in any fashion.

A frame is an array consisting of several regions for recording certain information. These regions are called **fields**. A frame may contain address, information, control, check, etc., fields. When combined, these fields form three basic frame types (Fig. 5.12): **header, body,** and **trailer.** The structure of these parts, which specifies the size and location of the different fields, is usually called the **frame format.**

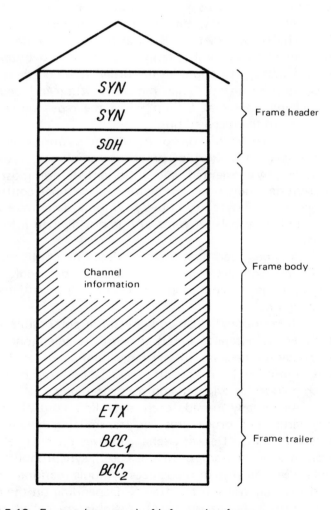

Fig. 5.12. Format (structure) of information frame.

Two types of frames, **information** and **control**, are transmitted in data links. The first of these is the primary one; its body contains packets transmitted by the upper (third) layer of the software structure of the network. The second are auxiliary and convey data required by the pair of systems in question for controlling the data link between them.

Earlier, there were no accepted international standards specifying data link control procedures. Therefore, different computer networks employed different types of bit-oriented procedures. Then the HDLC bit-oriented protocol appeared and was ratified by the CCITT [95] and approved by the International Standards Organization (ISO) [99]. However, it applies only to public computer networks. In government networks, therefore, new types of data link control protocols continue to appear.

Table 5.4 gives a list [90, 100–102] of the currently most widespread data link control protocols. Particularly important among them is the HDLC. In terms of structure, it is very similar to the SDLC protocol.

The appearance of the HDLC international standard has resulted in efforts to alter the existing protocols. For instance, it has been announced [90] that the ADCCP and BDLC protocols are compatible with HDLC. Control Data Corporation maintains [101] that its CDCCP protocol is also compatible with HDLC. Hewlett-Packard has accepted the HDLC protocol.

TABLE 5.4.

No.	Name of protocol	Company or organization that proposed it
1	HDLC (LAP B)	ISO, CCITT
2	SDLC	IBM
3	ADCCP	ANSI
4	CDCCP	CDC
5	UDLC	UNIVAC
6	DLC	NCR
7	DDCMP	DEC
8	BDLC	BURROUGHS

BSC protocol. The BSC protocol, developed by IBM, provides a set of rules that specify synchronous half-duplex data transmission over data links (see Fig. 5.11). In what follows, the BSC protocol will be briefly discussed while retaining the concepts of "frame" and "packet" introduced earlier to provide uniformity of presentation.

Frame format. The protocol provides for several modes of transmission of a packet received from the third layer of the software structure of the network. For example, the entire packet can be placed in the body of the frame (Fig. 5.12) and framed by symbols forming the header and trailer. The result is an information frame that transmits a packet over the data link. In addition, a packet may be divided into parts placed in separate frames that are transmitted independently. There is also the possibility of using control symbols to divide a packet in a frame into several parts (Fig. 5.13). The need for this arises when it is necessary to verify a long packet by parts or it is advisable to transmit a large data array without reversing the data link. It is also possible to transmit several interrelated packets that comprise parts of one message in this way.

In addition to information frames, the BSC protocol provides for the use of control frames, whose format (structure) is shown in Fig. 5.14. Control frames provide information on the beginning and end of a transmission session, and on the presence or absence of errors in transmitted packets; they can also require the next successive information frame to wait for transmission.

The eight-bit control symbols that are employed in the information and control frames of the BSC protocol can be divided into three groups:

a) Synchronizing symbol:

SYN: a symbol employed to synchronize systems connected by physical links, and also to fill up the time between adjacent frames; two successive such symbols (SYN SYN) indicate the beginning of the next successive frame;

b) Information-frame symbols:

SOH: symbol that precedes a packet heading,

STX: symbol that precedes a packet body,

ETX: symbol that follows the end of a packet,

ETB: symbol that follows the end of a heading or body of a packet,

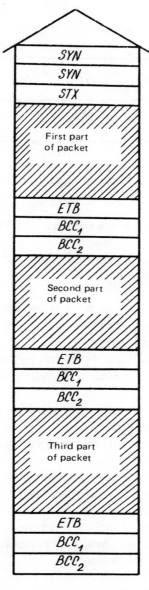

Fig. 5.13. Information frame with packet divided into parts.

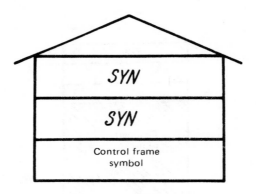

Fig. 5.14. Format of control frame.

ITB: symbol that follows the end of part of a packet (when the packet is divided into parts);

c) Control-frame symbols:

ENQ: symbol employed to request communications session, and also to request a repeat answer if the latter was late or arrived in distorted form,

ACK 0/1: alternating symbols that indicate correctness of a received information frame and readiness to receive the next frame,

WACK: received information frame is correct but that the receiving system is temporarily not ready to receive the next one,

NAK: received information frame contains an error and should be transmitted again,

RVI: received information frame is correct but that the transmitting system should cease operation,

EOT: end of communications session,

TTD: symbol transmitted by the system when it has nothing to transmit but does not wish to disconnect from the physical link and interrupt the session.

Each information frame terminates with a frame check sequence which provides for detection of errors in the information following its transmission over the physical link. In specific implementations the frame check sequence is formed in two basic ways. The LRC method is based on the generation of a check character by modulo 2 addition of the bits occupying the same digit positions in all characters of a packet. More efficient is the CRC method which involves the generation of a cyclic check sequence on the basis of a specified generator polynomial. In addition, when transmitting the information with the help of a seven-bit code, a parity bit is added to each character (VRC).

Control procedures. A communications session between a pair of systems connected by a data link is implemented in five stages, called **phases:**

1. Connection of channel. This phase is necessary when the connection between systems is effected via a switched telephone network. It becomes unnecessary when a leased communications channel is employed.

2. Request for transmission. For this a system that wishes to transmit one or more frames issues a request to the other system.

3. Frame transmission. Frames are transmitted over the data link in this phase. One of the systems becomes the transmitting system, the other the receiving system.

4. Completion of transmission. After the necessary number of frames have been transmitted, the transmitting system indicates that the session has ended.

5. Disconnection of channel. A switched channel is disconnected after use. When a leased channel is employed, this phase (like the first) ceases to be necessary.

Figure 5.15 shows an example of system interaction for the case of transmission of two packets packed into frames. Initially, system I sends a control frame to system II, requesting the initiation of a session. In response, system II transmits a control confirmation frame. Then system I sends system II an information frame containing packet A. Once it receives a control confirmation frame to the effect that the packet has been received error-free, system I sends an information frame with packet B. Upon receipt of confirmation that no errors appeared in this case either, system I sends a control frame indicating that the session is over.

When the receiving system detects an error in an information frame, it transmits a control frame (Fig. 5.16) containing the symbols SYN SYN NAK, asking for repeat transmission of the frame. The frame is then retransmitted over the channel to system II.

The BSC protocol provides for two modes of data representation in packets. In the first (normal) mode, all the information in

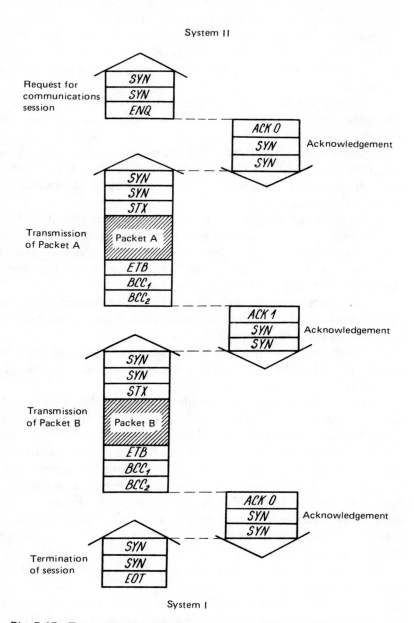

Fig. 5.15. Transmission procedure for two information frames over physical link.

System II

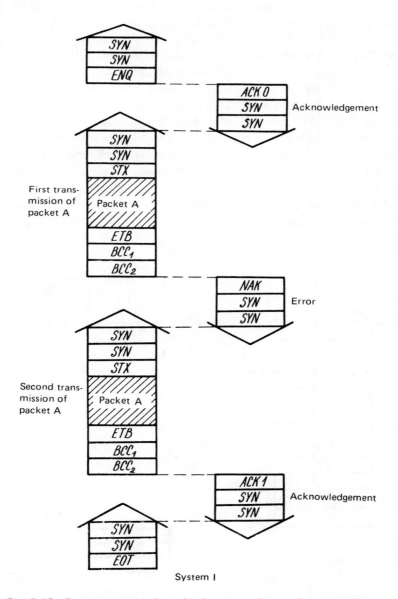

Fig. 5.16. Repeat transmission of information frame after appearance of error in it.

137

the packet is encoded in a certain definite way. In the second mode, the packet contents may be arbitrarily coded, but transparency is ensured by the use of special measures. The second mode is necessary to transmit floating-point data, blocks of digital data, programs written in machine language, and data obtained from experiments. As for control symbols in the headers and trailers of different frames, they are always encoded in definite fashion.

Transparency. To control the data link, the corresponding hardware should distinguish control symbols (STX, ETB, SYN, and so forth) from the contents of frames transmitted in their bodies. When the symbols of frame bodies are encoded arbitrarily, however, symbols having the same codes as control symbols may occur. In other words, symbols that are indistinguishable from control symbols may appear in the frame.

To distinguish frame-body symbols from control symbols, a special symbol (DLE) is introduced and the following procedure is executed (Fig. 5.17):

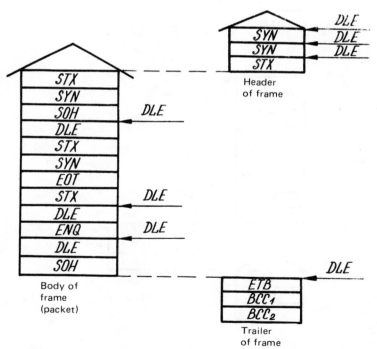

Fig. 5.17. Parts of information frame prior to assembly.

— DLE is added in front of each control symbol of the header and trailer;

— another DLE is added ahead of each DLE symbol in the body of the frame. This operation is called **byte-stuffing** (filling of frames by DLE bytes) and is performed prior to transfer of an information frame to the data link. After this frame is received from the channel, the reverse operation is performed, i.e., the DLE symbols that were previously inserted are eliminated.

Since DLE is not employed for other purposes, all control symbols becomes two-byte symbols after byte-stuffing is performed (Table 5.5). This yields the following algorithm for analyzing frames received from the channel. The appearance of DLE in a frame is a warning (Fig. 5.18) that the symbol to follow is a control symbol, if it is different from DLE. If, however, the symbol is identical to DLE, it is not a control symbol. As a result, regardless of the codes employed in the packet that forms the body of the frame, control symbols can be distinguished in the overall symbol flow.

An example of an information frame whose body contains a packet with arbitrarily coded symbols is provided by Figs. 5.17 and

TABLE 5.5.

No.	Symbol	Meaning
1	DLE STX	Initiation of transparent mode for next frame
2	DLE ETB	Ending of header or body of frame in transparent mode
3	DLE ETX	Ending of frame in transparent mode and transfer to operation in normal (nontransparent) mode
4	DLE SYN	Synchronization or filling of time between frames in transparent mode
5	DLE ENQ	Request to ignore transmitted frame and to change to normal mode
6	DLE ITB	Ending of intermediate transparent part of frame (in particular, when frame contains several parts of a packet)

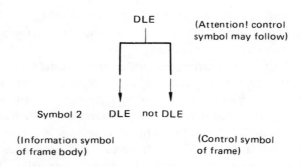

Fig. 5.18. Detection (extraction) algorithm for channel control symbols.

5.19. For convenience, we will consider the worst case in which the packet consists only of symbols that coincide with control symbols in the ordinary (nontransparent) mode. To transmit a frame with this packet, we add a DLE in front of all control symbols of the header and trailer, and also in front of DLE symbols in the body of the frame (see Fig. 5.17). As a result, we obtain a frame (Fig. 5.19) in which the control symbols are readily distinguishable. They are denoted by numbers 1–4 in Fig. 5.19. Naturally, everything in between them is the body of the frame into which the packet is packed. The control symbols in front of the body form the header, while the symbols after the body are part of the trailer.

After a frame is transmitted, the header and trailer are discarded in the receiving system, while one DLE is eliminated from each DLE DLE pair in the remaining part (body). As a result, the packet is restored to its original form, shown in Fig. 5.17.

HDLC protocol. Considerable experience gained through operation of data channels employing the BSC protocol enabled IBM to develop a new and improved protocol, called SDLC [103]. On the basis of this protocol, the ISO developed and approved an international data link control protocol called HDLC [104]. This protocol was subsequently accepted by the CCITT [95], with some modifications, and came to be known as the **LAP B protocol.**

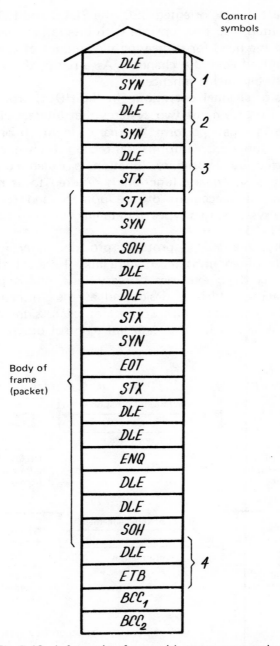

Fig. 5.19. Information frame with transparent packet.

Unlike the byte-oriented BSC, the SDLC and HDLC protocols are bit-oriented, i.e., they operate with bits rather than bytes. This stems from the need for decreasing the amount of control information transmitted over the channel. As a result, the utilization efficiency of the channel is enhanced.

Modes of channel operation. In the HDLC protocol, the data-link control programs of two systems that interact via the channel (see Fig. 5.11) may perform "primary" (control) or "secondary" (controlled) functions. Information related to channel control that is transmitted by a primary function is called **commands;** that supplied by a secondary function is referred to as **responses.** Depending on the placement of the primary and secondary functions in the systems, two types of data link (unbalanced or balanced) are created [105].

Initially, the HDLC protocol provided only for the unbalanced mode of an **unbalanced data-link.** Here the data link control program which executes primary functions is placed in one of the systems, which is designated as the "primary" one (Fig. 5.20). It is entrusted with control of all sessions conducted by the data link channel. The data link control program that imple-

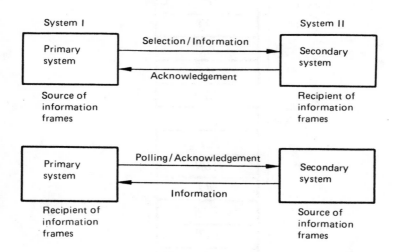

Fig. 5.20. Interaction of primary and secondary systems.

142

ments secondary functions is, in the second system, designated as the "secondary" one. In all sessions, it performs a system-controlled role.

The primary system provides execution of two methods of data link control. If the data source is the primary system (upper part of Fig. 5.20), then interaction with the secondary one is effected by selection commands (choice of necessary secondary system). If the secondary system becomes the source (lower part of Fig. 5.20), then the primary utilizes polling commands to interact with it.

As for the secondary system, HDLC provides two modes of operation: **normal** (NRM) and **asynchronous** (ARM). In the normal mode, the secondary system may initiate frame transmission only after being enabled or polled by the primary one, after which the secondary system must transmit one or more frames to the primary. When the last frame is transmitted, it must inform the primary to this effect. The secondary system then ceases to transmit.

In the asynchronous mode, the secondary system can initiate transmission without enablement by the primary. This transmission contains one or more frames and is used to transmit data or to indicate changes in the state of the secondary system (e.g., a change from a state of being ready to accept data to one of being busy, development of special situations, and so forth). Contention may appear in this mode, i.e., simultaneous transmission of a command (by the primary system) and a response (by the secondary). To eliminate contention, simultaneously appearing commands and responses are rejected. They may be repeated after specified time intervals. However, the time interval used by the secondary system is set to be much greater than that of the primary. Thus, contention is eliminated.

It should be pointed out that several physical links are connected to every communications system of a cellular computer network (Fig. 5.21). In relation to different channels, therefore, one and the same system may have a different status. For example, system III is primary (P) in relation to channels 3 and 4, but secondary (S) in relation to channel 2.

Distributed computer networks almost always involve systems of equal status. Subsequently, therefore, HDLC incorporated yet another mode of data-links operations, called **balanced** [94]. When this mode is employed, systems are not designated as "primary" and "secondary." All systems are of equal status and, by

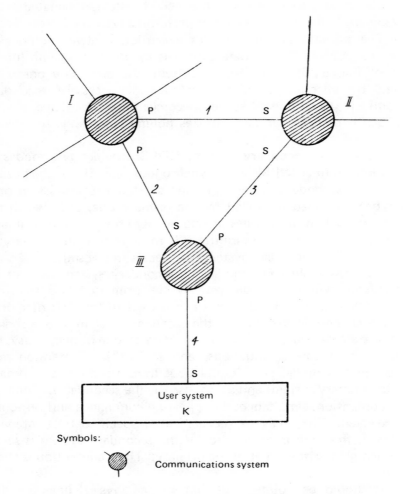

Symbols:

Communications system

Fig. 5.21. Status of systems relative to different channels.

controlling channel operation in an asynchronous mode, they can send both command frames and response frames to one another.

At present, therefore, the HDLC protocol specifies a set of procedures that are distributed among three classes:

— normal unbalanced;
— asynchronous unbalanced;
— balanced.

Similarly, the LAP B protocol approved by the CCITT provides for a **balanced data link.** Here each system performs

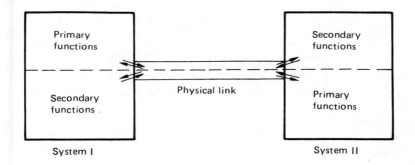

Fig. 5.22. Primary and secondary functions of systems.

both primary and secondary functions (Fig. 5.22), and thus, two asymmetrical data links are in effect merged into one symmetrical one. Correspondingly, everything concerning primary and secondary systems that has been said so far, and that will be said henceforth, applies equally to the primary and secondary functions of symmetrical (balanced) channels. It should only be borne in mind that the normal response mode (NRM) is not employed in LAP B, only the asynchronous balanced mode (ABM). Hence, there is no need for the secondary system to transmit information frames.

Information is exchanged in HDLC and LAP B by frame transmission. As in the BSC protocol, two types of frames are employed in this case: **information** and **control** frames. Each of the information frames is stored in the transmitting system until a confirmation is obtained from the receiving system that it has been transferred or received without error. HDLC provides synchronous transmission in both full-duplex and half-duplex modes; LAP B offers only the full-duplex mode.

Frame format. The frame structure (or, as it is called, the frame format) that is employed in the HDLC protocol is shown in Fig. 5.23. A frame consists of three parts: a three-byte (or, in special cases, four-byte) header, a body from 0 to N bytes in size, and a three-byte trailer. Each frame begins and ends with a flag, i.e., an eight-bit control symbol that separates frames from one another in the continuous flow of data through the data link.

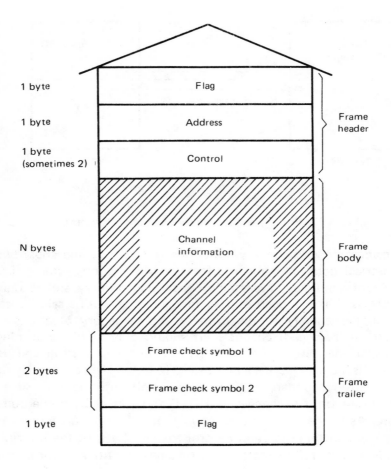

1 byte	Flag	
1 byte	Address	Frame header
1 byte (sometimes 2)	Control	
N bytes	Channel information	Frame body
2 bytes	Frame check symbol 1	Frame trailer
	Frame check symbol 2	
1 byte	Flag	

Fig. 5.23. Format (structure) of HDLC frame.

A flag at the beginning of a frame is called an **opening** flag, while one at the end of a frame is called a **closing** flag. One flag may be a closing flag for a preceding frame and an opening flag for a subsequent one. Each flag is represented in the frame by the eight-bit code 01111110.

The HDLC protocol provides for three types of frames, which define three phases (or stages) of operation of two systems that interact via a data link:

146

1. **Unnumbered frame** (U-frame), intended for performing the functions of the phase of establishment and termination of connection of the pair of systems connected by the data link (request to establish communication, acceptance of request; messages concerning errors in the frame format).

2. **Supervisory frame** (S-frame), which provides execution of the functions of the transmission-control phase (messages regarding readiness or nonreadiness for reception, appearance or absence of errors in frame content, requests for repeat frame transmission).

3. **Information frame** (I-frame), employed in the phase of data transmission via a data link from one system to another.

A data link between a pair of systems is used to transmit two opposite intermixing flows of information frames. Two counters are employed in each system (Fig. 5.24) to provide clearcut con-

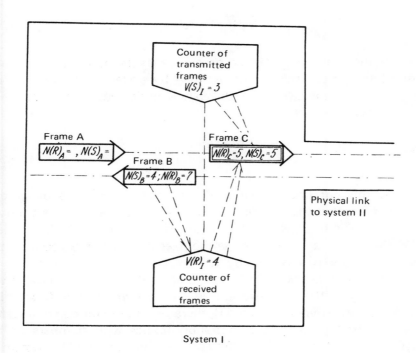

Fig. 5.24. Numbering of information frames.

trol of these flows and error-free frame identification. One of them tallies information frames transmitted by the system to the channel, while the other counts frames received by the system from the channel. The values yielded by these counters are denoted by $V(S)$ and $V(R)$, respectively. If the information frames have a normal control field (1 byte), then the counters issue cyclical values equal to 0,1,2,3,4,5,6,7,0,1, ... If, however, the frames employ an expanded control field (2 bytes), then the counter values are 0,1,2, . . ., 126, 127,0,1, ...

Immediately before an information frame is fed to the channel, the following numbers are entered into it:

$N(S)$, the number of the transmitted frame;

$N(R)$, the number of the expected frame (upon reception). These numbers are determined by the values provided by the counters of system I (e.g., frame C; see Fig. 5.24):

$$N(S)_C = V(S)_I, \qquad N(R)_C = V(R)_I. \tag{5.1}$$

If the frame transmission procedure is error-free, then the number of the transmitted frame assigned by system II (frame B, Fig. 5.24) should coincide with the values indicated by the received-frame counter in system I:

$$N(S)_B = V(R)_I. \tag{5.2}$$

If this condition is violated, the received frame is discarded, and system II sends a request for repeat transmission. The counter value $V(R)$ is unaltered in this case. If condition (5.2) is satisfied and the frame is transmitted without error, then it is accepted by system I and $V(R)$ is altered by 1.

In accordance with (5.1) and (5.2), in the transmitted frame we have $N(R)_C = N(S)_B + 1$ in the transmitted frame (frame C; see Fig. 5.24). Upon arriving at system II, therefore, the frame communicates via the $N(R)$ value that information frames with numbers up to $N(R) - 1$ have been transmitted correctly and accepted by system I.

Supervisory frames are also assigned numbers. Unlike information frames, however, only the number $N(R)$ of the supervisory frame that is expected (upon reception) is employed.

Transmission of unnumbered frames does not involve the counters — hence their name.

Frame header. A frame header (see Fig. 5.23) that is a channel heading in the hierarchy of headers (see Fig. 4.10) consists of three fields (or regions). The heading begins with a one-byte field that contains an opening flag. This is followed by a one-byte address field that contains the address of the secondary system or direction of frame transmission over the data link. A one-byte control field (two-byte in special cases) concludes the frame header. The codes entered here provide for the following:

— determination of frame type;
— communication of transmitted frame number $N(S)$ and expected frame number $N(R)$ (upon reception);
— transmission of command or response;
— introduction of poll/final function.

The formats of the control field of the three types of frames we have considered are shown in Table 5.6; it can be seen that a 0 in the first bit indicates that the frame in question is an information frame. The code 10 in the first and second bits identifies a supervisory frame, while an 11 in these bits represents an unnumbered frame. Bits 3 and 4 in supervisory frames, and also 3, 4, 6, 7, and 8 in unnumbered frames, are used to encode commands and responses. Frame numbers are entered into the control field of information frames (bits 2, 3, 4, 6, 7, 8) and supervisory frames (bits 6, 7, and 8).

Bit 5 in the control field of all types of frames is used to record a poll/final (P/F) bit: P for a frame containing a command, F for a

TABLE 5.6.

Type of frame	Bits of field							
	1	2	3	4	5	6	7	8
Information (I-frame)	0	Number $N(S)$ of transmitted frame			P/F	Number $N(R)$ of expected frame (upon reception)		
Supervisory (S-frame)	1	0	Command/response code		P/F	Number $N(R)$ of expected frame (upon reception)		
Unnumbered (U-frame)	1	1	Command/response code		P/F	Command/response code		

frame containing a response to a command. The bit in question may be used to execute the four functions shown in Table 5.7. Here the letter D indicates a function that can be executed in the full-duplex mode of the channel; H indicates the half-duplex mode. When it is necessary to execute the functions in the table, the command $P = 1$ is transmitted and the response $F = 1$ is received. Until the latter is received, the next successive command cannot be transmitted. If $P = 0$ in the command, there is no need for a response.

Table 5.8 gives the list of commands and responses employed in the HDLC protocol. Commands and responses indicated by asterisks are absent in LAP. Each unnumbered or supervisory frame transmits a command or response, thus ensuring control of the data link.

Each unnumbered frame includes one of five commands or one of two responses. The command SNRM is employed to request establishment of communication between systems in normal mode. Transmission of this command and subsequent receipt of the ac-knowledgement UA switches the data link from a passive to an active state so that transmission of information frames can begin. At this point, all the information-frame and supervisory-frame counters are set to zero.

The command SNRME is employed in special instances in which the size of the frame control field should be doubled and made equal to two bytes. This is necessary for frame numbering up to 128 (instead of 8) as a result of extension of the control field containing these numbers.

The command SARM is a request for establishment of com-munication in an asynchronous mode. After the acknowledgement

TABLE 5.7.

Function \ Purpose of frame	Mode of operation in which function is performed			
	normal		asynchronous	
	Command	Response	Command	Response
Request instruction	D, H			
Indicate last frame	H	D, H		
Call out unnumbered or supervisory response	D, H		D, H	
Indicate error	D, H	D, H	D, H	D, H

150

TABLE 5.8.

Type of frame	Commands	Response
Unnumbered	SNRM* establish communication in normal mode	UA acknowledgement
	SNRME* establish communication in normal mode with extended control field	CMDR rejection of execution of command
	SARM establish communication in asynchronous mode	
	SARME* establish communication in asynchronous mode with extended control field	
	DISC discontinue communication	
Supervisory	RR* receive ready	RR receive ready
	RNR* receive not ready	RNR receive not ready
	REJ* rejection of frames	REJ rejection of frames
	SREJ* selective rejection of frames	SREJ* selective rejection of frames
Information	I information	I* information

UA, the data link goes into the active state and the counters are reset to zero.

The command SARME is employed for the asynchronous mode with double-size control field.

The command DISC is used to halt operation of the channel in the mode specified by the command transmitted at the beginning of the session (SNRM, SNRME, SARM, SARME). The command is sustained by the response UA.

Response UA is employed to transmit information regarding a command received for execution in an unnumbered frame. The response CMDR is issued when a received command cannot be executed. This occurs in the following cases:

— reception of erroneous or unfamiliar command;
— reception of information frame with a packet whose size exceeds the stipulated standard;
— reception of a frame with an unacceptable number (number of a frame already received and confirmed, or out-of-sequence frame number).

151

Supervisory frames transmit one of four commands or one of four responses, indicated in Table 5.8. When fed to the channel, these frames are assigned numbers $N(R)$ that vary cyclically from 0 to 7 when a normal control field is employed, or from 0 to 127 when an extended control field is employed. They are needed to control the flow of supervisory frames in physical links. The commands (or responses) employed in supervisory format denote the following.

The command or response RR indicates that the system is ready to receive an information frame or is used to confirm receipt of earlier frames with numbers up to $N(R) - 1$.

The command or response RNR indicates that the receiving system temporarily cannot accept new information frames. Simultaneously, it acknowledges information frames numbered up to $N(R) - 1$ that have been received up to this point. Reception of the remaining frames is not acknowledged.

The command or response REJ is used to request repeat transmission of all information frames beginning with $N(R)$. Information frames with numbers up to $N(R) - 1$ are regarded as acknowledged. Additional frames waiting for transmission can be sent only after repeat transmission of the frames in question.

The command or response SREJ is employed to request repeat transmission of the single information frame with number $N(R)$. Receipt of frames with numbers up to $N(R) - 1$ is acknowledged.

The control field of information frames (frame 1) contains no commands, since the code of the frame itself is simultaneously a command indicating that the frame contains a packet received from a higher level of the network software structure.

It should be borne in mind that the HDLC protocol allows a certain amount of flexibility in the use of commands and responses. On the one hand, in transmitting information frames over the channel, it is not necessary to employ all the commands or responses indicated in Table 5.8. For example, one can operate only in normal mode and employ a one-byte control field. Then the commands SARM, SNRME, and SARME are unnecessary. On the other hand, the HDLC protocol provides the possibility of introducing new commands and responses in the future.

Body of frame. All information frames have a body that includes a packet received from a higher hierarchical level of the network software structure. It may be a packet containing user information, or one of the control packets used to control the communications network. In any of these cases, the size of the body of the frame is governed by that of the packet it contains. The contents of the packet may be arbitrarily coded, since special measures ensure its transmission over the channel regardless of the information codes employed.

Two operations must be performed to extract packets from frames (after transmission over the channel). The header (containing three bytes in the case of a normal control field, or four in the case of an expanded one) must be removed from the frame; then, reckoning from the end of the frame, the three-byte trailer must be discarded. The remaining part of the frame is the body, which contains the packet transmitted over the channel.

Unnumbered frames that transmit the command CMDR also have a body. The three-byte field of this body contains information regarding the reasons for not executing the instruction. Other unnumbered frames, and all supervisory frames, have no body (N = 0 in the frame structure shown in Fig. 5.23).

Trailer of frame. The trailer is the closing part of every frame. It consists of a two-byte frame check field and a one-byte field containing a closing flag (Fig. 5.23).

The frame check field, denoted by FCS in the protocol, contains information for checking the frame after transmission over the channel. The HDLC protocol does not standardize the checking method. The version of the protocol approved by the CCITT proposes a method in which the two-byte check symbol is the 1's complement of the (mod 2) sum of the following two terms: 1) the remainder from mod 2 division of the expression $X^k (X^{15} + X^{14} + \ldots$ $\ldots X^2 + X + 1)$ by the polynomial $X^{16} + X^{12} + X^5 + 1$, where k is the total number of bits of the address, control and information fields; 2) the remainder from multiplication by X^{16} and subsequent division modulo 2 of the contents of the address, control, and information fields by the polynomial $X^{16} + X^{12} + X^5 + 1$.

This checking algorithm seems fairly complicated. However, it can be implemented fairly simply by a special counter and provides a high degree of check reliability.

The frame check field is followed by a closing flag (Fig. 5.23) that terminates any frame (information or control). A frame not enclosed by flags or that has less than 32 bits between flags is considered **erroneous.** If a frame is not immediately followed by another frame, the space between them may be filled by a set of flags in succession.

Transparency. To feed a frame to the data link, the transmitted sequence must not contain any signal that coincides with a flag. Before sending the bit sequence specified by the frame, therefore, the transmitting system inspects the sequence and performs the operation of **bit-stuffing**: it inserts 0's after each five 1's in succession. Then the bit sequence specified by the frame does not contain any code that corresponds to a flag (01111110). The sequence is enclosed by flags and is fed to the channel. Upon reception of the bit sequence from the channel, the reverse operation is performed. The receiving system discards the flags, inspects the contents between flags, and eliminates every 0 encountered after five successive 1's.

Channel control procedure. As shown above, each system cyclically tallies the ordinal numbers $N(S)$ and $N(R)$ of the information frames it transmits and receives. Three bits are allocated in the normal control field of the heading (or seven in an expanded field) to record these numbers, thus providing a frame tally from 0 to 7 or from 0 to 127. Without waiting for acknowledgement, therefore, the transmitting system can feed up to 7 or 127 frames, respectively, into the channel.

Data links may be in one of two states, **active** or **passive**. Such channels are in the active state if a frame or sequence of flags that fill the gaps between adjacent frames is being transmitted over it. When the channel is in the active state, the system has the capability of immediately continuing frame transmission. Transmission of from 7 to 14 successive 1's in the active state indicates a request to cancel a transmitted frame.

Transmission of 15 or more successive 1's switches the channel from the active to the passive state. The passive state means that the transmitting system has terminated the communications session. In the passive state only a control frame containing one of the commands SNRM, SARM, SNRME, or SARME can be transmitted over the channel. Transmission of one of these commands and receipt of the response UA again puts the channel in the active state.

Interaction of two systems is characterized by three **phases** (or stages) of operation: establishment, maintenance, and termination of communication. Prior to establishment of communication, the data link is in the passive state, while the frame counters are set to zero. The primary system, upon desiring to establish communication, sends a control frame containing one of the commands SNRM, SARM, SNRME, or SARME to the secondary system,

154

thus proposing that a session be initiated in the corresponding mode. If the secondary system wishes to initiate a session, it communicates this by transmitting a continuous sequence of flags (request for transmission). The primary responds to this sequence by one of the above four commands. After the secondary has sent the acknowledgement UA in response, the establishment phase terminates and the channel switches from the passive to the active state. An example of the operation of a data link is shown in Fig. 5.25, where the primary system has transmitted an SNRM to initiate operation in normal mode and has received an acknowledgement UA to this effect from the secondary.

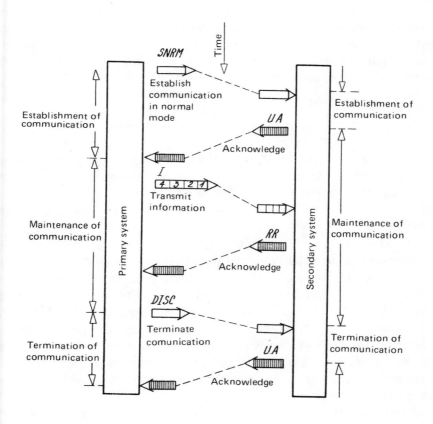

Fig. 5.25. Phases (stages) of interaction of two systems.

The maintenance phase is characterized by transmission of information frames in both directions, as well as of acknowledgements of correct receipt or requests for repeat transmission of frames in the event of errors in them. Prior to receipt of acknowledgement, groups containing from 1 to 7 or 127 information frames (depending on the size of the control field) may be transmitted.

To terminate a session, the primary system transmits the command DISC (Fig. 5.25). In response, the secondary sends a UA. When the secondary desires to terminate the connection, it ceases to feed flag sequences to the channel. The channel then goes from the active to the passive state, and the termination phase is thus completed.

Figure 5.25 shows an elementary communications session during which four information frames were transmitted in one direction, with no errors being found in them. In reality, a variety of highly diverse situations arise in data links. They can all be resolved by the commands and responses shown in Table 5.8.

5.7.

BROADCAST-CHANNEL CONTROL

As in the case of physical links (Fig. 5.11), broadcast-channel control makes it possible to create network channels. A network channel (Fig. 5.26) consists of a pair of interacting logical modules (2, 1), each of which provides **data-link control** and **broadcast-channel control.**

There is an important difference, however, between broadcast channels and physical links. In the latter case, each frame from the sender system reaches only the necessary addressee system. For broadcast channels, in contrast, each frame is transmitted to all user systems, not to just one. As a result, in addition to the functions described in §5.6, the data-link program must also perform frame filtering tasks. This means that upon receiving all frames, the data-link control program selects only those that are addressed to the system in which this program is located. The program eliminates the remaining frames.

It may happen in operation (Fig. 5.26) that frames from more than one user system are passed simultaneously to the broadcast channel. Thus, we encounter the problem of sharing channel resources. This can be dealt with by organizing special access to the

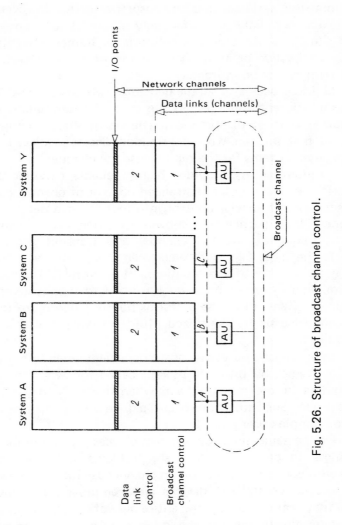

Fig. 5.26. Structure of broadcast channel control.

channel. Since large numbers of user systems are connected to broadcast channels, the type of access under consideration is called **multiple.** The situation in which two or more user systems wish to occupy a channel simultaneously for transmission is called **contention** of these systems. Contentions can be removed in two ways: by elimination or detection. **Elimination** involves the use of an access method such that only one user system can (in principle) transmit over the channel at one time. In contrast, the **detection** method allows contention to happen, i.e., it permits situations in which two or more user systems simultaneously transmit. However, measures are taken to rapidly and effectively eliminate the consequences of such situations. In this case **collisions** of frames transmitted simultaneously by two or more user systems are reduced to cases of ordinary error detection in frames.

Multiple access is subdivided into two basic types (Fig. 5.27), deterministic and random. In the case of **deterministic access,** the operating time of the broadcast channel is shared among the user systems that interact with it. **Random access** involves competition among user systems for the right to use the channel.

Random access provides highly reliable network operations, since it does not require centralized control of channel operation or transmission of special control information in order to utilize the channel. It is particularly convenient when user systems interact only infrequently via the channel and transmit short messages. This is the case, e.g., with electronic mail. However, the method also has a number of shortcomings. It is not suitable when different transmission priorities must be furnished to user systems, tasks, or terminals. Random access performs poorly when more than 30% of the channel capacity is utilized [106], or when real-time operation is required.

Deterministic access is most convenient when priority transmission of frames by different users is called for, when there are large computers in the network, and when relatively long messages are transmitted. Such situations occur, e.g., in remote distributed processing of complex user jobs.

At the same time, deterministic access has a number of shortcomings. In particular, there are problems of furnishing user systems with control information on channel use rights. In earlier methods, special centralized devices were employed for this purpose; when they malfunctioned, the entire network ceased to operate. The new deterministic methods no longer require centralized devices, but other methods of reliably transmitting enablement signals are needed.

Deterministic multiple access is divided into three groups (Fig. 5.27). In the case of **synchronous sharing,** the broadcast-channel operating time is cyclically divided into n intervals, where n is the number of user systems connected to the channel. Each i-th user system, X^k $(X^{15} + X^{14} + \ldots X^2 + X + 1)$ is given the i-th interval in a cycle, during which the system can use the channel for transmitting a data array (frame or group of frames). With this method, it fre-

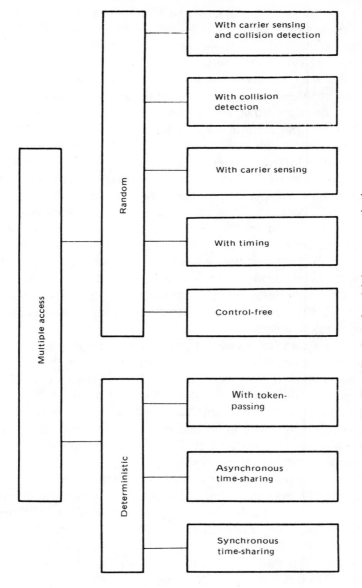

Fig. 5.27. Classification of multiple-access methods.

quently happens that in a given cycle some systems have nothing to transmit and the intervals allotted to them are not used, while other systems are unable to transmit everything they need to. Thus, the synchronous method is simple but can be utilized only when the number of user systems is small.

In the case of **asynchronous sharing,** a special procedure is introduced for determining statistics and for predicting on this basis the size of the data flows to the channel from the various user systems. The channel time is divided cyclically into unequal intervals in accordance with this prediction. The larger the data flow anticipated from the i-th user system, the greater the time interval allotted to him for transmission. The asynchronous method makes it possible to increase channel capacity somewhat, but not to a great extent.

Recently, particularly in conjunction with the increased manufacture of mini- and microcomputers, it has become necessary to connect many tens or even hundreds of user systems to one broadcast channel. With such numbers of systems, earlier modes of multiple access with time-sharing become inefficient. This has led to the creation of a new deterministic method that substantially enhances channel utilization efficiency. It has come to be known as **multiple access with token-passing.**

The algorithm for access with token-passing is very simple. Once it has received authorization, a user system transmits the number of frames allotted to it over the channel. Then it passes the token to another system specified in the algorithm. If the authorized system has nothing to transmit, it immediately passes the token to the next system. As a result, there is no loss of time associated with the fact that a user system has no data to transmit to another system at the time it becomes enabled to transmit.

When computer networks employ the method of token-passing, there are hardly ever any central devices to provide time-sharing of the channel. This enhances operating reliability, since it eliminates elements whose malfunctioning causes the entire network to cease operation. It should also be borne in mind that the method with token-passing furnishes user systems with several transmission priorities, and makes it possible to utilize adapters of simple design. At the same time, a shortcoming of the method is the possibility of **loss of authorization** by one of the user systems or **duplication of authorization** (transfer to two user systems simultaneously). Special methods are employed to avoid these possibilities. For example, if a given system has not received tokens over a specified time interval, it generates them and transmits them further down the network. Tokens may be transferred via the channel. Frequently, however, tokens are transmitted via a special **logical control circuit** so as not to load the channel. This circuit may be either open or closed.

An example of multiple access with token-passing is provided by a technique developed by IBM [107]. To ensure token-passing, the user systems are connected via an open one-way logical control network. This network performs disjunction of the signals (S) issued by the user systems. The channel access algorithm involves the following. If user system i needs to transmit a frame, it should do the following:

— issue the signals $S_i = 1$;

— wait the amount of time required for this signal to propagate through the entire logical control circuit;

— begin to transmit the frame as soon as the channel becomes free.

Random multiple access was first implemented in the ALOHA network [108], which was set up at the University of Hawaii for transmission of packets via a satellite radio channel. Figure 5.28 gives a description of the **control-free random multiple access** employed, which allows any types of frame collisions in the channel. The channel operates in an asynchronous mode, and any user system begins to transmit frames via the channel as soon as the need arises. Frames transmitted via the channel may contain errors as a result of the following factors:

— simultaneous transmission of frames by two or more user systems (frame collision);

— hardware malfunctions;

— transmission noise.

Therefore, the addressee system must give a positive acknowledgement that the frame or frame sequence has been received and is error-free. The correctness of each received frame is determined by means of a check sequence at the end of the frame. The number of frames after correct reception of which an acknowledgement is sent, is established by the administration of the monorouting network. If no confirmation has been dispatched to the sender system after the time established by the administration, the frame is repeated.

The control-free access method is extremely simple. It should be recalled, however, that the frequency of errors that appear in

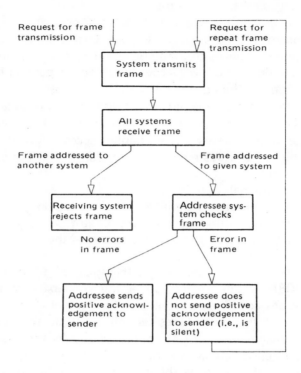

Fig. 5.28. Control-free random multiple access method (ALOHA method).

frames as a result of impermissible simultaneous transmission over the channel by two or more user systems (frame collision) depends on the number of user systems and on the overall volume of data transmitted over the channel.

Three ways of improving the control-free access method have been proposed to increase broadcast-channel capacity:

— timing of channel operation;

— checking of the channel prior to transmission;

— checking of the channel during transmission.

Any set of these methods, or all of them, can be employed.

Random multiple access with timing of channel operation means that the network has an electronic clock which ensures a synchronous mode of operation by generating a clock pulse over the time interval required by any user system to transmit one frame.

162

Regardless of when it has become necessary for the system in question to transmit frames, it can begin to do so only at the instant a clock pulse appears. As a result, frame collision in the channel cannot occur arbitrarily, as in control-free access, but only at the instants of appearance of a clock pulse. Then, after the user system has begun to transmit a frame, everything is the same as in the control free method.

Random multiple access with carrier sensing means that each user system can monitor the symbols that appear in the broadcast channel. When it becomes necessary to transmit a frame, the user system checks the channel, and begins to transmit only if the channel is free. If another user system is already transmitting over the channel, the system in question waits for the transmission to end. In this case, frame collision can occur only when two or more user systems begin to transmit simultaneously. If a user system has taken up the channel, nothing can prevent it from transmitting frames.

Channel monitoring by the sender system during transmission avoids useless frame transmission if frames directed to other user systems appear in the channel. Thus, **random multiple access with collision detection** appeared. When this method is employed, if several users transmit simultaneously, they all cease transmission and begin again at different time intervals (which are specified for them). This method also increases channel capacity, since the need for completing transmission of a frame is obviated if it is already known that there will be errors in it.

As already noted, any set of the above three ways of improving control-free access may be employed. The most frequent procedure is the combined use of two of them: carrier sensing and collision detection [108—110].

Figure 5.29 shows an arrangement with **multiple access with carrier sensing and collision detection.** Analysis of this arrangement shows that it greatly increases the relative channel capacity.

As usual, packets are transmitted between user systems over a broadcast channel (Fig. 5.26). They are transported by frames, into which (like containers) the packets are packed. The frame structure in this instance is roughly the same as in the case of physical links (Fig. 5.23). However, frames should have two addresses, namely, that of the sender and that of the recipient.

The need for specifying two addresses stems from the following. Any physical link connects two systems (Fig. 5.30). Therefore,

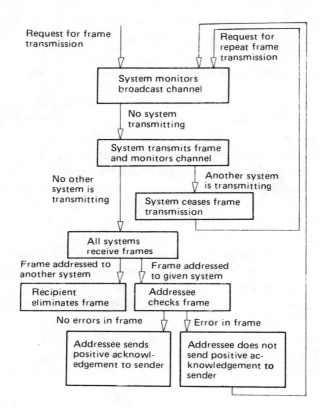

Fig. 5.29. Multiple access with carrier sensing and collision detection.

if a frame arrives at any system (e.g., system B) via a physical link, the addressee is certain of the sender (system N). However, more than two systems are connected to a broadcast channel. In this case, therefore (Fig. 5.30), the recipient (e.g., system B) does not know who sent the frame. If the sender is unknown, then the channel level of the addressee cannot inform him that the frame has been received and does not (or does) contain errors.

Figure 5.31 shows a typical structure of an information frame transmitted over a broadcast channel. The beginning and end of the frame are marked by special symbols, called **flags**. The frame header includes not only the address of the destination but also that of the

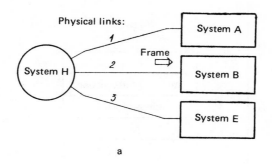

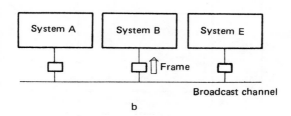

Fig. 5.30. Scheme of frame transmission.

sender. Each address is one or two bytes long [111, 112], thus specifying 256 or 65,536 user addresses, respectively. Information needed
to control frame transmission closes out the header. The body of
the frame is made up of the packet to be transmitted. Its limiting
size fluctuates in different networks from 128 to 1024 bytes [112,
113]. The trailer of the frame incorporates a 2-byte or 4-byte (for
greater reliability) check sequence [111, 113]. Both information
frames (containing user information) and control frames are transmitted via the broadcast channel.

As in the case of physical links, developments are under way
aimed at employing Recommendation X.25 [114, 115] and the
HDLC channel control procedures [113] in broadcast channels. For
example, in an experimental satellite network set up in Japan, the
channel control satisfies the requirements of the HDLC procedure
[115]. A balanced mode is employed, in which error correction is
performed both in the frame sequence and in individual frames.

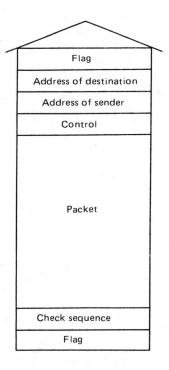

Fig. 5.31. Structure of frame in broadcast-channel computer network.

Each broadcast channel which has been created has its own set of standards, which frequently differ from one another only in terms of unimportant parameters and characteristics. This results in reduced efficiency of the associated hardware and software, and makes network operation more complicated and expensive. Therefore, research aimed at developing standard broadcast channels is under way in many countries.

5.8.
THE IEEE 802 STANDARD

The most serious and thorough analysis of broadcast channels and physical links employed in local computer networks was performed by the Institute of Electrical and Electronic Engineers (IEEE) in the United States. This institute developed **Standard 802** [116—120], which specifies recommendations on architecture, procedures, parameters, and terminology of broadcast channels and physical links used in broadcast-channel and ring-shaped networks, respectively. The basic features of this standard will be considered below.

Architecturally, Standard 802 follows the overall organization and principles of the Reference Model of Open Systems Architecture. It is also based on a seven-layer protocol hierarchy, but describes only the two lowest layers (data-link and physical).

The logical structure of the data-link and physical layers (2 and 1) can be represented as shown in Fig. 5.32. Points of interaction of the network and data-link layers are called here **points of access to service** furnished by the lower layers. The data-link layer is divided into two sublevels: logical channel control and control of access to physical connection facilities. Physical connection facilities are ring-shaped or broadcast-channel communications networks (Fig. 4.2.).

Logical channel control functions determine the data-link layer protocol, while the functions that control access to physical connection facilities determine the method of access to these facilities. Standard 802 offers a choice of one of two access methods. The first of these involves carrier sensing and collision detection; the second is characterized by token-passing.

As is customary, user systems transmit control and information frames to one another. They are created and analyzed at the two data-link sublevels and physical layer of the systems under consideration. Correspondingly, three forms of data blocks, shown in Fig. 5.33, are introduced.

The LCC block is created by the logical channel control sublevel. For this purpose, three fields are added to the packet received by this sublevel from the network layer of the user system. The first two contain addresses of the initial and final points of access to service between which the packet in question is transmitted. The third field contains information needed to ensure interaction of the logical channel control sublevels in different user systems. This information determines the commands and responses which the systems in question transmit to one another. Each of these fields is one byte in size. The size of the data field of the LCC block where the packet is located may arbitrary. However, this field should always contain an integer number of bytes. As a result, the LCC block is declared to be invalid if

— its length is not a multiple of 8 bits;

167

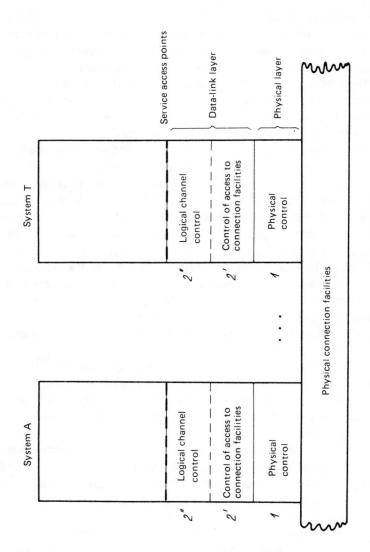

Fig. 5.32. Logical structure of control.

— it has fewer than two address and one control field;
— its overall length is less than three bytes.

The LCC block that is established is transferred from the logical channel control sublevel (Fig. 5.32) to the sublevel of control of access to physical connection facilities. Here three fields of a new header and one trailer field are added to the LCC block (Fig. 5.33), the result being a CAR block. The first of these fields ensures control of access to physical connection facilities. The next

168

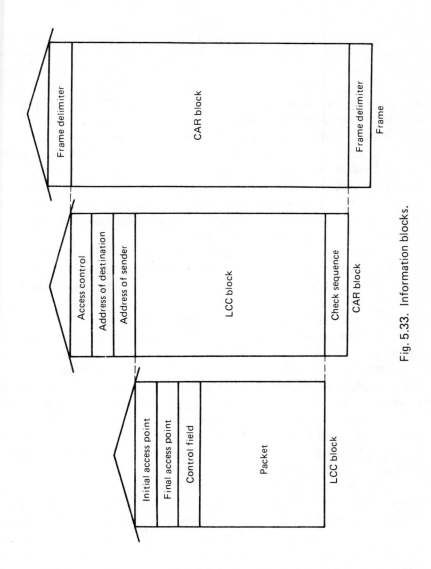

Fig. 5.33. Information blocks.

two fields indicate the addresses of the sender system of the CAR block and of the addressee system of this block. Three types of destination addresses are provided for: global, group, and individual. A **global address** specifies that the given CAR block is intended for all user systems of the local network. A **group address** singles out the set of user systems for whom the CAR block with this address is intended. Finally, an **individual address** specifies only one user system to which the CAR block is to be transmitted.

The data field of the CAR block (Fig. 5.33) contains the LCC block obtained from the logical channel control sublevel, or control information of the sublevel of control of access to physical connection facilities. The size of this field is arbitrary but equal to an integer number of bytes. The end of the CAR block contains a check sequence for determining errors that arise upon transmission. The result is the creation of a CAR block that is directed to the physical layer of the user system (Fig. 5.32). When access with token-passing is employed, the access control field increases. It cannot be less than four bytes in size. A CAR block is declared to be invalid if its length is not equal to an integer number of bytes, or it does not have two address fields and a check-sequence field. There need be no data field in a CAR block.

Initial and final delimiters are added to the resultant CAR block on the physical level (Fig. 5.33). They are needed to separate frames from one another in the overall data flow through the physical connection facilities. Frames obtained as a result of all the above procedures are transmitted via the physical communications facilities from one user system to another. This is done by sending all the bits making up a frame one at a time.

After a frame has been received, the addressee system begins to disassemble and analyze it in an order that is the reverse of the one described above. As a result, packets are transmitted via access service points to the network level of the addressee system. Thus, packets are transferred from the network level of one user system to that of another. Packets are transmitted in the form of sequences or one at a time (datagrams).

Two requirements are introduced in order to make it easier to check frames after transmission. The first is that the size of any information or control frame is determined by the smallest dimensions of the fields in it. The second requirement is that when a frame is created, it is always made up of a multiple of eight bits. Frames that do not satisfy one of the above requirements are declared to be **invalid**.

The **logical channel control sublevel** is the upper part of the data-link layer (Fig. 5.32). It ensures execution of two types of channel service: without and with establishment of a logical channel.

The first form of service is intended for networks in which, so as to maximally simplify the protocol and methods of implementing it, it is advisable to specify only the minimum necessary functions.

In operating with this type of service, frames are exchanged between the data-link layers of user systems without establishment of a logical channel between two points of access to service. Delivery of transmitted frames is not confirmed. There are no flow control procedures and errors occurring in lower layers are not corrected. All functions are transferred to higher-level protocols. In the addressee system, this protocol assembles and reconstructs packets in the same order in which they were transmitted by the sender system.

When the second form of service is employed, a logical channel is established between points of access to service prior to data exchange. Flow control and error correction are provided on the lower level. Packets that are packed into frames are transmitted over the logical channels. The data-link level interaction protocol is analogous to the asynchronous balanced mode of the HDLC standard. Packets transmitted in frames in each logical channel are numbered cyclically from 0 to 7. Packets are delivered to the addressee system in the same order in which they were transmitted by the sender system. The software of the logical channel control sublevel of each user system provides for transmission of both commands and responses.

The **sublevel of control of access** to connection facilities is the lower part of the data-link layer (Fig. 5.32). It is intended for controlling the complex component that the physical connection facilities constitute. Unlike the logical channel control sublevel, the structure of this sublevel is closely related to the specific features of the chosen connection facilities. The level should provide one of two access methods: random (with carrier sensing and collision detection) or deterministic (with token-passing).

The access control sublevel executes the following procedures:
— assembly/disassembly of CAR blocks;
— addressing of information source and recipient;
— checking of destination address and determination of whether or not a frame is intended for the system in question;
— error detection in received frames;
— elimination of frames whose length is less than the permissible value;
— delay of transmission of next frame in sequence to create a time interval between frames.

When access with carrier sensing and collision detection is employed, the sublevel also provides the following:

— immediate cessation of transmission upon detection of collisions of frames transmitted by more than one user system in the broadcast channel;

— generation of the command CONGESTION for the broadcast channel, indicating that frame collision has been detected in it;

— preparation of restart after appearance of collisions.

The **physical layer** of the user system provides interfacing (Fig. 5.32) with the physical connection facilities to transmit frames in the form of bit sequences and to receive these sequences from the facilities in question. A procedure called **Manchester encoding** is performed at the physical level. Its essential feature is that data signals and transmission synchronization signals are combined into a common flow for transmission over a serial channel.

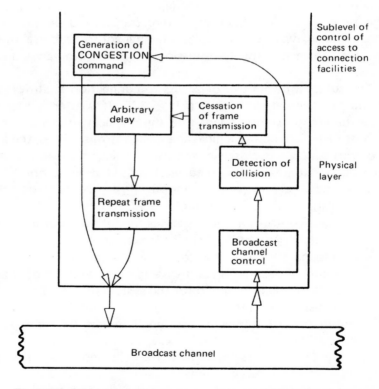

Fig. 5.34. Generation and transmission of CONGESTION signal.

As already noted, in the case of access with carrier sensing and collision detection the sublevel of control of access to connection facilities and the physical layer perform complex functions associated with prevention of competition of several user systems in attempting to transmit frames simultaneously via the channel. To avoid collisions, the procedures outlined in Fig. 5.34 are carried out. The command CONGESTION is transmitted to the broadcast channel to inform all user systems that a collision has been detected.

As for the receiving end, or addressee, measures are taken to distinguish the **bit burst** received in a collision from a frame. A bit burst that appears as a result of interference of several frames is always shorter than a normal frame, since transmission ceases when a collision is detected. This allows user systems to readily determine and eliminate bit bursts. Since sender systems monitor the channel before initiating frame transmission, collisions can occur only when systems begin to transmit simultaneously. If the initial part of a frame has already "gone through," then no collisions will occur subsequently.

It should be pointed out that Standard 802 specifies several different types of local computer networks. Different possible parameters and characteristics are indicated for each type of network. We cannot speak, therefore, of compatibility of computers and other hardware "in conformity with Standard 802." The designation of a standard involves something different, namely, principles that provides for creation of various local networks and effective control of information transmission.

CHAPTER 6

TRANSPORT SERVICE

In the preceding chapter we considered a logical entity called a network channel, which provides data transmission between adjacent communications and user systems connected by physical links. This transmission is described by the protocols of the two lowest layers of the software structure of the network, which specify information channel control and physical link control. In this chapter we will consider a second, higher-lying logical entity that makes it possible to organize data transmission from a process in one user system to a process in another. This logical entity, described by the transmission and network control protocols, creates the **transport service** of the network.

6.1.
STRUCTURE OF TRANSPORT SERVICE

The **transport service** incorporates the transport and network levels of all systems in the network. The latter is based (Fig. 4.2) on a cellular, ring-shaped, or broadcast-channel communications network. Correspondingly, cellular, ring-shaped, or broadcast-channel transport services are set up. The task of each of them is to create logical channels linking processes in different user systems.

Figure 6.1 shows the structure of a **cellular transport service.** It incorporates the transmission control levels (4) and network control levels (3) of all the systems of the networks. The upper levels (4–7) of the communications systems are intended only for supporting the administrative functions of the network and are not involved in transmission of data between user-system processes. Therefore, they are not shown in Fig. 6.1 and the subsequent figures.

At the top, the transport service connects to processes, while at the bottom it is based upon the network channels created in the data-link (2) and physical (1) layers. The points of connection of the service to processes are called **process ports.**

In considering the transport service, we should point out that there are various types of logical channels in computer networks. They are shown in Fig. 6.2. The name of each of them derives

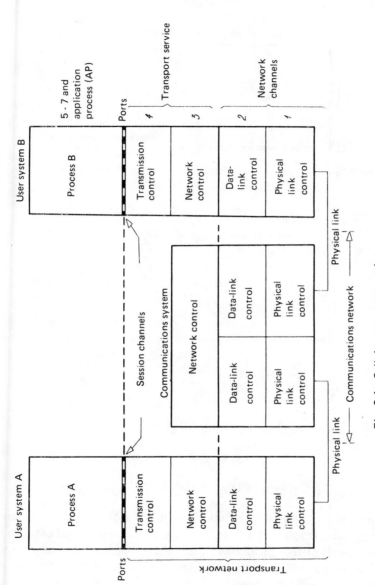

Fig. 6.1. Cellular transport service.

175

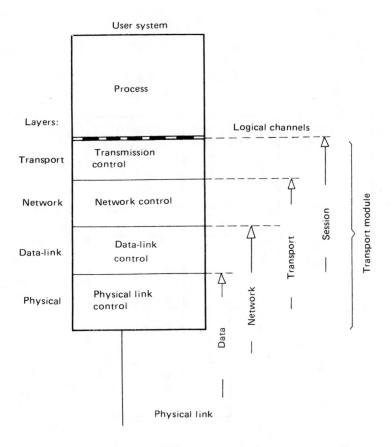

Fig. 6.2. Types of logical channels.

from the network layer whose logical module controls this channel. For example, the operation of the transport channel is supported by the transmission control programs in the transport layers. The entity consisting of transmission, network, data-link, and physical-link control programs in the user system will be called a **transport module.**

The transport modules of interacting systems together with all logical modules of communications systems and physical links between these user systems make up a **session logical channel** (Fig. 6.1). The ends of this channel determine the interacting process ports.

176

In a cellular transport network, information is transmitted in stages from a process in one user system to a process is another. Prior to delivery to each physical link, a packet is packed into an information frame, while after transmission over the link it is extracted from the frame. In this manner, moving like a relay baton from the transmitting transport module, and traversing communications systems and physical links, the packet reaches the receiving transport module that is its addressee. For example (Fig. 6.3), a packet is transmitted from a port of group K to one of the

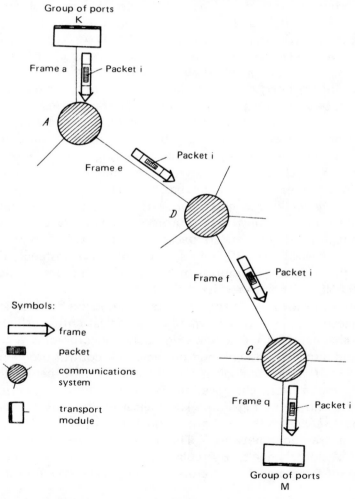

Fig. 6.3. Packet transmission by transport service.

ports of group M. For this the communications network should have several routes. Here packet i is transmitted via communications systems A, D, and G. Initially, packet i is packed into frame **a** and is passed to communications system A. Here packet i is extracted from frame **a** and is checked to establish that there are no errors, and the address of the destination is analyzed. In accordance with this address, one of the communications systems to which packet i should then be passed on is selected. Then packet i is inserted into frame e and is passed on to commuciations system D. Here i is again extracted from the frame and checked, and in accordance with the destination it is directed to communications system G, except that it is now packed into frame **f.** All the above is again performed in G, after which packet i, now inserted in frame g, finally reaches the transport module with the ports of group M.

In this manner, packets containing not only user data but also transport-service control information can be transmitted.

As noted earlier, the network protocols are relatively independent of one another. As a result, it becomes possible to alter the software structure of one layer without altering that of another. In transmitting packets via the network, this makes it possible to pack them into frames of different types. The HDLC protocol is an efficient and generally recognized one. However, there are still many data links that employ the BSC protocol. Therefore, cases are fairly frequent in which packets are packed into HDLC frames in one part of the path and into BSC frames in another. For instance, Fig. 6.4 shows the formats (structures) of frames of both types, employed in the TRANSPAC computer network [121].

As was shown in Chapter 5, data transmission between any pair of adjacent systems is performed by a logical entity called a network channel. This channel (Fig. 5.11) incorporates a physical link, and also the data-link and physical link control programs at its ends. Each of these logical entities operates independently. By introducing network channels into Fig. 6.1, therefore, we obtain the structure shown in Fig. 6.5. The logical entity that connects the transport service to the network channels that interact with it will be called a **transport network.** The latter furnishes processes with logical session channels. By replacing the transport network in Fig. 6.5 by session channels, therefore, we obtain the structure shown in Fig. 6.6.

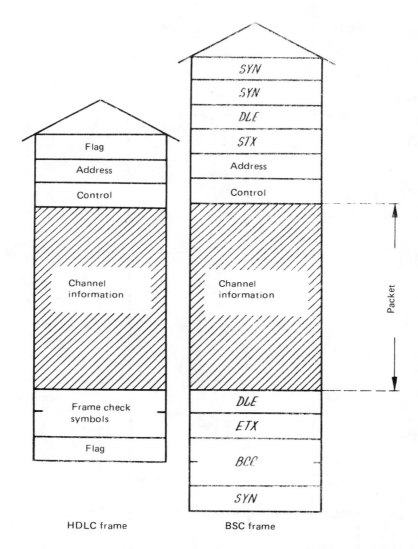

HDLC frame	BSC frame
Flag	SYN
Address	SYN
Control	DLE
Channel information	STX
Frame check symbols	Address
Flag	Control
	Channel information
	DLE
	ETX
	BCC
	SYN

Packet

Fig. 6.4. Different types of frames that support transmission of the same packets.

Session channels may be permanent or temporary (furnished to processes only for the duration of one communications session). These channels should have characteristics that can ensure any necessary forms of process interaction.

Figure 6.7 shows the structure of a **broadcast-channel transport service.** It differs from the cellular case (Fig. 6.1) in that there are no communications systems and the set of physical links is replaced by

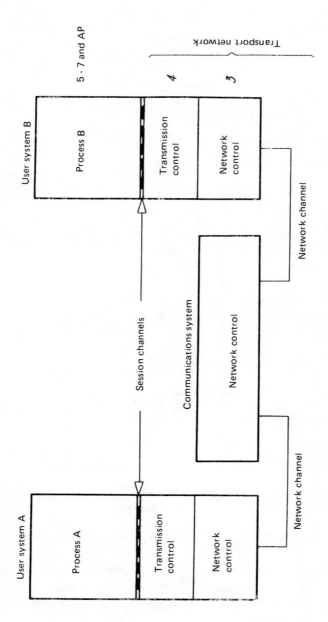

Fig. 6.5. Structure of control of network channels.

180

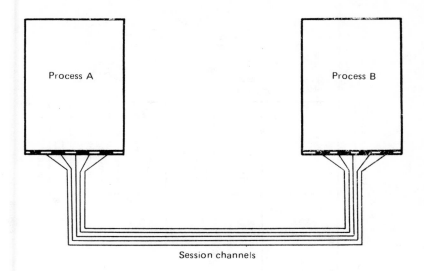

Fig. 6.6. Logical equivalent of transport network.

a single broadcast channel. **Ring-shaped transport services,** in principle, can be based on the structures shown in Figs. 6.1 or 6.7.

In a broadcast-channel transport service (Fig. 6.7) we make the same changes as in a cellular service (changeover from Fig. 6.1 to Fig. 6.5); as a result, we obtain the structure of a broadcast-channel transport service with network channels. It is shown in Fig. 6.8. Here, as in Fig. 6.5, the combination of a transport service and network channels makes it possible to create a transport network. If in Fig. 6.8 we replace the transport network by session channels, we obtain the arrangement shown in Fig. 6.6. Thus, cellular and broadcast-channel transport services generally perform the same tasks: creation of session channels linking processes in different user systems.

Transport services should satisfy a large number of diverse requirements, the principal ones being:
  — transmission of packets with an upper bound on their size (usually not more than 2000 bits);
  — small delay in packet transmission (less than 0.5 sec);
  — low error levels (around 10^{-10} per bit);
  — packet safety (loss or duplication of packets not greater than 10^{-4} per packet);

181

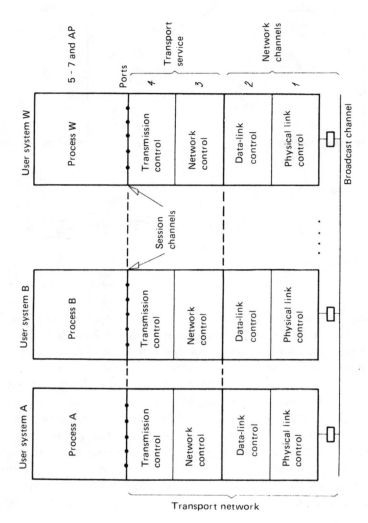

Fig. 6.7. Broadcast-channel transport service.

— allowance for inclusion of any bit combinations (information codes) in packets, i.e., it should be transparent for all packets.

The commands employed by the transport service define the **network control language.**

Two processes are linked by sending data arrays over logical channels from one port to another. The transported packets can be divided into two groups, namely, information and control. An

182

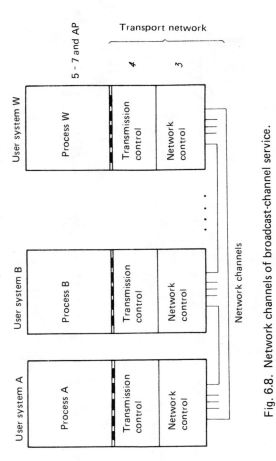

Transport network

User system W

Process W

Transmission control

Network control

User system B

Process B

Transmission control

Network control

User system A

Process A

Transmission control

Network control

Network channels

Fig. 6.8. Network channels of broadcast-channel service.

information packet is one that contains user information transmitted by one process to another. **Control** packets do not contain user information but transmit information needed for control. Therefore, control packets are much shorter than information ones.

Computer networks are frequently based on an **association** of several interconnected transport networks, rather than on just one such network. This is necessary when several networks are being combined, or when already existing terminal installations or computers whose software does not correspond to the network protocols are incorporated into a computer network with the status of additional (local) networks.

183

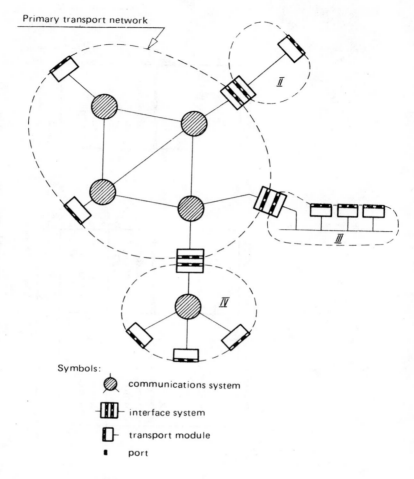

Fig. 6.9. Association of transport services.

An example of an association of four transport networks is shown in Fig. 6.9; the figure indicates the connection between the primary transport network and three additional ones (II, III, and IV). Since the protocols of the upper levels of the software structure of these networks are different, **interface systems** must be installed at the points of connection.

Physical implementation of a transport network involves the installment of logical modules in the computers. Each of the latter may implement one or more logical modules. Therefore, the arrangement of the modules in the computers is dictated by the size of the computers and by their software (i.e., the operating systems and methods of remote data processing).

Depending on how information packets are transmitted in transport networks, the networks are divided into datagram and virtual networks. If a transport network (see Figs. 6.1 and 6.7) provides transmission of only separate, mutually unrelated packets (from the standpoint of the network), it is called a **datagram** network, while the self-contained packets transmitted over it are called **datagrams.** The manner of operation of a datagram transport network is similar to that of a mail service, dispatching separate letters (packets) to addressees in the transmission control modules. To be sure, a datagram network is much faster, since it transmits each packet in fractions of a second.

The second type of network is a **virtual circuit** network, in which sequences (or strings) of interrelated packets are transmitted. The operation of this network is analogous to that of a telephone network that directly connects two users (ports) who can exchange whatever information they wish. In this analogy, it is entirely unimportant that in telephone networks two users are furnished with a sequence of physical links, as a result of circuit switching, while user interaction in virtual circuit networks is provided by other methods. The only important point is that in a

TABLE 6.1.

Characteristic	Type of transport network	
	datagram	virtual
Transmitted entities	Separate, mutually unrelated packets (from the standpoint of the network)	Sequences (strings) of interrelated packets
Order of delivery of packets	Random	Specified
Measures for protecting network from packet overflow	Expulsion of packets at appropriate point of network	Inhibition of transmission of next packet sequence
Reliability of packet delivery	Not guaranteed	Guaranteed
Structure of communications systems	Relatively simple	More complicated
Structure of transport module	More complicated	Relatively simple

185

virtual circuit transport network two user systems may interact via a logical channel in almost the same way as if they were directly connected in the form of a physical link.

Table 6.1 gives the basic features of datagram and virtual transport networks. As we know, processes in user systems process and exchange messages whose lengths may be arbitrarily large. As a rule, therefore, messages must be divided into sequences of blocks prior to transmission over a transport network, and then reassembled after transmission. Virtual transport networks transmit the entire sequence of packets intact. Therefore, the order of the packets is unaltered and there is no need for packet ordering. In a datagram transport network, however, each packet is transmitted independently of the others. Therefore, they may not necessarily arrive in the order in which they were sent. As a result, after transmission via a datagram network the packets must be ordered for subsequent assembly into messages, i.e., they must be arranged in the same order that they were in before the message was divided into blocks.

In the preceding chapter we described methods employed by every network channel to protect against packet error and packet loss. Similar measures are taken in transport services to ensure high transmission reliability.

In a datagram service, however, some modules or communications systems may overflow with packets, which are simply discarded in this case. This requires that measures be taken for repeat transmission of lost packets. In the case of virtual services, packet flow control is provided, and therefore virtual services do not overflow. However, packets may also be lost as a result of various errors in virtual services (as in datagram services). Moreover, erroneous duplicates of packets may appear.

In comparing datagram and virtual circuit transport networks, it should be borne in mind that they both perform the same tasks globally, but by different methods. Datagram networks simplify the structure of communications systems and packet transmission procedures, but require relatively complex transport modules. In contrast, virtual circuit transport networks can greatly simplify the structure of transport modules, but result in increased complexity of the communications systems and packet transmission procedures.

All information and control packets transmitted via datagram or virtual transport networks have destination addresses. These addresses should be multistage addresses. For example, to transmit

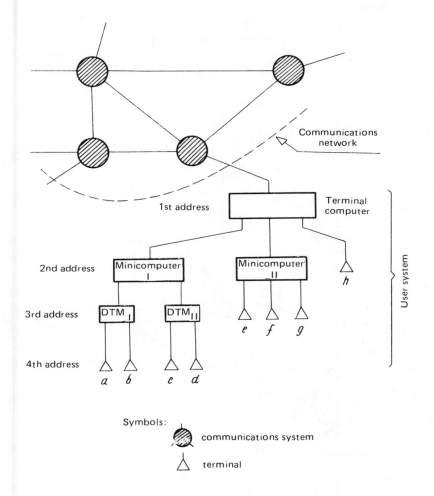

1st address

2nd address

3rd address

4th address

Communications
network

Terminal
computer

Minicomputer
I

Minicomputer
II

h

DTM$_I$

DTM$_{II}$

e f g

a b c d

User system

Symbols:

communications system

terminal

Fig. 6.10. Four-level packet addressing.

packets via the cellular network in Fig. 6.10 to terminal h, it is sufficient to specify two addresses. For terminal **a,** however, four addresses are required: those of the terminal computer, minicomputer I, the data transmission multiplexer (DTM$_I$), and terminal **a.**

As indicated previously, cellular networks should have several routes for delivering packets from one port to another. For example, in the network in Fig. 6.11, a packet from user system I can be delivered to user system II via various routes formed by combinations of nine physical links (1—9).

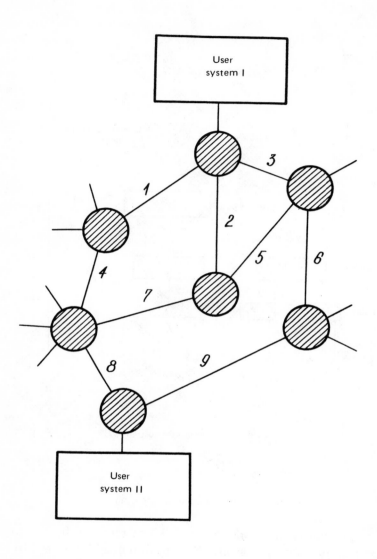

 communications system

Fig. 6.11. Packet delivery routes from user system I to user system II.

The abundance of physical links in cellular transport networks gives rise to a problem of efficient **packet routing.** There are several routing methods. The simplest involves the fact that each communications system (see Fig. 6.11) has a fixed list of possible physical links via which it can transmit a packet with a specified address. This list is compiled with allowance for the link order of preference. A more efficient but more complicated method is adaptive routing. In this case the communications system analyzes the statistics of use of different routes and selects the one that is optimal with respect to a specified criterion (packet delivery time, physical link loading, and so forth).

In practice, every computer network that has been created has its own standards and protocols. This results in complicated problems of efficiency of networks and of their interaction. In recent years, therefore, a number of international organizations have developed standards, protocols, and terminology which could be adopted by all countries.

6.2.

THE X.25/3 NETWORK PROTOCOL

Recommendation X.25/3 of the CCITT, henceforth called the **X.25/3 protocol,** specifes the network control level of a virtual-datagram transport service [95, 131] : "packet format and control procedures for exchanging packets containing control information and user data." The protocol employs experience gained from existing computer networks and initiates the first phase of development of international standards [105] . The developers of TELENET [132] , and also representatives of the Ministries of Communication of England, France, and Canada, helped to create this protocol. At present, the X.25/3 protocol is employed by TELENET (USA), DATAPAC (Canada), TRANSPAC (France), EURONET (Western Europe), and others [132, 133] .

Logical channels. The X.25/3 protocol specifies the interface between user and communications systems and transmission via this interface of packet sequences or individual datagram packets. Depending on the packet format (structure), each sequence contains up to 8 or 128 (depending on the chosen limit) successively numbered packets.

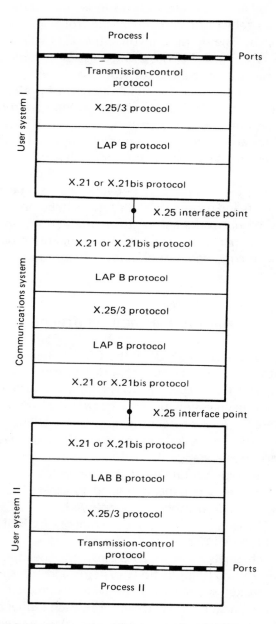

Fig. 6.12. Connection of ports in two user systems.

For simplicity, we will assume that in the virtual-datagram transport service the ports are implemented in the user systems (Fig. 6.12). Everything to follow, however, will apply equally to cases in which the ports are in the interface systems (see Fig. 6.9), terminal concentrators, microprogrammed display controllers, and so forth.

Bearing in mind the above, the "arrangement" of protocols in the user and communications systems assumes the form shown in Fig. 6.12. Here protocols X.21 or X.21bis define the characteristics of physical link control. The LAP B protocol describes information-channel control procedures. Finally, the X.25/3 protocol defines the network control functions (see Fig. 6.5). All three levels (X.21, LAP B, and X.25/3) characterize the interface at points between the user and communications systems.

Protocol X.25/3 describes the creation of both **temporary** logical channels (for one session) and **permanent** channels. The decision to employ a temporary or permanent channel is based on the necessary dynamics of communication and the frequency of information exchange between specific user systems. In the X.25/3 protocol, a temporary logical channel is called a **virtual call**, while a permanent one is called a **virtual circuit.** Each virtual call or virtual circuit is assigned a logical channel group number (from 0 to 15) and a logical channel number (from 0 to 255). Virtual circuits are permanent, and therefore the numbers of these circuits refer to all sessions conducted via them.

The basic tasks that the X.25/3 protocol is intended to fulfill are the following:

— support of procedures associated with the creation and use of logical channels;

— simultaneous operation of a large number of virtual connections;

— assurance of completeness and accuracy of information delivery.

Packet formats. The X.25/3 protocol is unbalanced, since, upon interacting with one another, the user system and communications network perform different tasks (Fig. 6.13). Each of the user systems is an information source of consumer, while the communications network is the facility for transmitting it. Unlike the network, therefore, a user system initiates sessions, numbers packets, controls packet-sequence flows, and so forth.

191

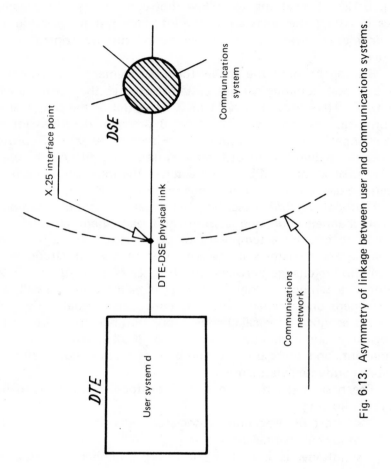

X.25 interface point

DSE

Communications system

DTE-DSE physical link

Communications network

DTE

User system d

Fig. 6.13. Asymmetry of linkage between user and communications systems.

To provide data transmission, the X.25/3 protocol utilizes 19 types of packets (Table 6.2), both in the direction from the user system to the communications network and in the reverse direction. Two of these packets, called Data and Datagram, are information packets, since they contain user information. The remaining packets provide control of the transport service, executing the following functions:

    — establishment of virtual connection;

    — maintenance of (any) virtual connection;

TABLE 6.2.

No.	Type of packet	
	From communications to user system (DSE → DTE)	From user to communications system (DTE → DSE)
	Call and disconnection	
1	Incoming call	Call request
2	Call established	Call received
3	Indicate disconnection	Request disconnection
4	Acknowledge disconnection	Acknowledge disconnection
	Data, datagrams, and interrupts	
5	Data	Data
6	Datagram	Datagram
7	Signal of datagram service	
8	Interrupt	Interrupt
9	Acknowledge interrupt	Acknowledge interrupt
	Flow control and clear	
10	Receive ready	Receive ready
11	Receive not ready	Receive not ready
12		Packet refusal*
13	Indicate clear	Request clear
14	Acknowledge clear	Acknowledge clear
15	Receive ready (modulo 128)*	Receive ready (modulo 128)*
16	Receive not ready (modulo 128)*	Receive not ready (modulo 128)*
17		Packet refusal (modulo 128)*
	Restart	
18	Indicate restart	Request restart
19	Acknowledge restart	Acknowledge restart

— data transmission;
— packet flow control;
— restart (repeat organization of virtual connections).
Packets indicated by asterisks in Table 6.2 need not be used.

Figure 6.14 shows two forms of the Data packet. They differ in that one of them (the upper one) has three-byte header, while the second (lower) one has a four-byte header. These headers consist of seven information fields.

The left half of the first byte (bits 8—5) is called the general format identifier field of the overall packet format. This four-bit

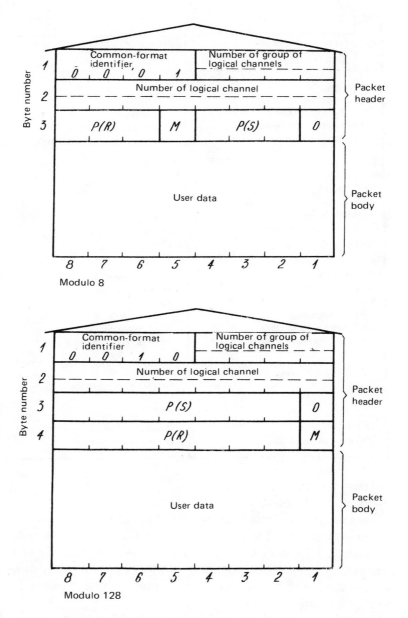

Fig. 6.14. Format of Data packet.

194

field contains a code that indicates the type of overall format of the remaining part of the heading. If the Data packets are numbered cyclically from 0 to 7 (modulo 8), then the identifier of all the types of packets indicated in Table 6.2 contains the code 0001. If the numbering of Data packets is cyclical from 0 to 127 (modulo 128), then the identifier contains the code 0010. The right half of the first byte (bits 4—1) specifies the field in which the number of the group of logical channels is entered. The field furnished by the second byte of the packet heading is for recording the number of the logical channel over which the user information and information needed for packet transmission control should be transmitted. The first (rightmost) bit of the third byte contains a 0, that distinguishes information packets, and also signal packets of a datagram service from among all 19 packets. For the remaining (control) 16 packets, a 1 is entered into this bit.

Each Data packet in any direction of transmission over a temporary logical channel (virtual call) or permanent channel (virtual circuit) is numbered successively. For the case of cyclical numbering from 0 to 7 (modulo 8), a Data packet is assigned a three-bit ordinal packet transmission number $P(S)$. For checking purposes, this same (third) byte contains a three-bit ordinal packet reception number $P(R)$. The signal $M = 1$ indicates that an intermediate packet is being transmitted and that the transmission of Data packets is not yet complete. If $M = 0$, then the Data packet is the last one in the sequence under consideration.

If packets are numbered cyclically from 0 to 127 (modulo 128), then the ordinal numbers $P(S)$ and $P(R)$ become seven-bit. Therefore, the information fields in the third byte of the packet shown in the upper part of Fig. 6.14 are increased and occupy the third and fourth bytes of the packet shown in the lower part of this figure.

Another type of information packet specified by the X.25/3 protocol is the Datagram [131]. The structure of this type of packet, with numbering from 0 to 7 (modulo 8) is shown in Fig. 6.15. If the numbering is from 0 to 127 (modulo 128), then, as in Fig. 6.14, the third byte of the Datagram is replaced by two bytes. As a comparison of Figs. 6.14 and 6.15 indicates, the heading in a Datagram packet is several times larger than in a Data packet, but a Datagram is transmitted over the communications network independently of other packets.

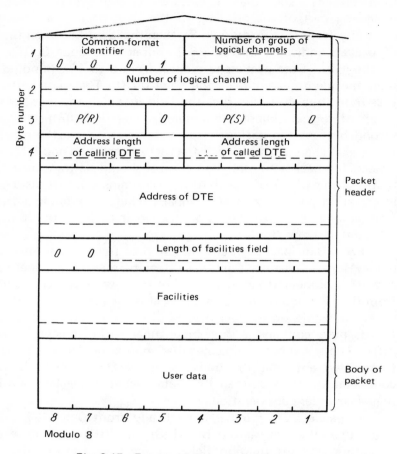

Fig. 6.15. Format of Datagram packet.

The bodies of Data and Datagram packets contain information transmitted by the transmission control program (see Fig. 4.10). The X.25/3 protocol stipulates that the maximum size of the body of these packets should be 128 bytes. At the same time, the protocol allows the administration of the communications network to introduce other limiting packet sizes, i.e., up to 16, 32, 64, 256, 512, and 1024 bytes.

The order of Data packets in each sequence (string) remains unaltered upon transmission over the communications network. Therefore, the sequence is delivered to the recipient user system intact and in the same order in which it was sent by the sender system.

196

The order of delivery of Datagram packets after transmission through the network may be arbitrary.

Information packets are transmitted by the transport service in accordance with the scheme shown in Fig. 6.16. In the sender system (system I), process A issues in block form the information that is to be transmitted to process B in the receiving system (system II). The transmission control program adds a header, and the resultant fragment is passed on. The programs that implement the X.25/3 protocol add a packet header (X.25/3 header) to the fragment. The result is a Data or Datagram packet. This packet is delivered to a program specified by the LAP B protocol. Here a channel header (LAP B header) and channel trailer (LAP B trailer) are added to the packet. As a result, an information frame is generated. This frame is transferred to the physical link via the physical link control program (X.21 or X.21bis), and thus enters the communications system.

In the communications system, the frame passes again through the physical link control program (X.21 or X.21bis) and is handed over to a program that implements the LAP B protocol. This program removes the channel header (LAP B header) and trailer (LAP B trailer) and checks the contents of the packet. If errors have appeared in the packet after transmission over the information channel, the received frame (together with the packet) is discarded and a request for repeat transmission of the frame is sent. If there are no errors, the packet is accepted and is passed on to a program that implements the network control protocol (X.25/3 protocol). The latter reads the destination address of the packet and determines the next successive network channel over which the packet should be transmitted. The packet is handed over to a program that executes the LAP B protocol, which packs it into a frame and passes it on to the physical link via the physical link control program.

Then the frame goes to the next communications system, or, if there is none (as shown in Fig. 6.16), to the user system that is its destination. After passing through the physical link control program (X.21 or X.21bis), the frame is handed to a program that implements the LAP B protocol, and is checked and unpacked. The resultant Data or Datagram packet is given to a program that executes the network control protocol (X.25/3 protocol). Here the fragment is extracted from the packet and is passed on to the transmission control program; the information is then delivered via a port to the addressed process B (process in user system II).

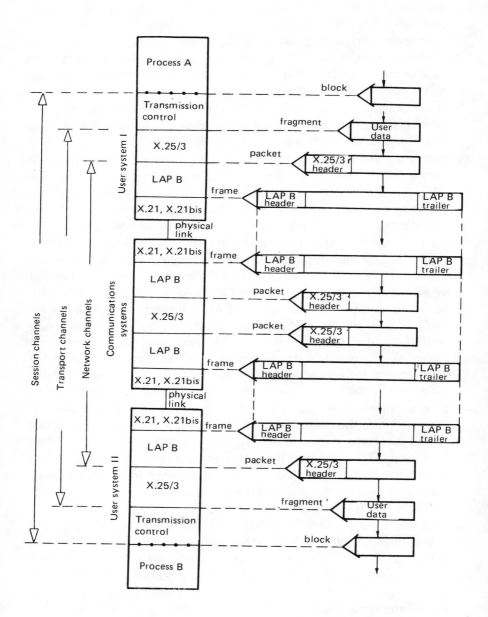

Fig. 6.16. Information transmission by transport service.

198

Protocol X.25/3 also specifies the format (structure) of the control packets enumerated in Table 6.2. One of these packets is shown in Fig. 6.17. Depending on the direction of transmission over the physical DTE/DSE link (see Fig. 6.13), this packet has two names. If it is sent by the user system, it is called Call Request; if it is sent by the communications system, it is called Incoming Call.

The first two bytes of a Call Request/Incoming Call packet have the same fields as all other packets (see Fig. 6.14). The field of the third byte in a Call Request/Incoming Call packet contains an identifier of the type of packet, i.e., the code assigned to this packet. Then the packet indicates the addresses of user systems (DTE) whose ports must be connected by a logical channel (addresses of the calling and called DTE). Since the X.25/3 protocol does not standardize the sizes of these addresses, two fields are allotted in the fourth byte for information on the size of these addresses.

When necessary, the X.25/3 protocol allows a Call Request/ Incoming Call packet to be supplemented by fields of user facilities and user call data. The first field indicates the sizes of the fields of facilities; the second enumerates the necessary additional user facilities (programs, devices). The size of this field is not greater than 62 bytes. The third field contains information (up to 16 bytes) which the user wishes to communicate to a user system during call establishment.

Thus, transmission of a Call Request/Incoming Call control packet is not only a proposal to establish a logical channel but also a signal containing additional information that may be required upon calling.

Transmission of any control packet via the communications service is very similar to the arrangement for transporting Data and Datagram packets (see Fig. 6.16). In both cases, the sources and recipients are programs specified by the X.25/3 protocol that implement network control procedures. It should only be borne in mind that information packets can be transmitted either in the form of sequences or one at a time. As for control packets, they are transmitted only one at a time. Moreover, every control packet is a command for the network control program of the receiving user system.

Control procedure. The X.25/3 protocol specifies the following phases (or stages) of operation of a virtual-circuit network:

199

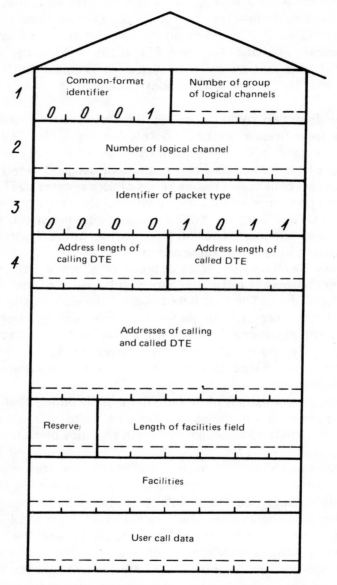

Fig. 6.17. Format of Call Request/Incoming Call packet.

200

— virtual call;
— data transmission;
— flow control;
— reset of logical channel;
— restart;
— clearing.

If it becomes necessary for one of the user systems to transmit information to another user system, the former sends a Call Request control packet to the physical DTE/DSE link (Fig. 6.18). It passes through the entire communications network and arrives at the addressed user system. Upon delivery from the communications network, however, the packet is no longer termed Call Request but Incoming Call. This is done so that, when one physical DTE/DSE link contains packets in both directions simultaneously, it is possible to distinguish them from one another.

Figure 6.19 shows a diagram of the **call phase.** If there are no calls, then the network control module is in the Ready state. If it becomes necessary for the communications system (DSE) to establish a logical channel to transmit information, it sends an Incoming Call control packet via the DTE/DSE link (see Fig. 6.18).* If, however, the user system (DTE) wishes to establish a logical channel for information transmission, then it sends a Call Request packet. At this point a Waiting state occurs (either the DTE or DSE is waiting, depending on the packet source). The Call Request/Incoming Call packet is processed during this state. Upon completion of this procedure, a Call Established or Call Accepted packet, respectively, is sent. The first of these is the DSE's response to the DTE call request, while the second is the DTE's response to a call from the DSE. As a result, there is a transition to the Data Transmission state (see Fig. 6.19).

If, during the procedure for processing a request from the DTE or DSE, a request appears from the other member of the pair in question, then a Collision state arises (see Fig. 6.19), in which both systems (DTE and DSE) wish to transmit information. In this case as well, there is a transition to the Data Transmission state.

---

*This is actually a call request from a remote user system. After passing through the network, however, it becomes a communications- system request.

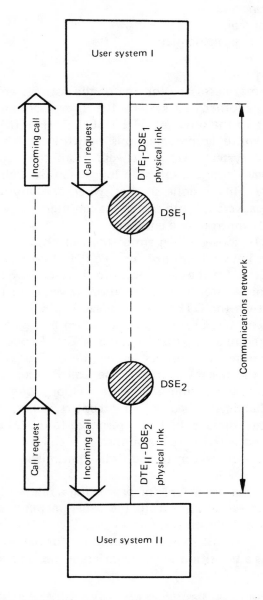

Fig. 6.18. Transit of Call Request/Incoming Call packet through communications network.

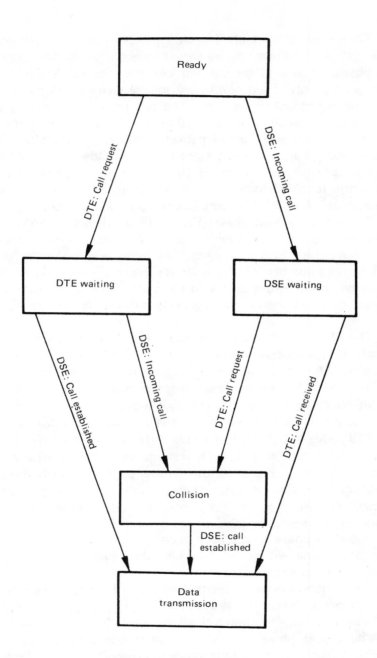

Fig. 6.19. Call phase.

203

Transition to the Data Transmission state signifies termination of the call establishment phase and changeover to the **data transmission phase.** It should be pointed out that the call establishment phase occurs only when temporary logical channels (for one communications session) are set up. The call phase is unnecessary for permanent logical channels, since they are always ready to transmit both information and control packets. Packets of the Data, Flow Control and Clear, and Restart groups are employed to control the data transition phase (see Table 6.2). These packets are employed to request the receiver's permission to transmit, to transmit Data and Datagram packets, to interrupt transmission, and so forth.

The **disconnection phase** (Fig. 6.20) involves the execution of procedures associated with termination of a communications session over a temporary logical channel. Disconnection is also performed when a called number is busy, when the order of packet transmission is violated, when errors appear in the control and transmission procedures, or when the communications network is overloaded with packets.

The phase begins by transmission of a Request Disconnection/ Indicate Disconnection packet by the initiating system (see Table 6.2), after which there is a transition from the Data Transmission state to the DTE Requests Disconnection or DSE Requests Disconnection state, respectively. Arrival of a request for disconnection from another system connected to the physical DTE/DSE link (see Fig. 6.18) does not affect this state. After an Acknowledge Disconnection packet has been received from an adjacent system, there is a transition (see Fig. 6.20) to the Ready state, in which the communications network is again ready to create a temporary logical channel. The functions of the control packets used in the call and disconnection phases are given in Table 6.3.

The **clear phase** is necessary to continue operation of both temporary and permanent logical channels after the appearance of certain error in the transport service:

— violation of order in the transmission of a packet sequence;
— errors in the control procedure;
— overflow of the communications network.

The **restart phase** is used to restore operation of all logical channels directly after the appearance of errors (Fig. 6.21). Exchange of control packets leads to an intermediate DTE Requests Restart or DSE Requests Restart state, and then to the final Ready state.

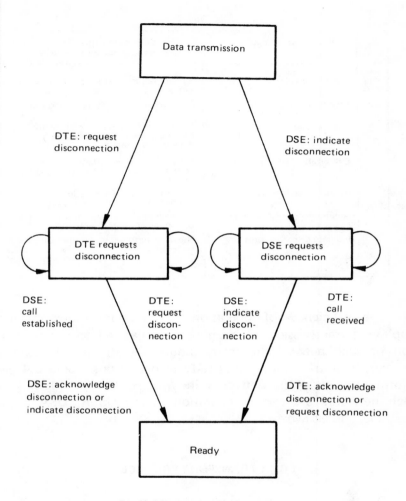

Fig. 6.20. Disconnection phase.

Figure 6.22 shows the interaction of the three operating phases of the transport service, namely, call, data transmission, and disconnection. Here we should point out that most control packets change name after passage through the communications network (see Table 6.2).

In concluding, we should mention that the X.25/3 protocol is a large assortment of procedures, many of which may not necessarily be employed in a particular computer network.

TABLE 6.3.

No.	Name of packet	Control information transmitted by packet
1	Call request	System requests communication with network
2	Incoming call	Network agrees to system's request
3	Call received	System informs network of forth-coming transmission of data or datagram packets
4	Call established	Network informs system of forth-coming reception of data or datagram packets
5	Request disconnection	System requests termination of communication with network
6	Acknowledge disconnection	Network indicates readiness to terminate communication with system
7	Indicate disconnection	Network terminates communication with system
8	Acknowledge disconnection	System terminates communication with network

The efficiency of operation of communications networks employing transmission of X.25 packets has led to the construction of such networks in many industrially developed countries. In many countries they are already in operation. Table 6.4 gives information on X.25 networks in Western Europe [135–138]. Such networks are also in operation in the USSR, USA, Japan, Australia, and elsewhere.

6.3.
ECMA TRANSPORT PROTOCOL

On the basis of the structures shown in Figs. 6.1, 6.2, and 6.7, the upper part of the transport service can be depicted in the form shown in Fig. 6.23. Here all the logical transmission control modules are interconnected by logical **transport channels.** It should be pointed out that the arrangement in Fig. 6.23 reflects equally the operation of cellular, ring-shaped, and broadcast-channel transport services (Figs. 6.1 and 6.8).

The European Computer Manufacturers Association (ECMA) has developed a transport protocol [146] that describes the transmission control level of the transport service shown in Fig. 6.23.

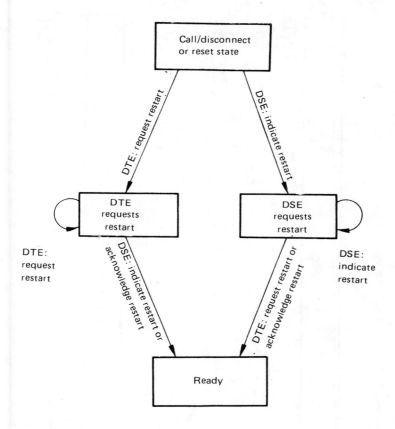

Fig. 6.21. Restart phase.

The ECMA protocol provides a universal transport service (i.e., one that is suitable for arbitrary forms of process interaction) that provides transparent transmission of blocks from one process to another. Use of this protocol frees processes from any need to worry about the details of their interaction in the computer network.

As a result of the ECMA protocol, the transmission control modules in different user systems communicate with one another, establishing transport channels. Between each pair of such modules, there may be one or more channels (Fig. 6.23 shows one channel each). Data arrays called **fragments** are transmitted over transport channels.

The processes for ensuring mutual interaction require that the transport level establish linking logical session channels.

207

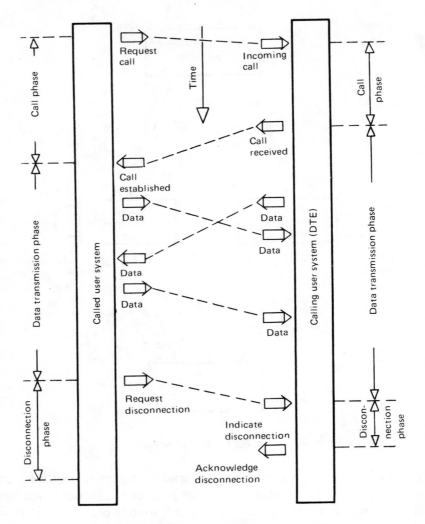

Fig. 6.22. Interrelationship of the three phases.

The processes communicate the following to their transmission control modules:
- the addresses of the source and recipient processes;
- the quality-of-service requirements;
- a list of necessary nonobligatory services.

The ECMA protocol performs for processes a wide assortment of functions associated with information transmission. These func-

TABLE 6.4.

No.	Country	Beginning of operation	Number of communications systems in 1980
1.	Austria	1982	
2.	Belgium	1980	3
3.	Denmark	1981-1983	1
4.	England	1980	9
5.	Fed. Rep. of Ger.	1980	1
6.	Finland	1983	
7.	France	1978	25
8.	Holland	1979	3
9.	Ireland	1982	6
10.	Italy	1981-1982	
11.	Luxembourg	1982	3
12.	Norway	1981-1983	7
13.	Portugal	1983	1
14.	Spain	1980	
15.	Sweden	1981	
16.	Switzerland	1982	1

tions may be divided into three groups: establishment of session channel, data transmission, and termination of session channel.

The following procedures are carried out in establishing a session channel:
— conversion of block addresses into fragment addresses;
— choice of transmission mechanisms;
— channel identification;
— multiplexing (if necessary) of transport channels.

Data transmission involves the following procedures:
— error detection and correction;
— segmenting of blocks and combination of fragments into one block;
— control of the flow of segments;
— transmission of priority and ordinary fragments;
— purge of transport channels.

Transmission of fragments over transport channels is duplex (i.e., simultaneously in both directions). Both ordinary and priority fragments are transmitted over the channels. The latter are employed to transmit information on the state of the communications session.

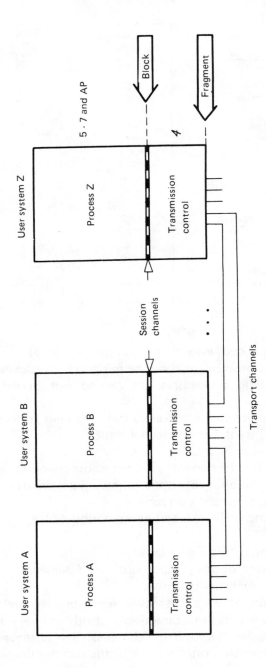

Fig. 6.23. Structure of operation of transport level.

210

The ECMA protocol ensures control of the flows of fragments transmitted over all transport channels. As a result, the recipient process can receive blocks at the most convenient rate.

To ensure reliable operation, the transmission control module checks the received fragments and passes on to its process only those blocks in which there are no errors. If a received fragment contains errors, it is transmitted a second time over the transport channel. In the event that any misunderstandings arise in the transport channel, the ECMA protocol performs a purge, eliminating all fragments and bits of erroneous information from the channel.

The functions performed by the ECMA protocol can be divided into four classes. The **principal class** (class 1) ensures the creation of simple session channels with a minimum number of procedures to be performed. It is employed for the simplest user systems that do not require multiplexing and flow-control operations.

The **flow-control class** (class 2) provides flow control so as to avoid overloads that occur in transport channels and destination ports. It is employed when there are large uniform flows of transmitted fragments, and also when there is intensive multiplexing.

The **error-correction class** (class 3) adds error-detecting and error-correcting procedures to the functions of classes 1 and 2. This class is selected by the process when it is necessary to ensure high reliability of transmission over session channels.

The **error-detection and restoration class** (class 4) executes auxiliary functions. In particular, these functions ensure ordering of fragments when a datagram transport service is employed. In addition, these functions perform top-down multiplexing (of one session channel into several transport channels). This yields exceptionally high reliability of block transport and extended transmission bandwidth. The class under consideration is intended for controlling large information flows between large-scale user systems.

The ECMA protocol provides the following set of commands for transmission control (Fig. 6.23):

— request for establishment of channel;
— acknowledgement of connection;
— request for channel disconnection;
— acknowledgement of disconnection;
— data transmission;
— priority data transmission;
— acknowledgement of data receipt;

211

— acknowledgement of priority data receipt;
— refusal to accept fragments;
— request for channel purge;
— acknowledgement of channel purge.

By using these commands, the logical transmission control modules can effectively coordinate operations and transmit data.

Commands and data are transmitted by sending the appropriate types of fragments. For example, information (text) from one process to another is transmitted in Data fragments. Figure 6.24 shows the

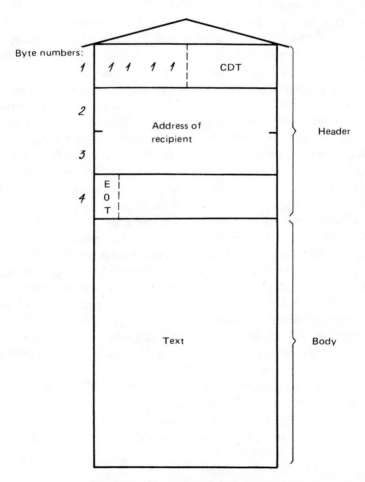

Fig. 6.24. Structure of Data fragment.

structure of this type of fragment. As the figure indicates, a Data fragment has four fields. They are control fields (bytes 1—4) and form the heading of the fragment. The body of the fragment contains the text, i.e., information coming from one of the processes.

The command code is to be found in the left part of byte 1. For a Data fragment, this code is 1111. The right side of byte 1 contains the credit (CDT), i.e., the number of fragments that the receiving transmission control module authorizes to be transmitted. Its address is entered into bytes 2 and 3 of the header. Byte 4 consists of two parts. Its left side (EOT) contains a 1 if the Data fragment under consideration is the last one; otherwise, there is a 0. The right side of byte 4 contains the number of the transmitted Data fragment. The size of the Text in the fragment is unrestricted, but is equal to an integer number of bytes.

6.4.
DATAGRAM TRANSPORT SERVICES

As already noted, transport services can transmit individual packets called **datagrams.** Use of datagram transport services can simplify functions associated with information transmission between user systems. As a result, datagram services have been developed in a substantial number of computer networks (ARPANET, NPL, CYCLADES, etc.). Operation of these services, however, has also revealed major shortcomings.

The advantages and shortcomings in this type of transport service are such that at present there is no unity of opinion among computer network development engineers as to the optimum structure of these services. Table 6.5 shows the types of services employed by major organizations and developers [61,90,96,122—129]. Most of them (including CCITT and IBM) prefer virtual services. At the same time, many organizations are developing protocols for combined virtual circuit and datagram services that provide operation in both the datagram and virtual circuit devices. In principle, a service of this type is virtual. However, the heading of the sending network control module may contain a symbol that indicates that the given packet is unique (i.e., a datagram) and that there is no need to carry out procedures associated with preparation for reception of subsequent packets and formation of a packet sequence. The virtual circuit-datagram method is being investigated experimentally in ARPANET [90].

TABLE 6.5.

Organization or network	Type of transport service	
	datagram	virtual
CCITT	Yes	Yes, X.25
ISO	Yes	Yes, X.25
ANSI	Yes	Yes, X.25
IFIP	Yes	
IBM		Yes
PIX		Yes, X.25
ARPA	Yes	Yes
CYCLADES	Yes	
SITA	Yes	
TELENET		Yes, X.25
DATAPAC		Yes, X.25
PSS		Yes, X.25
TRANSPAC		Yes, X.25
EURONET		Yes, X.25

In analyzing a datagram transport service, it should be pointed out that when datagrams are transmitted through a communications network, the situations shown in Fig. 6.25 arise. For example, let us say it is necessary to transmit a message from user system A to user system B. For this purpose, the message is divided in A into a group of individual datagram packets. Each datagram is transmitted independently (not via a virtual channel provided to a sequence of packets) over the communications network. Because the shortest path is occupied at the instant of transmission, the first datagram comprising the message may travel the long path shown on the left in Fig. 6.25. The shortest path becomes free by the time that datagram 2 is transmitted, and thus, this datagram follows the route shown on the right in Fig. 6.25.

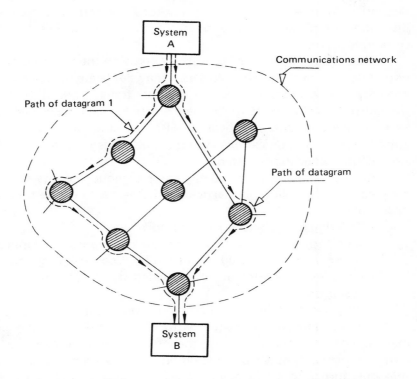

Fig. 6.25. Transmission of datagrams via communications network.

As a result, user system B receives datagram 2 first, and datagram 1 second. The group of datagrams that conveys the message does not arrive at system B in the same order in which system A transmitted it. Before assembling the message, therefore, the transmission control program (Fig. 6.23) must order the sequences of datagrams. Since a given datagram is sent independently, rather than via a virtual circuit, it has a much larger heading than a packet. Hence, redundant control information is transmitted over the channels.

In addition, the use of datagrams entails problems associated with information flow control. When there are virtual circuits in the communications network, it is possible to control packet flow over any of these circuits (and in both directions). If a large high-speed computer sends data to a small slow one, the latter restricts the

215

packet flow in accordance with its capabilities. When datagrams are employed, there are no virtual circuits in the communications network. In this case, therefore, packet flow control amounts to discarding of packets at any point of the network where critical situations occur.

Thus, datagram transmission bases itself on the fact that packet switching networks may be imperfect, may duplicate or lose packets, and may mix up the order in which they are transmitted. If, however, the network is allowed to make these errors, it ceases to be necessary to implement functions associated with the creation of virtual circuits in each communications system. This leads to some simplification of communications systems.

At the same time, the datagram technique has major shortcomings. These include, in particular, the necessity of the following operations:

 — ordering of packets at the transport level;

 — monitoring of packet loss and of appearance of duplicated packets not authorized by the network control programs;

 — complex flow control not provided by the communications systems;

 — long datagram headings (as compared to packets).

The advantages associated with simplification of the communications systems are outweighed by the shortcomings, which result in increased data-transmission costs. This stems from the fact that microprocessors and main storage are becoming cheaper much more rapidly than physical links. As a result, datagrams are less and less frequently used in communications networks.

The creation and development of the X.25 packet switching network known as TELENET in the United States provides a case in point. This network originally employed datagrams for transmission between communications systems [134]. Comparison of virtual circuits and datagrams, however, established that the former have significant advantages.

Packet headings are equal to 3 bytes, while in TELENET datagrams they are 16 bytes. Moreover, computer networks are making more and more use of interactive (or dialog) modes of user-system interaction. Therefore, the mean statistical message length is steadily decreasing. Moreover, routing in communications networks on the basis of virtual circuits provides more efficient allocation of the loading of physical links and communications systems. In contrast, when datagrams are employed the memory of the communications systems may overflow, since the systems do not provide information about what is happening at the network inputs.

Loss of a datagram in the network resulted in repeat transmission by the sender system after a time-out of approximately 6 sec. Each repeat transmission caused a temporary interruption in transmission equal to this time-out. When virtual circuits were introduced and datagrams were not used, time-outs from repeat transmissions disappeared. Hence, the operation of the communications network became more stable. Now a failure of a physical link or communications system is detected by an adjacent communications system, which disconnects the channel and initiates repeat connection.

The TELENET analysis showed that conversion from datagrams to virtual circuits offers major advantages and savings in communications network operation. As a result, datagram transmission in TELENET has been replaced by transmission based on virtual circuits.

This replacement yielded a number of advantages, the principal ones being the following:
   — unproductive operations in packet (datagram) transmission were eliminated;
   — the cost of data transmission was reduced;
   — capabilities for management of communications network resources were improved;
   — flow control which did not permit network overflow became possible;
   — the architecture of the communications network became simpler and more uniform.

6.5.
COMMUNICATIONS SYSTEMS

Figure 6.26 shows the logical structure of a communications system. The system must simultaneously execute p identical processes, defined by the physical and data-link protocols (1 and 2) and by part of the network protocol (3′). In this process the physical and data-link protocols describe interfacing with and control of the physical link, while the part of the network control protocol describes control of the logical channels created in one physical link. One common process, associated with the second part (3″) of the net-

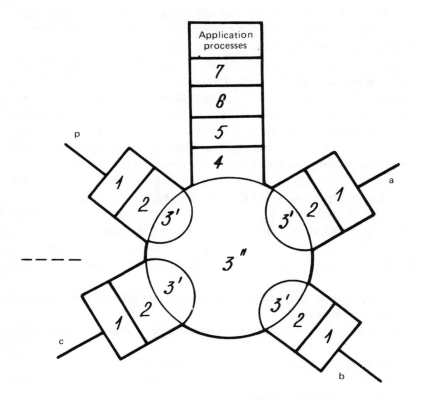

Fig. 6.26. Logical structure of communications systems.

work control protocol, is added to the parallel processes p under consideration. This process provides packet switching on the basis of the available routing table.

For reliable, fast, and efficient operation, any modern communications system is a multiprocessor system. Therefore, it is advisable to modify the overall logical structure of the communications system in Fig. 6.26 in such a way that it provides for multiprocessor implementation.

Two different versions of such a structure are shown in Figs. 6.27 and 6.28. Here each of the $p + q + 2$ rectangles specifies a group of functions to be implemented by one processor. Functions specified by layers 4—7 describe administrative management and are not related to primary control associated with packet switching and routing. In the subsequent analysis, therefore, they will be disregarded.

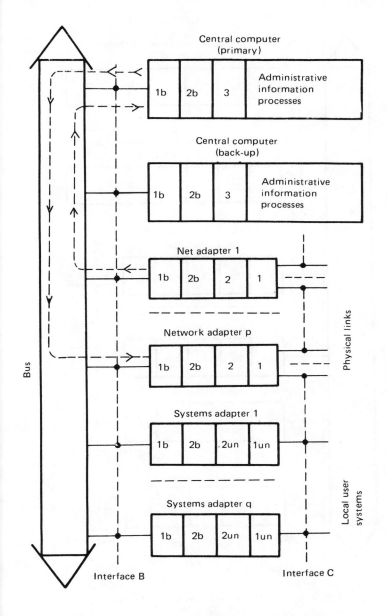

Fig. 6.27. Centralized communications system.

219

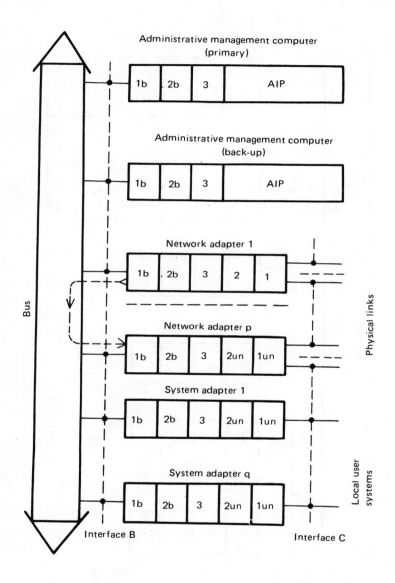

Fig. 6.28. Decentralized communications system.

The structures in Figs. 6.27 and 6.28 assume the existence of p + q + 2 processors that interact via a common physical connection called a **bus**. The primary and back-up central computers (if they are used in the system), p network adapters, and q systems adapters are connected to it. **Network adapters** provide interaction between physical channels and the bus, while **systems adapters** link user systems at moderate distances (usually 15—30 m) to the bus.

In the structure in Fig. 6.27, the functions of the channel and physical levels of the communications system are implemented in p + q identical processors, while the network-level functions are concentrated in two processors (primary and back-up). Therefore, the p + q processors interact via the central computer, which has a table of routes (the interaction path of the processors of network adapters 1 and p is shown in Fig. 6.27). This type of communications system will be called a **centralized** system.

In contrast, in Fig. 6.28 the functions of the network (third) layer are repeated in the p + q processors. Accordingly, information routing is performed by all processors of the network and systems adapters. Here there is no central computer; any pair of processors of adapters can interact directly with one another via the bus. For this purpose, all processors have routing tables. This type of communications system will be called a **decentralized** system.

The processors are connected to the bus in accordance with a common standard called a **bus interface** (B). The interfacing to and control of the bus is determined by levels 1b and 2b. In addition, the processors of the network adapters implement a **physical link interface** (C), characterized by levels 1 and 2. This interface may be a unified one for all channels. Frequently, however, a communications system involves channels of different types. In these cases the physical link interface is represented by a group of standards that specifies the possible channel types (and characteristics).

Similarly, the interface of the systems adapters depends on the types of channels or busses of the computers going to local user systems and connected to these adapters. For example, if Unified System or SM computers are connected directly (without physical links) to the communications system, two types of C interface (specified by the standards of the Unified System channels and SM bus) are employed.

In a **centralized communications system** (Fig. 6.27), the network level (3) is implemented by the processor of the central computer. This same processor executes administrative information processes. In the event the primary computer breaks down or is being repaired, it is replaced by the back-up. The lower layers of the protocols (1 and 2) are implemented by network microprocessor adapters. Multiplexers are added to the adapters for channels with modest data transmission rates. Then one adapter can control up to 4—8 channels simultaneously.

Figure 6.28 shows a **decentralized communications system.** In this system there is an administrative management computer (processor) that executes administrative information processes (AIP). Functions of the network level (3) are repeated in all network microprocessor adapters. As in Fig. 6.27, multiplexers are added to the adapters for physical links that operate at low rates.

The structure of the communications system is highly reliable, since there is no single central point that determines transmission reliability. The reliability of the decentralized system is especially high. Here (Fig. 6.28) there are no central computers at all, and malfunctioning of the adapter (if the necessary switchings are lacking) can lead only to malfunctioning of one or more physical links. As for the administrative-management computer, it is not involved in primary control associated with packet switching and routing. Therefore, a decentralized communications system can operate when both computers (i.e., the primary and the back-up) break down. In a decentralized communications system, for convenience of servicing, the computer and adapters are based on the same type of microprocessor.

To summarize, the communications systems that are becoming most widespread are decentralized ones based on large numbers of microcomputers that interact via one or more busses. Figure 6.29 shows a typical structure of such a system. The system consists of a set of microcomputers of the same type, specialized for performing four types of operations (1—4). They differ from one another only in terms of software and controllers. Microcomputers of the first type (1) have controllers for connecting floppy disks and, if necessary, displays with printers. Microcomputers of the second type (2) contain controllers that provide interfacing to LAP B channels (first and second layers of Recommendations X.25 or X.75). Machines of the third and fourth type (3, 4) are equipped with controllers for connection to channels to nonstandard user systems and terminals.

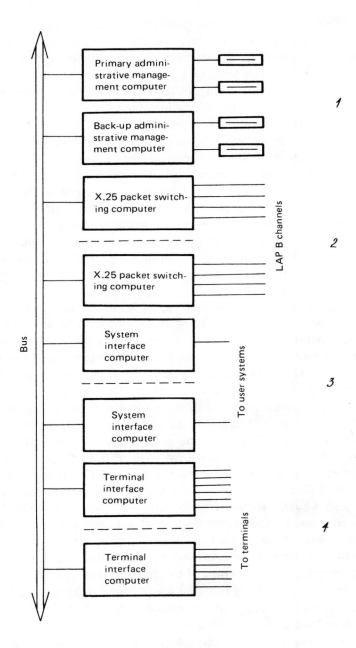

Fig. 6.29. Structure of decentralized system.

The first type of microcomputer provides administrative management of the communications system and connection to the administrative management systems of the communications network. Microcomputers of the second type are primary, since they perform all functions associated with packet switching. Microcomputers of the third type support the X.25 interface for user systems that do not have it. Finally, interface microcomputers of the fourth type provide connection of (asynchronous or synchronous) terminals.

Frequently, to enhance communications system reliability, not only the administrative control computers but also the microprocessors of the adapters and even the busses are made redundant. Figure 6.30 shows an example of such a system [136]. Here h network microprocessor adapters, each with a primary and a back-up microprocessor, are connected to the primary and back-up busses. The microprocessors operate with a common main storage and interact with the physical links via controllers $K_1 - K_h$. Up to 32 adapters may be connected to the busses.

Figure 6.31 shows another example of a microcomputer communications system [141]. Here the types of microprocessor controllers depend on the types of physical links used. The communications controllers have direct access to the memory of the central computers. The arrangement has a high degree of redundancy (central computer, communications controller, bus).

A multimicroprocessor communications system may also consist of a group of virtually identical microcomputers connected to two ring busses [142, 143]. The structure of such a system, whose capacity is 200 kbits/sec, is shown in Fig. 6.32. Up to 64 microcomputers may be connected to the busses. Of these, two are of type A and 62 of type K. Each computer has a main storage of from 64 to 256 kbytes; they differ in terms of their controllers. Computers of type A have controllers that support connection of one or two floppy disks to each of them. The disks are not involved in primary control; they are used to load programs and to assemble statistics on the operation of the communications system. Unlike computers of type A, those of type K have linking controllers to physical links. In addition, of course, the two different types of computers have different software.

Microcomputers of type A (primary and back-up) are required for administrative management of the communications system. In performing these functions, they interact with the administrative network control system.

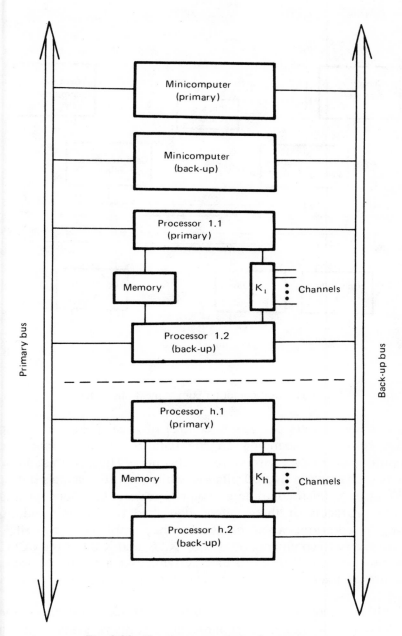

Fig. 6.30. Two-bus communications system.

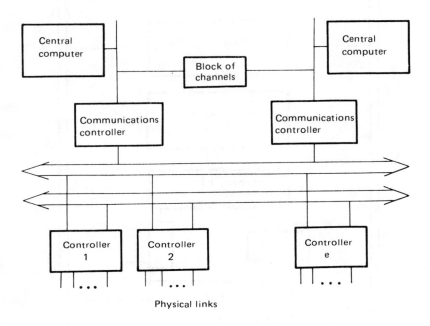

Fig. 6.31. Multicomputer communications system.

Microcomputers of type K control physical links and provide packet routing. Depending on the data transmission rate, each computer can interact with up to 16 channels. The transmission rate over two channels is 64,000 bits/sec, while over 16 channels it drops to 50 bits/sec. Microcomputers of type K perform functions specified by the protocols of three layers, described by Recommendation X.25. In addition, when necessary, they implement the HDLC protocols and Recommendations X.3, X.28, and X.29 of the CCITT; they also emulate IBM 3270 user systems. As a result, the logical structure of microcomputers of type K assumes the form shown in Fig. 6.33.

All microcomputers interact with the primary and back-up via ring busses. For modest communications systems, simple but relatively slow busses are employed, each with a data transmission rate of 100 kbits/sec. Large communications systems employ complex high-speed busses that operate at 8 Mbits/sec.

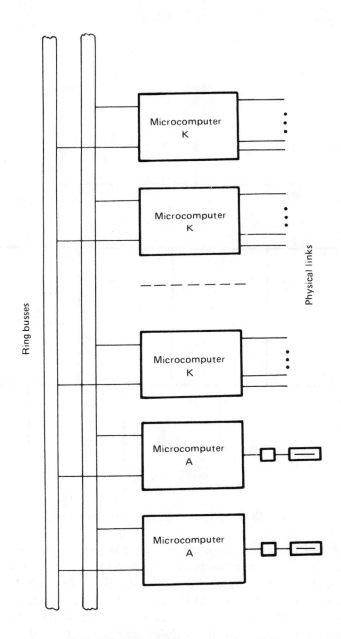

Fig. 6.32. Multimicroprocessor system.

227

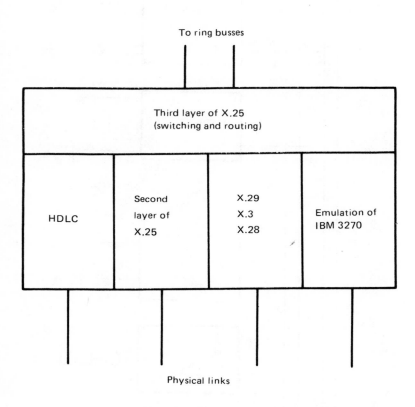

To ring busses

Third layer of X.25
(switching and routing)

| HDLC | Second layer of X.25 | X.29 X.3 X.28 | Emulation of IBM 3270 |

Physical links

Fig. 6.33. Logical structure of microcomputer.

The XPRO large-scale communications system has been developed by Tran Telecommunications [144, 145]. The overall operating speed of this system is 300 kbits/sec. Sixty-four physical links are employed for packet switching, as specified by Recommendation X.25. Up to 1500 virtual circuits can be set up in these links; 100 connections are made and up to 800 packets transmitted per second via these circuits. The system also executes interface functions that provide for connection of terminals via BSC channels (up to 64 kbits/sec) and asynchronous channels (up to 9600 bits/sec).

6.6.
DATA EXCHANGE BETWEEN NETWORKS

At present there are dozens of computer networks operating with different protocol hierarchies. Manufacturers continue to produce many thousands of large computers whose remote-processing standards differ substantially from the protocols of the networks to which they are connected. This requires the development of methods providing data exchange between networks, so that users can interact with systems united by associations of transport services.

When it is necessary to connect two packet switching networks described by relatively similar sets of protocols, the connection may be effected via an interface system that performs the function of **internetwork communications systems** (Fig. 6.34). In these cases the result is a common transport network that links all user systems of computer networks A and B.

An interface system in the form of a communications system that is common to two computer networks (Fig. 6.35) has a fairly complicated structure, including emulation models for the communications systems of the two networks, two types of translators, and a common functional conversion module. The last of these performs formatting, routing, fragmenting, and assembly/disassembly of packets.

An internetwork communications system is relatively complex, since it must represent and mutually convert the protocols of the two communications networks. The more the networks differ from one another, the more complicated the structure of the internetwork communications system. This method also requires universal addressing of the systems and ports of both networks; otherwise the interface system must analyze the addresses and perform readdressing. But in that case it must implement protocols which are usually not executed by communications systems.

A more universal way of connecting two computer networks involves their interaction via an interface system that constitutes a common user system incorporated into the two networks (Fig. 6.36). When this methods is employed, it is possible to set up any kind of internetwork communication, without specifically dealing with the protocols that are employed in the connected networks. Therefore, this method is the one most frequently employed.

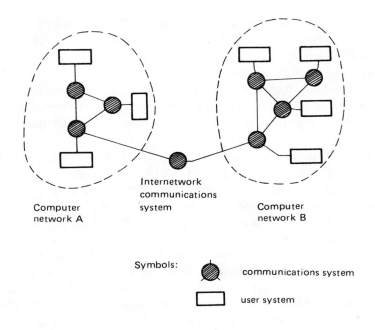

Symbols: ◍ communications system

            ▭ user system

Fig. 6.34. Structure of link between two computer networks via a common communications systems.

Figure 6.37 shows the structure of an interface system that emulates user systems of the two networks. In this case, a module that performs common protocol-conversion functions is placed between the emulators of the two systems.

The price of the universality of the connection method under consideration is complexity of the modules that implement it and the need for utilizing relatively large information and computing resources. Frequently, therefore, yet another network connection method is employed.

This third method involves the creation of an interface system that is a serial converter of information [140]. The converter is connected (Fig. 6.38) to the user systems (I and II) of the networks being joined. Its logical structure is shown in Fig. 6.39.

In the method under consideration, all the protocols of both networks are implemented in user systems I and II, while the inter-

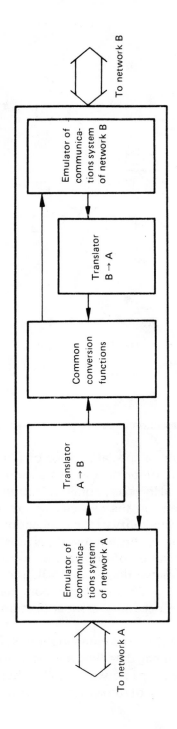

Fig. 6.35. Block diagram of internetwork communications system.

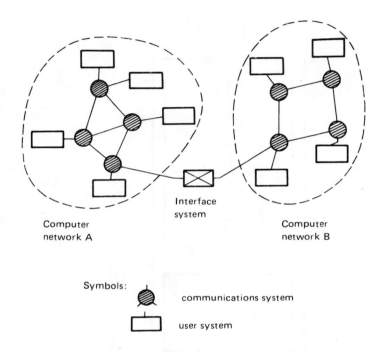

Symbols:

⊘ communications system

▢ user system

Fig. 6.36. Structure of interaction of computer networks via interface system.

face system performs only a special process of linking these systems via a simplified local set of protocols. This simplifies the software of the interface system. However, communication between the networks becomes dependent on the capacity and reliability of the two user systems. Also, the flexibility of the connection upon modernization of the protocols of one or both networks is substantially impaired.

To ensure standardization of information exchange between different communications networks (Fig. 6.40), the CCITT has introduced Recommendation X.75 [139]. Recommendation X.121 is intended to provide the necessary standardization of the addresses of the user systems.

As in the case of X.25, **Recommendation X.75** describes functions of three layers (physical, data-link, and network) at the interface points of the communications networks. The physical layer of X.75 specifies the characteristics of the interface with synchronous full-

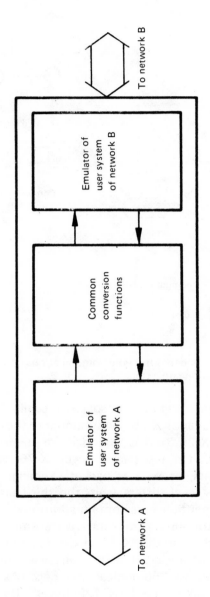

Fig. 6.37 Block diagram of interface system.

233

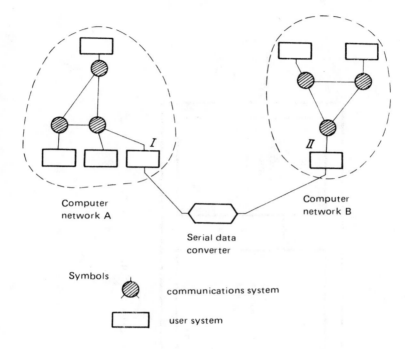

Computer
network A

Computer
network B

Serial data
converter

Symbols

communications system

user system

Fig. 6.38. Structure of link between two communications networks via
serial information converter.

duplex physical links operating at high speeds (usually 50 kbits/sec
or more). The data-link layer of X.75 is very similar to the corresponding layer specified by X.25, and is intended for describing frame
transmission procedures. On the packet level, X.75 describes the
packet types and formats, as well as packet exchange procedures
between networks. This level differs from the third layer of X.25
in that the call establishment packets contain additional information.

Control and data-containing packets are transmitted between
communications networks via the X.75 network. Here up to 16
groups of logical channels are created in a physical link. Each of
these groups contains up to 256 logical channels. As in Recommendation X.25, the packet length is 128 bytes. By agreement
between networks, however, packets of greater or smaller size are
allowed.

234

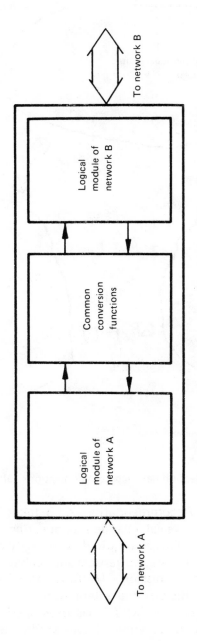

Fig. 6.39. Block diagram of serial information converter.

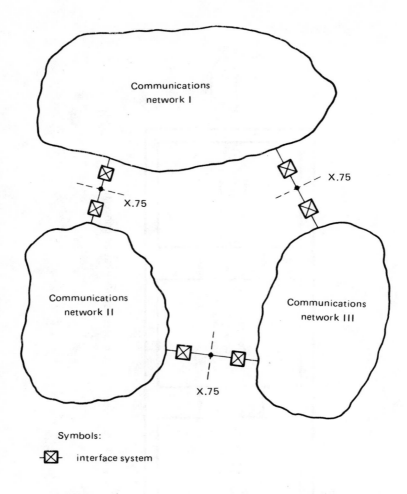

Symbols:

—⊠— interface system

Fig. 6.40. Interaction between communications networks.

The structure of Recommendation X.75 takes account of the need for using long physical channels connecting different communications networks. This is required when networks are linked via communications satellites or transoceanic cables, and there are substantial delays in transmission. Malfunction of a physical link between networks can disrupt the interaction of large numbers of user systems. Therefore, the CCITT has developed a multichannel protocol that provides for running of logical channels over several physical links between two networks.

Recommendation X.75 is widely used for interconnecting nationwide X.25 packet switching networks. Here each network can be regarded as a component of an international network. This makes it possible to set up an international X.75 packet switching network. An example of such a network is shown in Fig. 6.41. The figure depicts three **international communications systems,** forming (together with the physical channels) an international X.75 network. Four component nationwide X.25 packet switching networks are connected to it. The logical channels involved are specified by means of 12-bit numbers.

Figure 6.42 shows an example of an international X.75 packet switching network that is currently being set up [137]. To simplify the figure, the internetwork interface systems are now shown. The network now has four international communications systems, in North America (United States and Canada), Europe (London), and Asia (Japan). Nationwide X.25 packet switching networks are connected to these points. In addition, the association includes EURONET, which joins user systems in France, the FRG, Italy, Denmark, Holland, Belgium, Luxembourg, Ireland, and England. Future inclusion of networks in Australia, Norway, Ireland, Hong Kong, and Singapore is planned.

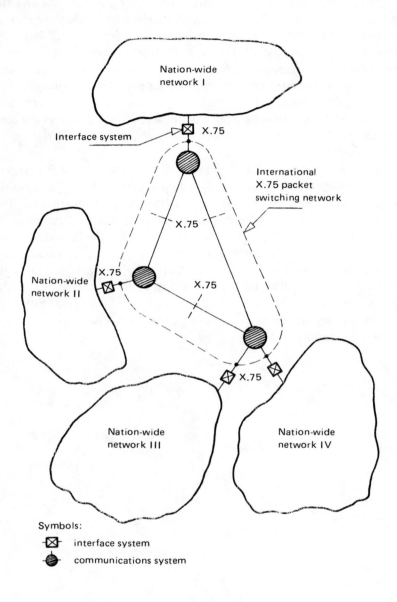

Nation-wide
network I

Interface system

X.75

International
X.75 packet
switching network

X.75

Nation-wide
network II

X.75

X.75

X.75

Nation-wide
network III

Nation-wide
network IV

Symbols:

interface system

communications system

Fig. 6.41. Structure of international network.

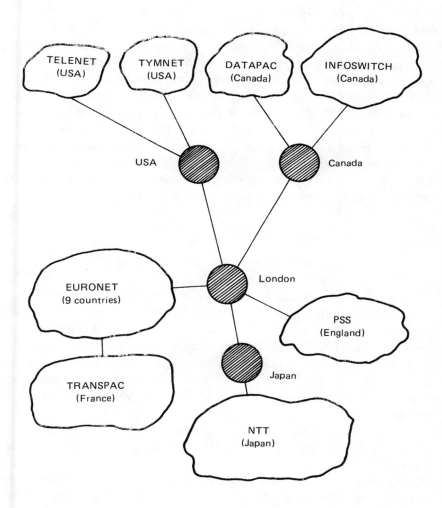

Fig. 6.42. International packet switching network.

CHAPTER 7

PROCESSES

In the sixth chapter we considered a logical entity called a transport service. Its tasks included the creation of logical session channels providing transmission of data units between ports of processes. Transport service operation is described by the middle pair of protocols, namely, network and transmission control (see Figs. 6.1 and 6.7). In this chapter we will consider a third logical entity that specifies methods of process interaction via logical session channels furnished by the transport service. The procedures of this entity are described by the three higher-level protocols, namely session, presentation, and application-process control (Fig. 1.5). These protocols define the standards that provide distributed data processing for extensive groups of users.

7.1.
ACCESS TO APPLICATION PROCESSES

A transport service with its set of network channels forms a **transport network** (Figs. 6.5 and 6.8), through which processes interact with one another. As for processes, we distinguish two parts in them: the first is determined by application processes (Fig. 1.5), while the second provides access to application processes. The second part is described by the application, presentation, and session-level protocols. In what follows, we will refer to it as **network elements.**

In the general case, each user system has M network elements, each with its own port. Thus, system I in Fig. 7.1 has seven network elements.

There are one or more application processes, each connected to one or more network elements, in a user system. The ports of these elements are interconnected through the transport network by logical session channels. Two of them (from port a to port b and from port c to port d) are shown in Fig. 7.1. It should be borne in mind that during network operation, the list of communications systems and physical links through which each of the logical channels runs may change.

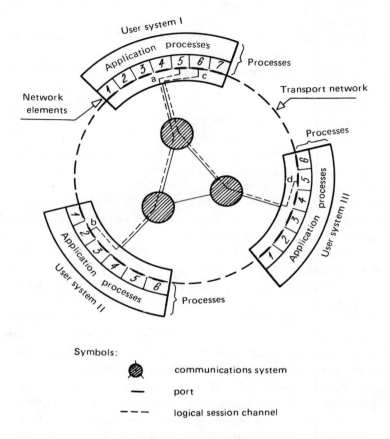

Symbols:

    communications system

—   port

– – –   logical session channel

Fig. 7.1. Interrelationship of application processes.

Pairs of network elements interact during communications sessions. A session begins when it becomes necessary to transmit information and ends after transmission has been completed.

The session and presentation control programs execute two basic groups of functions, associated with control of data flow and information conversion. Flow control generally includes the following procedures:

- control of transmission of tasks (questions) and solutions (answers);
- elimination of contention when several network elements simultaneously access one element;

— initialization and termination of communications sessions;
— temporary halting and restoration of transmission during sessions;
— repeat transmission of data units eliminated as a result of errors in them.

Information conversion involves primarily the need for the following functions:
— separation of messages into sequences of blocks, and assembly of blocks into messages;
— format and code conversion.

Application-process control programs provide direct communication with these processes, furnishing them with interaction services with other application processes.

Interaction with the transport network (transmission of commands and information) may be performed not only by application processes but also by operators at the consoles (or terminals) of user systems. Therefore, it is said that the concept of application processes encompasses not only user programs but also human operators. Programs and operators are combined into the general concept of **users.**

Because of the multilevel structure of computer networks and the independent operation of transport networks, users may interact with one another via logical channels without becoming involved in transmission control procedures via the communications systems and logical channels connecting ports of network elements.

Interaction of two users is governed by a group consisting of three protocols, namely, application-process, presentation, and session control. Each computer network has a set of functionally oriented groups of these protocols which specify various modes of joint user operation. Theoretically, the number of different protocol groups in a computer network may be equal to the number of user pairs. In practice, however, it is from three to five. The most frequent groups are those that specify the following:
— transmission of files;
— remote job I/O for purposes of computation;
— interactive (dialog) interaction between terminals and data banks and information systems;
— electronic mail.

The last of these protocols is for sending texts ("letters") from one operator to another.

The session, presentation, and application protocols are divided into **bilateral** and **multilateral** protocols. A bilateral protocol supports communication between two user systems, so that two network users (user programs or operators) can interact. These protocols are the simplest and most widespread. Universal multilateral protocols that support interaction between one user and many others are more complex.

The principal tasks entrusted to these protocols are as follows:
— organization of user interaction;
— session control;
— conversion of messages into sequences of blocks and, conversely, assembly of messages from sets of blocks;
— multiplexing and demultiplexing of information flows.

The hierarchy of the software structure of a computer network (see (Fig. 1.5) not only divides its operation into quasi-independent levels, but also makes it possible to construct interfacing "trees" for large numbers of users to one physical link. Thus, data units travelling along physical link A (Fig. 7.2) are allocated among D physical links in the communications system. Upon arriving at a user system, these units are directed to different resources. As they proceed, they are handed over to different network elements, each of which interacts with a certain application process. The result is the "tree" of information allocation that is shown in Fig. 7.3. Moving in the opposite direction (from the "branches" to the "trunk"), information coming through the ports is assembled and transmitted over physical links.

In this process, data units are processed (Fig. 7.4), and their structure and names change. Thus, a block issued by a process becomes a frame at the output of a user system, with four headers and a trailer.

The channel header is generated in the data link control layer (see Chapter 5), while the packet and transmission headers are added by the transport-service programs (see Chapter 6). As for the process header, it is created and utilized by the session and presentation control protocols. This header includes control information that users exchange with one another, usually the following:
— an enumeration of operations which must be performed with the information that follows the header;
— specification of indicators that determine the meaning of the codes;

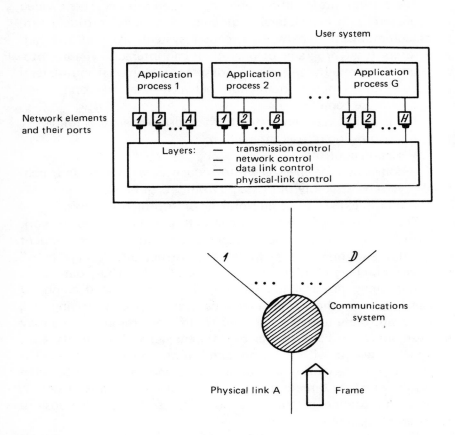

Fig. 7.2. Interface between physical channel and users.

— information on whether or not it is possible or necessary to reverse the logical channel to change the direction of transmission;

— information on the location of the block in the transmitted message (first, intermediate, or last);

— indication of need (or lack of it) for acknowledging receipt of block.

Application processes exchange commands with network elements, thus enabling them to activate ports, make the necessary arrangements for the transport network, and control information flows over the logical channels. Table 7.1 gives a list of commands most widely used in networks. Seven commands are described here; they are not always fully utilized. For example, some computer net-

244

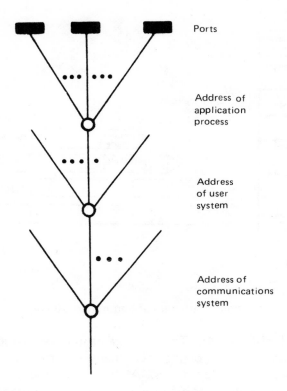

Ports

Address of
application
process

Address
of user
system

Address of
communications
system

Fig. 7.3. "Tree" of information distribution.

works assume that it is sufficient to have a set comprising commands 1, 2, 6, and 7.

Users exchange information over logical channels during sessions. Each session comprises three basic phases: establishment of communication between processes, information transmission, and termination of session.

7.2.
EXECUTION OF APPLICATION PROCESSES

Application processes, which comprise various user programs, are at the highest hierarchical level of the software structure of com-

245

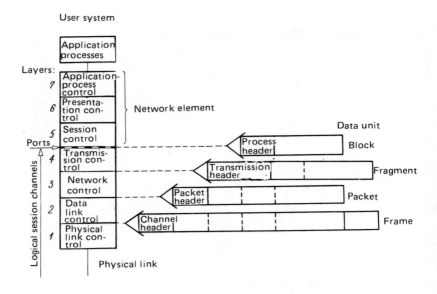

User system

Layers:

Fig. 7.4. Alteration of structure of transmitted data units.

puter networks (see Fig. 7.4). These programs may be characterized by their frequency of use. For instance, many programs written by scientists are used only a few times. At the same time, there is an enormous set of programs that are used repeatedly, over many years. These include most programs related to sectors of the national economy, e.g.,
  — inventory and accounting;
  — banking and financial;
  — urban transport control;
  — airline and train reservations;
  — distribution of medical supplies to pharmacies.

User programs are connected to the transport network by network elements.

Depending on the manner of location of user programs in user systems, these systems are divided into **multipurpose** and **specialized** systems. Multipurpose systems typically contain large numbers of different user programs. Such systems are widely employed in scientific research and development. In contrast, specialized systems

TABLE 7.1.

No.	Name of command	Meaning of command
1	Open port	Request to activate port, i.e., to prepare it for session with designated network element (addressee)
2	Send block	Transmission of message block over logical channel that has been set up
3	Interrupt transmission	Temporary interruption of transmission without termination of session
4	Clear channel	Elimination (after the appearance of a malfunction) of all information in the logical channel
5	Resume transmission	Continuation of transmission of blocks after temporary interruption
6	Receive block	Transmission of message block to user
7	Close port	Indication of end of session

have only one user program, accessed by large numbers of network users. An example can be provided by a system that implements an urban information and reference service. Many specialized systems are used to create data banks in nuclear physics, power engineering, and so forth.

The structure and set of external devices of a specialized system conform closely to the nature of the problem being solved. Therefore, the operation of specialized systems is always characterized by high efficiency. Multipurpose systems, in contrast, are intended for solving a wide range of problems. Therefore, the utilization efficiency of the hardware and software is generally low.

In self-contained operation, most computers are multipurpose, since each of them must support execution of various user programs (or tasks). When computers are combined into networks, this requirements creases to operate. After they are connected to networks, therefore, many multipurpose computers become specialized for certain tasks.

Special components, namely, programs for administrative management of the computer network, are added to the set of ordinary programs in user systems. One of these is the **network control component,** while the remaining ones are **local control components.** These components are connected to the transport network by network elements that are usually given the same names. The interconnection between network control and local control components via the transport network (Fig. 7.5) forms a distributed entity that controls the logical (software) and physical resources of the entire network.

The network control component may be located in a user system together with ordinary user programs. Lately, however, this component is more frequently placed in a separate user system.

Local control components are present in all user systems in the network (one in each), or in part of them. At the same time, a determination is made of the part of the network whose administrative management (within the framework of certain rights and obligations) is entrusted to each of the local control components.

Depending on the nature of administrative management, computer networks are subdivided into centralized and decentralized networks. They all have the same management structure (see Fig. 7.5), but they differ in terms of how functions are allocated between the network control component and the associated local control components. In a network with centralized control, the network control component is the sole "boss" of the network, and performs the following basic functions:

- creation and elimination of logical channels;
- management of the organization of user sessions;
- activation and deactivation of logical and technical network resources;
- alteration of packet routing algorithms;
- reconfiguration of the transport network in the event of breakdown or repair or modification of the structure;
- assembly of statistics and records on the use of logical and technical network resources.

In **networks with centralized control,** the network control component authorizes each session between application processes and makes decisions regarding all other issues associated with network operation. The local control components are allotted only secondary functions of gathering information on the operation of the network

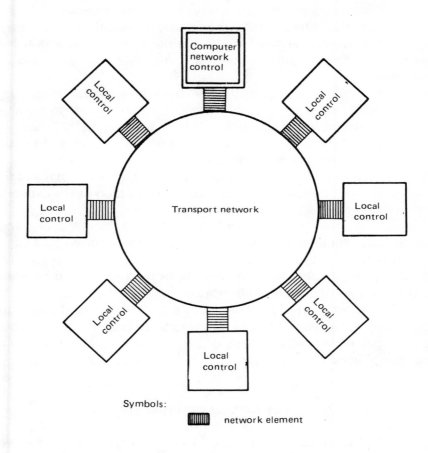

Symbols:

▦ network element

Fig. 7.5. Structure of network control processes.

segment allotted to each of them and of carrying out the instructions of the network control component on this segment.

In **networks with decentralized control,** a substantial part of the functions that are carried out by the network control component in the case of centralized control are transferred to the local control components. In this case the network control component executes only the following functions:

— furnishing or withdrawal of permanent logical channels;
— planned structural changes in the transport network or packet routing algorithm;

249

— maintenance of an information service regarding the network configuration and resources (software and hardware);
— statistical data and reports on network operation.

The local control components in a network with decentralized control perform a great many tasks, including the following in particular:

— assembly of statistics and reports on the operation of the allocated network segment, and transmission of these to the network control component;
— management of the logical and technical resources of the allotted network segment;
— keeping the network control component informed of malfunctions or changes in resources or configuration of the network segment.

As computer networks increase in size, and their reliability and dynamicity requirements become more and more stringent, the number of networks utilizing decentralized control will increase rapidly. At the same time, the structure and forms of decentralized network control will become more sophisticated.

At present there are no standards specifying levels of access to application processes. In what follows, therefore, we will consider some examples of higher layers of software structure, created by a number of network developers.

7.3.

INTERACTION OF APPLICATION PROCESSES IN SNA

The IBM Corporation has created a systems network architecture known as SNA [147—151]. This architecture embodies current conceptions of multicomputer associations. The methods do not place constraints on the forms of network architecture. However, the VTAM version of the remote-access method that was initially made available by IBM worked only with tree structures of the transport network. At the end of 1976, there appeared an expansion of VTAM called the Advanced Communications Function (ACF) [152, 156]. Its use together with VTAM makes it possible to support interaction of several principal user systems, each forming its own tree-like computer network.

At the same time, IBM is collaborating with the CCITT along the lines of using and improving the X.25 protocols [154-156]. The firm has announced the development of an interface that makes it possible to connect principal user systems and terminals of IBM to the TELENET, TRANSPAC, and DATAPAC networks, which utilize the X.25 recommendations. Adaptation of SNA to the X.25 protocols involves primarily a reworking of the network control program, implemented by a 3705 communications computer.

Logical structure. The logical structure of the SNA network is shown in Fig. 7.6. Here the principal user system and terminal systems have three consolidated network software structure layers, one above the other.

In the principal system, the transmission layer is implemented the VTAM remote-access method. A set of IBM-developed systems programs (middle layer) interacts with it. These include, in particular, IMS, CICS, TSO, RES, and JES. These programs constitute the **function management layer** in SNA.

Above the function management layer there are users. In SNA, **users** are understood to mean not only user programs and operators (as is customary), but also external devices (disks, tape, punchcard input devices, and so forth).

In a terminal system, the two lowest layers of the software structure are implemented by special systems control programs. As in the principal system, the top layer includes the users.

The **transmission layer** determines the transport network that supports packet transmission. It consists of three layers:

— transmission control;
— network (path) control;
— data link control.

These sublevels are quasi-independent and support the operation of the transport networks. The analogous protocol layers are described in Chapters 5 and 6. The transport network in question is a virtual one.

The **function management layer** performs two principal tasks: control of format conversion of transmitted data units and control of data exchange procedures between users. The need for format conversion stems from the fact that users operate with data units in different formats. Therefore, the network provides for mutual conversion of these units.

The **application-process layer** includes user programs that implement user-specified data processing algorithms. Terminal operators and external devices of user systems are also at this level.

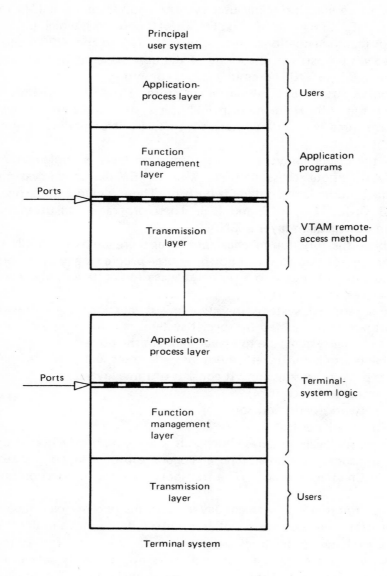

Fig. 7.6. Logical structure of SNA network.

Function management. The function management layer supports user interaction via the transport network. In the SNA network, the tasks of this layer are as follows:
- planning of data transmission;
- organization of user sessions;
- management of physical and logical resources of the network;
- diagnostics and statistics regarding network operation.

This layer is made up of three components (Table 7.2), called **programmable network units.** Network units link users to the transport network that provides data transmission between these elements (Fig. 7.7).

As already noted, SNA networks usually have a tree structure. The principal user system is the basic element (Fig. 7.8). It is the starting-point for one or more "trees" made up of physical links, communications, terminal, and terminal-communications systems, and also terminals.

Centralized control of network operation is implemented in SNA networks. Therefore, the system services control point is located in the principal system (Fig. 7.9). There is a local control unit (called a physical unit in this case) in each system, including network (packet) terminals. Logical units providing communication with users are located in user and terminal systems. Their number is equal to the number of users of each system.

The system services control point is at the top of the hierarchy of network units. This unit is linked to all physical and logical units, and controls their operation.

The computer network is divided into subareas, with their own addresses. In each of these subareas, all network units (and their ports) also have addresses assigned to them. As a result, each network unit obtains a 16-bit address, consisting of two parts. The first part contains the address of the subarea, while the second contains the address of the units. The number of bits of the address field (out of the 16 available) allocated to each of these parts is specified by the network administration. A subarea may be a principal user system, terminal system, terminal-communications system with associated group of terminals, and so forth.

Network units in systems connected to the network by leased (dedicated) physical links are assigned a permanent address. Addresses of user-system units connected via switched channels are assigned when a connection is established, and only for one session.

TABLE 7.2.

Name of component	Functions performed by component
System services control point	Control of physical and logical resources of network
Physical unit	Control of physical configuration of system and of physical links connected to it
Logical unit	Control of interaction of user programs or terminal operators

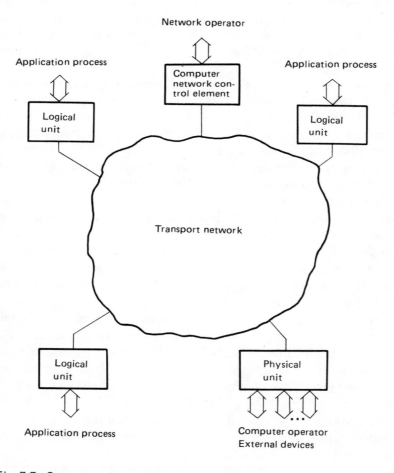

Fig. 7.7. Structure of user linkage via network units and transport network.

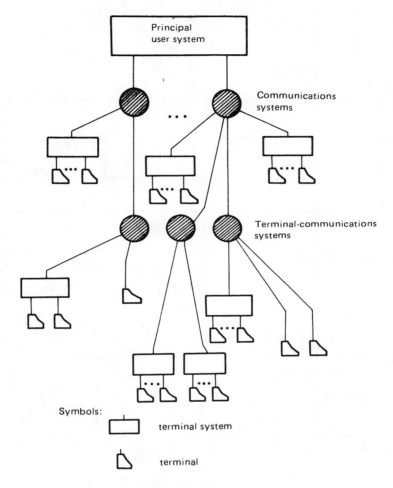

Symbols:

| terminal system

terminal

Fig. 7.8. Physical structure of SNA network.

Network units interact with one another by means of communications sessions. For each session, the necessary network resources (user programs, physical links, buffer storage, processors, and so forth) are allocated. To conduct a session, a user must have an agreement with the functional control layer regarding data format, type of communication over the logical channel (full-duplex or half-duplex), and method of monitoring the intensity of data transmission.

The **system services control point** performs a large number of functions associated with the use of the logical and physical resources of the network. These include, in particular, the following:

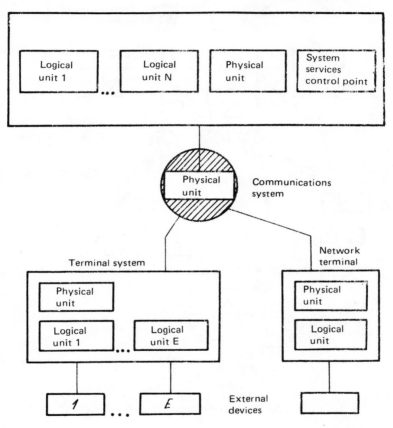

Fig. 7.9. Arrangement of network units in user systems of SNA.

— management of the operation of all physical and logical units of the network;
— management of communication of operators of different systems;
— management of network configuration;
— start-up of the network or of parts of it;
— assembly of statistics regarding network operation;
— authorization of sessions between network units.

The system services control point manages physical and logical units distributed throughout the network (see Fig. 7.9). In turn, these units provide the system services control point with the information necessary for decision-making and for issuing commands to the physical and logical units. This mutual exchange of information is conducted via logical channels provided by the transport network. An exception involves communication with the physical and logical units of the principal system, with which the system services control point interacts via internal connections in this system.

Figure 7.10 shows the structure of the system services control points. The core of this structure consists of the control components for the physical and logical units of the entire network. The physical-unit control component includes configuration-control and operating-service programs. To control the physical resources, these programs contain generators of the commands that are sent throughout the network.

The configuration control program provides overall management of network resources and generates information regarding network addresses and the status of network units. Each of the latter may be activated at the request of an operator or as a result of initialization of associated devices.

The operating-service program controls the checking of network operation. For this purpose, it conducts communication sessions with all physical units, and assembles statistical data on the operation of the systems and other network hardware.

The logical-unit control component manages sessions between all logical units in user systems.

The core of the system services control point interacts with the operating system of the principal system, on the one hand, and with the transport network on the other. The operator interface component emulates the systems console of the operator of the principal system.

By means of bit-encoded commands, the formatted-system control component effects communication between the core of the system services control point and physical and logical units in other systems. Since unformatted commands are used for communication with terminal operators, a recording-system control component is included in the structure of the system services control point.

Physical unit. This unit provides control of all physical resources of the system in which it is located, and of the physical links adjoining this system. For this purpose, a physical unit performs the following functions:

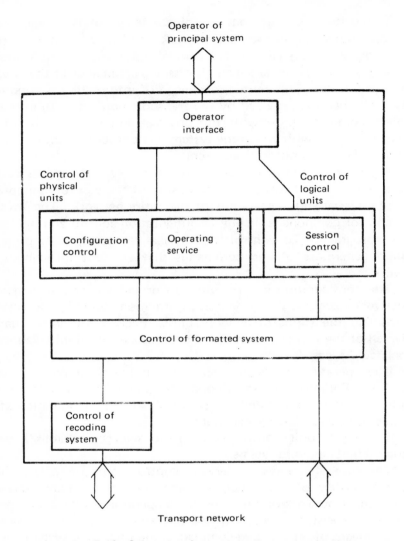

Operator of
principal system

Operator
interface

Control of
physical
units

Control of
logical
units

Configuration
control

Operating
service

Session
control

Control of formatted system

Control of
recoding
system

Transport network

Fig. 7.10. Structure of system services control point.

— management of physical resources of the system (connection
   and disconnection of computer devices, adapters, controllers,
   and physical links);
— initialization and deinitialization of adjoining physical links;
— involvement (together with the system services control point)
   in recovery of the controlled part of the network after
   damage to it;

258

- assembly of statistics on operation of the system and associated hardware;
- analysis of certain errors in system operation and of the possibilities of eliminating them;
- connection to the system operator in critical situations; supply to the operator of needed information regarding operation of the system and associated hardware.

Figure 7.11 shows the structure of the physical unit. The unit consists of a number of independent components. The logical-channel control component performs functions that support communication of ports via the transport network. The physical-link interface component supports communication between this element and a physical link. Finally, the component called the boundary function transforms network addresses into addresses of specific terminal systems and terminals. It also allocates buffers for packet flows. The physical-unit service component generates commands that control the physical links to the system in question. The functions performed by the command-generator, routing, and data-flow control components are clear from their names.

Logical unit. The task of a logical unit is to support user interaction via the transport network. Each logical unit performs the following operations:
- forwarding of requests for establishment of logical channels between ports of logical elements;
- transmission of data between users via logical channels;
- control of data flows;
- transmission of requests for initiation and termination of communications sessions.

Logical units are divided into primary and secondary units. A **primary** unit is one that can initiate user interaction. A unit that cannot initiate a session is called **secondary**. The transport network of SNA allows simultaneous communication only between one primary logical unit and one secondary unit.

Logical units also check received blocks. If an error is detected in a block, the logical unit requests that it be repeated. If the error is not corrected, the unit informs the users to this effect.

A logical unit consists of five components (Fig. 7.12) that support user communication, via the transport network, with other logical units and with the network control unit.

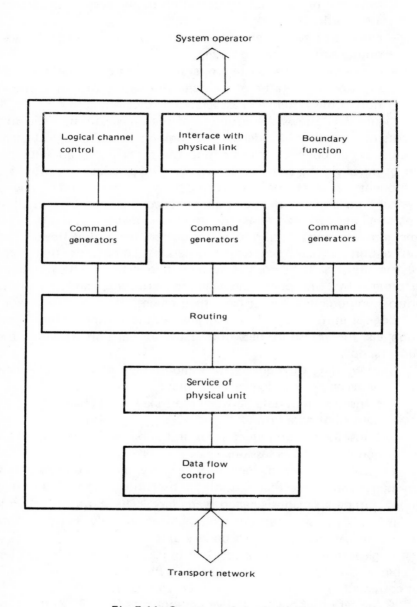

Fig. 7.11. Structure of physical unit.

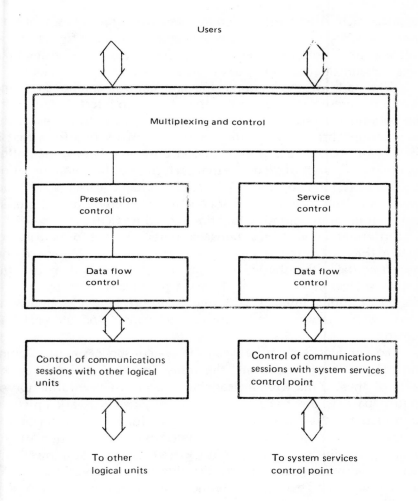

Users

Multiplexing and control

Presentation control

Service control

Data flow control

Data flow control

Control of communications sessions with other logical units

Control of communications sessions with system services control point

To other logical units

To system services control point

Fig. 7.12. Structure of logical unit.

The data-flow control component interacts directly with the session control component that organizes sessions between logical units. The task of the latter component is to regulate the manner and rate at which data are transferred to the transport network. The data-flow control component converts long messages into sequences of blocks.

The service control component matches the pace of block transmission (the number of blocks that can be transmitted without waiting for acknowledgement) with the network control unit, and supports each session with its component that organizes sessions between network units. The latter manages the queues to the logical unit and does not permit any user system involved in setting up a logical channel between network units to overflow with blocks.

The task of the multiplexing and control components, and also of the presentation control component, is to interface users with the data-flow control component, and, conversely, to represent the information obtained from the transport network in a form that is convenient for the user. Each logical unit may have **presentation functions,** i.e., a set of programs that perform specific communication requirements for two users. This set is chosen for each session between two logical units. The VTAM access method provides users with a group of presentation functions called RECORD.

Information exchange between units. In the principal user system (Fig. 7.13), all N logical units are primary. Moreover, this system contains the physical unit that controls the system, and the system services control point. The system services control point and the logical units interact with the transport network supporting transmission, network, and information channel and physical link control.

To conduct sessions between the system services control point and physical or logical units, the transport network furnishes the ports of these units with logical channels via which information or control packets are transmitted. However, two network units are connected by the transport network only for the duration of the session; the logical session is eliminated upon termination of the session. Usually, a receiving network unit operates at a lower rate than a transmitting one (receiving units must analyze the blocks they received). Therefore, intermediate storage buffers are employed to match the transmission rate between them.

The SNA network provides three types of sessions, which are determined by the following types of interaction:

- system services control point/physical unit (control of system configuration);
- system services control point/logical unit (activation and deactivation of logical units);
- logical unit/logical unit (transmission of information between users).

Interaction between physical and logical units is not provided for in SNA. Of the above three types of interaction between network

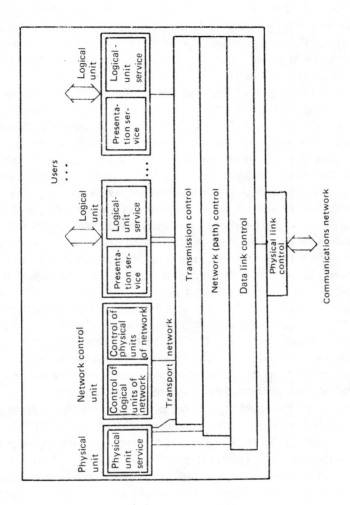

Fig. 7.13. Logical structure of principal user system.

units, exchange between logical units is the basic one. The other two types are necessary for reliable basic exchange.

When necessary to initiate a session between one of the three types of pairs of network units, a user (program, external device, or operator) issues the command BIND to the associated unit. Then the subsets of information-flow and session control procedures are chosen. They are determined by sets of commands exchanged by logical units connected by a logical channel. To access the logical unit that interacts with it, the user program employs macros of the VTAM access method, and also macros of terminal systems.

When a long message is to be transmitted between logical units, it is divided into a sequence of interconnected blocks. After all the information has been transmitted, the user sends the command END SESSION to his logical unit.

Figure 7.14 shows the interaction procedure of a triad of network units during a session. The logical unit at which a need for data transmission has arisen becomes a block source. The logical unit to which this information is addressed is a block recipient. The source unit sends the command INITIATE, which constitutes a request for authorization of a session (Table 7.3), to the system services control point. If the system services control point receives a request for a session from two logical units simultaneously, it authorizes only one of them. Once authorization has been received, the command BIND is used to initiate the session. The source unit communicates this to the system services control point. Then transmission of blocks from the logical source unit to the logical recipient unit begins. In the transmission process, the source unit divides the message into parts, adds a process header (process control header; Fig. 7.15) to each part, and creates a **block.** The block is passed on to the transport network. The recipient, after receiving the block from the network, discards the header and passes on the user information (body of the block) to the addressee user. The process header contains all the information needed by the recipient unit. Upon termination of the session, the recipient informs the system services control point to this effect by the command TERMINATE. Using the command CONTROL TERMINATE, the system services control point authorizes the termination of the session. Then the session termination procedure is carried out. To each of the above commands, the receiving network unit issues an acknowledgement in the form of the command RSP.

The RECORD presentation class. The RECORD system of **presentation functions** is an assortment of components that support interaction between a user and a logical unit. The components of RECORD operate with various application programs. They interact particularly well, however, with IMS and CICS programs.

The RECORD presentation class makes it possible to employ three macrocommands:

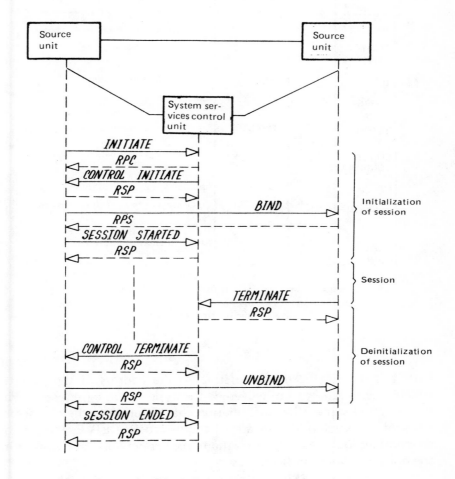

Fig. 7.14. Diagram of interaction of network elements.

— SEND (send data blocks to the indicated logical unit);
— RECEIVE (receive data block);
— SESSION C (organize session).

Transmission of these macros makes it possible to generate commands for organizing and conducting sessions between network units.

Upon receiving the macro SEND, a logical unit receives a data unit from a user (Fig. 7.15), converting it into a block. Together

TABLE 7.3.

Name of command	Source/ recipient	Meaning
INITIATE	S → SSCP	Request for authorization for session
CONTROL INITIATE	SSCP → S	Authorization for session
BIND	S → R	Request to begin session
SESSION STARTED	R → SSCP	Indication that session has begun
TERMINATE	R → SSCP	Indication of receipt of last packet in session
CONTROL TERMINATE	SSCP → S	Indication of termination of session
UNBIND	S → R	Proposal to terminate session
SESSION	S → SSCP	Indication of termination of session
RSP		Acknowledgement of receipt of all preceding commands

Remarks: here S represents the logical source unit;
R the recipient unit;
and SSCP the system services control point.

with this macro, the user also supplies the address of the port to which this unit is to be delivered, the type of unit (request or response), and some other information that determines the characteristics of the session. By means of the macro RECEIVE, the logical element accepts the block from the transport network and sends it in the opposite direction (to the user).

The macro SESSION C makes it possible to affect the way in which sessions are conducted. This macro includes three commands. In cases in which, upon checking or processing of malfunctions or recovering portions of the network, it is necessary to conduct a selective check, the command SET AND TEST SEQUENCE NUMBERS is transmitted. It requires setting and testing of sequence numbers of the transmitted blocks. When errors or malfunctions arise, it becomes necessary to clear out the entire logical channel connecting the ports of two network units. The command CLEAR is

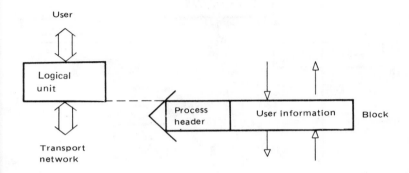

User

Logical
unit

Process
header

User information

Block

Transport
network

Fig. 7.15. Conversion of data array.

employed for this purpose; it eliminates all data in the logical channel. After it has become possible to conduct a session, the command
START DATA TRAFFIC is transmitted. Once this command has
been sent, data transmission resumes over the cleared-out logical
channel.

The process control level that is implemented in SNA networks
provides efficient interaction of highly diverse users. They are given
the capability of operating with data banks, remote job I/O, interactive interaction, file exchange. Problems of false diagnostics
and of control of the logical and physical resources of the network
have also been thoroughly worked out.

7.4.
ACCESS TO APPLICATION PROCESSES OF RPCNET

In Italy, a group of scientific institutions and institutes of
higher learning, headed by the Centro Nazionale Universitario di
Calcole Elaboratore (CNUCE) of the National Research Council
has created the RPCNET computer network [157—160]. The IBM
Research Center in Pisa has also been a participant. The RPCNET
network is architecturally very similar to SNA. At the same time,
RPCNET has a distributed (rather than a tree-like) topology,

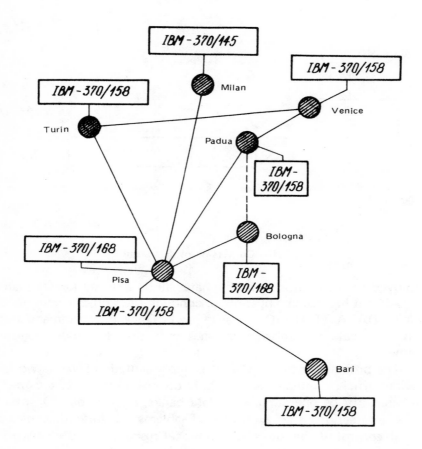

Fig. 7.16. Structure of RPCNET network.

incorporating several user systems (Fig. 7.16). As in SNA, the logical structure is divided into three levels (see Fig. 7.6). Instead of the VTAM remote-access method, however, RPCNET employs a new method called RNAM.

Figure 7.17 shows the structure of the user system of RPCNET. Components belonging to the transport network receive and route blocks, and direct them to the application-process control layer. This layer supports the interface between users and the transport network; therefore, it is also called the functional-interface layer.

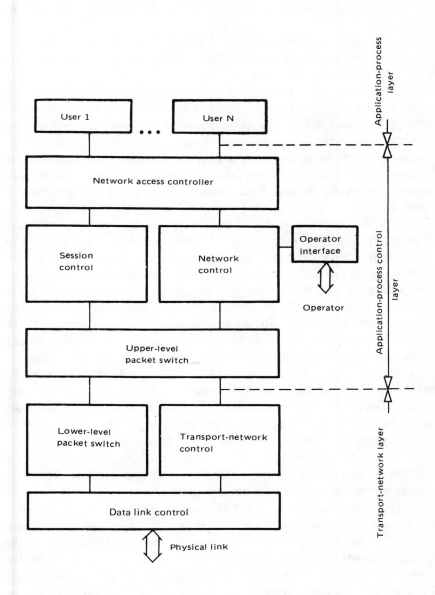

Fig. 7.17. Structure of user system.

The principal tasks of the application-process control layer are as follows:
— opening and elimination of ports of the transport network;
— servicing of users (messages to them; responses to their questions).

The access controller to the network is intended for linking users to the session control component. As in SNA, a user in the RPCNET network is understood to mean an application program, operator, or external user-system device. A component called the top-level switch converts messages issued by users into sequences of blocks for transmission to the transport network, and assembles messages from blocks before dispatching them to users in the same user system.

RPCNET embodies distributed network control. For this purpose, each user system contains a network control element (see Fig. 7.17) that implements the administrative tasks confronted by the application-process control layer. It also matches the data transmission rate over logical channels and the measures that must be taken in the event that blocks are lost. Network control elements receive information on changes in the configuration of the transport network, and inform the session control component to this effect. These elements also perform error detection and restoration of transmission in the event that blocks are lost or duplicate blocks are received. Figure 7.18 shows the structure of a network control element. The element contains five different services, whose tasks are listed in Table 7.4. Network control elements are linked to operators via an operator interface.

Table 7.5 offers a list of macros that users can employ in RPCNET. They fall into five different groups, which determine the modes of user interaction via the transport network.

There are no permanent logical channels in RPCNET. When a need for transmission arises, therefore, a user must request a logical channel. For this he sends the macrocommand OPENLU to the logical element. Upon termination of the session, the user issues the macro CLOSELU, which frees up the logical channel for other users. In addition, two commands are employed for exchanging service data. The macro INQUIRE is employed to inquire about the network structure at the current point in time. The command MAIL is provided for controlling transmission of service messages.

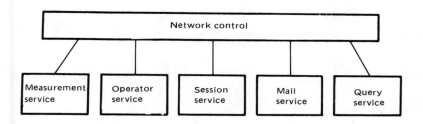

Fig. 7.18. Structure of network control element.

TABLE 7.4.

Name of service	Functions performed
Measurement	Measurements and monitoring required for statistics
Operator	Communication with operator
Session	Organization of beginning and end of sessions
Mail	Control of transmission of auxiliary messages between logical elements
Query	Determination of current state of network structure and resources

Users can transmit three macros via logical channels. The macro INVITE is the user request for data transmission. The macro BIND is employed to communicate the beginning of transmission; when transmission is completed, the user sends the macro UNBIND.

Data is exchanged between users in communications sessions. To control data flows, the session control component (see Fig. 7.17) operates with the linking and data I/O macros (see Table 7.5).

Logical channels permit only one session to be conducted at a time, with data transmitted in one direction. For the receiving end to be able to transmit data in the opposite direction, it is necessary to reverse the channel by means of the macro BREAK.

Logical channels are checked by the TESTLC operation. This operation activates procedures for determining whether blocks arrived

TABLE 7.5.

Designation of macro	Instruction transmitted by macro
Macros related to engagement and freeing of logical elements	
OPENLU	Open port
CLOSELU	Close port
Service macros	
INQUIRE	Transmission inquiry
MAIL	Mail communication
Communication macros	
INVITE	Invitation for session
BIND	Begin session
UNBIND	End session
Data I/O macros	
SEND	Transmit information
RECEIVE	Receive information
BREAK	Interrupt transmission
Macros for maintenance of transmission	
TESTLC	Test logical channel
CANCEL	Cancel what has been transmitted

at the other end of the channel. The transmitting end then receives the appropriate confirmation. The macro CANCEL clears logical channels of unnecessary or erroneous data after malfunctions have occurred or portions of the transport network have ceased operation.

Work aimed at improvement of the higher-level protocols in RPCNET is continuing. Conversion to international protocols is being implemented, as are provisions for connecting computers of different manufacturers to the network. It is planned that RPCNET will become the network of the organizations in the National Research Council.

7.5.
USER INFORMATION CONTROL

To create a convenient interface with application processes and to free them from the need for writing complex terminal-system, terminal, and physical-link control programs, the IBM Corporation has created the **Customer Information Control System,** or CICS. CICS is linked to users, on the one hand (Fig. 7.19); on the other, it interacts with the transport network. It is a programmable network unit that consists of two components. The first of these components specifies the basic representation facilities whose task is to support interaction with users; the second supports terminal control.

Figure 7.20 shows the structure of interconnection between terminals and CICS. Each terminal that interacts with CICS has its own logical unit (there are five of them in Fig. 7.20), through which it is incorporated into the transport network. There are CICS programs at the other ends of the logical channels. Through the use of CICS, the terminal operator is able to gain access to needed application processes in the principal user system. These processes, by interacting with the data banks in this computer, ensure execution of jobs.

CICS can perform a broad range of operations (Table 7.6). Its location in the user system is shown in Fig. 7.21. CICS control is effected by the operating system of the computer. In turn, CICS controls the operation of application processes, allowing them to communicate with terminals and to interact with user data banks.

Figure 7.22 shows the logical structure of CICS [161]. In CICS, a logical line called a task is created for each communications session with a terminal. Interaction with a terminal. Interaction with these lines is performed by the task control component. Macrocommands are employed to link this component to application processes. The basic functions of the task control component are as follows:

— task generation at the request of the terminal control component, and placing of the task in queue;
— completion (termination) of a task and its elimination from the list of active tasks;
— task control, involving completion of operations in sequence and transfer of the task to execution of subsequent operations;
— alteration of task priority and appropriate rearrangement of the task in queue;
— provision of computer resources in accordance with user programs;

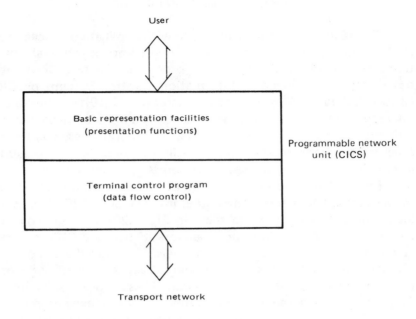

User

Basic representation facilities
(presentation functions)

Programmable network
unit (CICS)

Terminal control program
(data flow control)

Transport network

Fig. 7.19. Main components of CICS.

— temporary halting of tasks so as to optimize overall data processing and to transfer tasks from the active state to the queue of postponed tasks;

— renewal of task processing and transfer of tasks to the active queue.

The main storage occupied by CICS in the user system is divided into separate sections called buffers. Operations with them are performed by the storage control component. Since each task exists only for the duration of a session, buffers that are freed up are transferred to other tasks. Requests for allocation of buffers and messages that buffers have been freed up are sent to the storage control component in the form of macros.

User programs cannot all be placed in the main memory of the principal user system. Therefore, they are placed in disk storage and are transferred to the main memory of the principal system when a need for interacting with one or more terminals arises. These operations are performed by the program control component. The

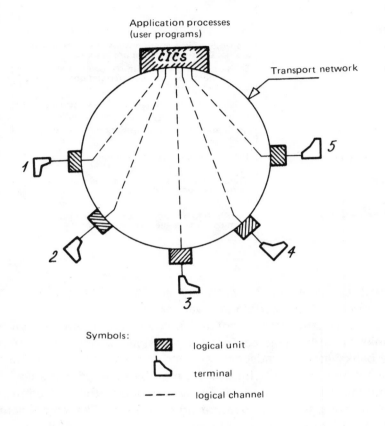

Application processes
(user programs)

Transport network

Symbols:

▨ logical unit

⌐ terminal

— — — logical channel

Fig. 7.20. Structure of interaction between CICS and terminals.

macros of this component are employed to load programs into main memory, to link programs to one another, and to remove loaded programs. The component operates with user programs, ensuring their simultaneous use by several tasks. A library of user programs, in which users may have their own personal libraries, is organized in the disk storage.

The interval control component detects and eliminates blockings that appear when the main memory of the system is full and appearance of new high-priority tasks is impossible. In such cases, low-priority tasks are eliminated from main memory. In addition,

TABLE 7.6.

Name of task	Functions performed
Issue information	Retrieval of information against specified features
Scan	Retrieval of information whose formal features are not clearly defined or are unknown
File control	Division of information into individual entries, whose identification and interrelationships are specified by users
Computation	Calculations in accordance with user program
Message input	Input and editing of information in dialog mode
Data input	Input of data needed for job execution
Mail	Transmission of auxiliary messages from one terminal to one or more other terminals
Message distribution	Distribution of information inputted from terminal to several other terminals

component indicates the time of day and can initiate tasks at a specified time or after a certain interval has elapsed.

The file control component is employed for interaction with data banks on disk. This component reads and writes information in these banks, gathers statistical data, and requests and obtains main memory for working with files. Files may be of fixed, variable, or indeterminate length. Upon receiving a request, the file control component finds the files that the user requires. The component also enters data into the data banks and updates old data in them.

The terminal control component is intended for linking terminals with user programs. This is done by means of the VTAM remote-access method, interacting with the communications network control program (NCP). The terminal control component provides polling of terminals, reading of data from terminals, and transmission of data to them. The desired polling interval is specified by the user. In addition, by using the facilities of the system and the users, this component detects errors that arise upon input and output of data.

All operations associated with temporary data storage in main memory are performed by the temporary storage control component.

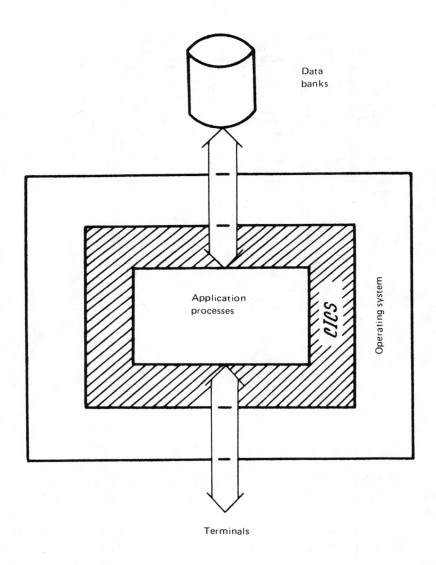

Fig. 7.21. Access of terminals to application processes.

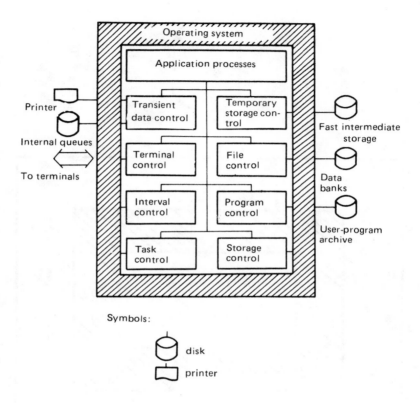

Fig. 7.22. Structure of CICS.

For this the component furnishes temporary storage that is used to accumulate data or to store them in the event of a temporary halt in a task.

The transient-data control component performs functions associated with internal transport of data — primarily organization of data queues, task initiation, and opening and closing of destination points of data sets.

CICS performs the function of a logical element in SNA. The partner of CICS is a logical-unit program in the terminal system. The latter is linked to CICS via a logical channel, on the one hand, and to a terminal forming part of a terminal system on the other.

As already noted, logical elements interact by means of communications sessions.

CICS requires that it be given in advance a list of all terminals with which it is to operate, specification of the features of the logical units linked to the terminals, the necessary reliability of interaction, and the priority levels.

In addition to the primary functions, CICS maintains an account of user operation and gathers statistics. The following items are recorded:

— number of tasks in CICS at any point in time;
— number of active tasks;
— number of accesses to user programs;
— number of requests for data retrieval;
— number of messages sent to terminals;
— number of errors in tasks, and so forth.

CICS ensures efficient and convenient real-time interaction between many terminals and large numbers of user programs. The functions performed by CICS free the developers of data-processing installations from many problems associated with control. They can then focus their attention on the creation of the user programs themselves that form part of the set of application processes. CICS offers extensive capabilities for development as the requirements of network users evolve further.

7.6.
ARRANGEMENTS FOR CONNECTING USER SYSTEMS TO NETWORKS

The processes whose interaction a computer network is meant to support are located in user systems and interact with the transport network (Fig. 7.1). To provide the proper operation, each user system should be connected to a communications network. This can be done in several ways; Fig. 7.23 shows three of them. In the first case the ports of the processes are located in the user system itself, which is linked directly to the communications system (a). In the second case, an interface system (d) is placed between the communications system (b) and user system. In the third case, the interface and communications systems are combined into a single interface-communications system (c), to which the user system is connected.

The first method is employed when there is a user system whose hardware and software were created specially for the network in question.

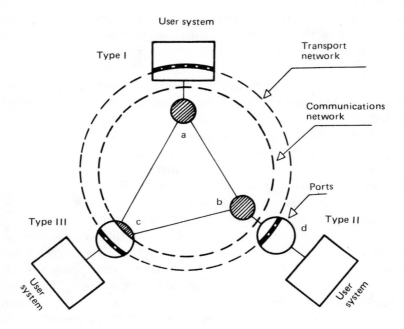

User system

Type I

Transport network

Communications network

a

Ports

b

Type III

c

d

Type II

User system

User system

Fig. 7.23. Forms of linkage between user systems and communications network.

At the same time, there are frequent instances in which a system that is incompatible with the network protocols must be connected to a computer network. Connections II or III are employed in these cases. The last method is employed only when the interface-communications system is a multiprocessor system or when the number of physical links to it is small and loading by communication or interface functions is relatively modest.

Computers or computer installations may form part of user systems in computer networks. At present there is no clear-cut classification of these data-processing devices. A device with one or more universal processors that interact with a common main memory is generally called a **computer**. If, however, the device contains several processors that operate with different main-memory devices, it is called a **computer installation**. Recently, as a result of the rapid development of microelectronics and the extensive use of microprocessors and solid-state main memories, virtually any large or medium-sized computer can be called an installation. Moreover, even single-processor computers with remote-processing hardware have begun to be called installations. From the standpoint of computer networks, this classification makes no difference. Therefore, all such data-processing devices are generally called computers [162, 163].

Computer networks generally employ various types of computers, since this provides users with highly diverse resources. For example, ARPANET includes CDC 7600, UNIVAC 1108, PDP-11, GEC 4080, ICL 470, H-68/80, B-5500, IBM 370, IBM 360, ECLIPSE, and other computers.

Computer networks include large numbers of terminals, connected in one of the ways shown in Fig. 7.24. The first and third methods are employed in user systems that already have their own terminal installations when connected to the network. In addition, the first method is widely employed in terminal systems, where it is called primary.

The second or fourth methods are preferable in large user systems, since their use entails increased reliability of interaction between terminals and the network (they continue to operate when the system breaks down or is being repaired). In addition, when these methods are employed the user system is not occupied with inefficient tasks of terminal control and data transmission between terminals and the transport network. However, the second or fourth methods require a terminal-communications or terminal-interface system with special hardware and software for interaction with available terminals or with terminals to be acquired.

With the development of microelectronics, the cost of mini-processors has become comparable to that of a terminal, while microprocessors have become substantially cheaper than terminals. Thus, many terminals linked to their own terminal processors (Fig. 7.25) have appeared. Interacting terminal/processor pairs are called **virtual terminals.** Usually, a computer network interacts with a large number of different terminals; this greatly complicates the software and manner of operation. Use of virtual terminals radically alters the situation. In this case the virtual terminals include various real terminals, but, because of the terminal processors, they all interact with the computer network in the same way, transmitting and receiving packets that are standardized for the network.

Virtual terminals may be connected not only to communications systems but also to computers. Therefore, in cases in which a

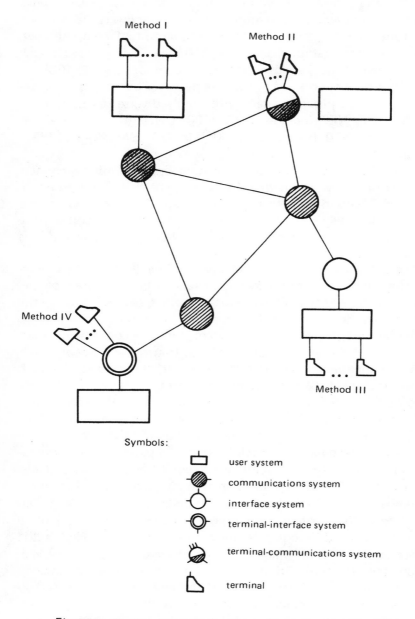

Method I

Method II

Method IV

Method III

Symbols:

user system

communications system

interface system

terminal-interface system

terminal-communications system

terminal

Fig. 7.24. Modes of connecting terminals to computer network.

282

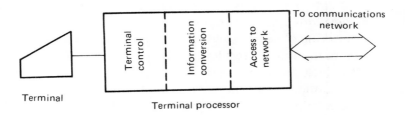

Fig. 7.25. Structure of virtual terminal.

virtual terminal is connected directly to a communications network, it is called a **network** terminal. Network terminals must process the same levels of the network software structure as user systems. This requires that terminal processors have a main memory with a capacity of 24—32 kbytes [90] .

It is by no means obligatory that each virtual or network terminal have its own terminal processor. This function can be performed by programs in a fairly powerful processor that interacts with several terminals. Physically, therefore, a terminal processor can be placed within a terminal or in a user system.

7.7.
ADMINISTRATIVE SYSTEMS

Administrative systems are intended for executing tasks associated with control of all or part of a computer network. In what follows, we will consider administrative systems that control communications networks. The structure of all administrative systems is identical to that of user systems. In administrative systems, however, application processes do not handle any and all tasks, but only network control functions.

A communications network consisting of communications systems and interconnecting physical links is a complex entity that requires support of the tasks associated with its operation. These functions are performed by the communications-network control system. It includes checking of network operations and technical and administrative network management.

Control of network operation involves the following:

— determination of the state of communications systems and links;
— compilation of statistics and reports on operation of communications systems and links;
— monitoring of user systems connected to the network;
— presentation of the resultant data.

Control includes localization of detected faults, alteration of the network configuration, and allocation of software in the network. In addition, administrative management provides servicing of data banks associated with network operation, and generation of reports regarding this operation.

The data banks that support operation of the network should have all information associated with its operation. This includes, in particular, the following:

— data on the state of the network (lists of working user and communications systems, links, and so forth);
— information on characteristics of network components (systems, links);
— duplicates of software;
— statistical data on network operation;
— information for network management personnel (a list of managers, their rights and obligations, telephone numbers, and so forth).

Information in these banks can be divided into static and dynamic information. Static information defines the network in its ideal state, i.e., when all the hardware and software in the network is operational. Dynamic information specifies the actual state of the network at a given point in time. It indicates malfunctions or departures from the ideal state (breakdowns, revisions, repairs, and so forth).

Communications networks are controlled by one or more administrative user systems. If more than one such system is employed in a network, an allocation of responsibility among them is specified, and one of the systems is designated as the principal one.

Administrative and communications systems can interact on the basis of the same protocols used to link user systems with one another. At the same time, it is not required that the administrative and communications systems interact with the remaining (non-administrative) user systems. From the standpoint of administrative management, therefore, a communications network together with the administrative system can be regarded as a special subnetwork with its own higher-level (layers 4—7) protocols. This considerably simplifies the protocols, and hence the software of the administrative and communications systems in the network.

CHAPTER 8

WIDE-AREA COMPUTER NETWORKS

The advantages provided by multicomputer associations have resulted in efforts to create large wide-area computer networks in a considerable number of countries. At present, the number of large networks that utilized packet switching is already reckoned in the dozens. Table 8.1 shows the largest of them [90, 157, 164]. Several networks are being set up in a number of countries; such parallelism, however, is by no means always justifiable.

Most networks currently in operation are sponsored by government agencies (ARPANET, NPL, EURONET) and are intended for certain groups of organizations. At the same time, networks with a wide scope of use are being set up (TELENET, DATAPAC, TRANS-PAC).

The networks that have been created differ substantially in terms of their structure and have differing protocol hierarchies. However, they embody two important common principles. First, they all have a multilayer software structure. Second, each network uses a unified method (for any forms of process interaction) of transporting information between all the user systems.

Present-day wide-area networks have the following characteristic features:

— inexpensive and simple communications systems;
— maximum utilization of expensive communications channels;
— transport stations in user or interface systems;
— monitoring of data transmission via physical links and logical channels;
— high transmission rates that can support dialog modes.

As for control of wide-area networks, the latter can be divided into two groups. One group employs complex administrative systems (one in each network) that manage all the network resources. The other group employs distributed control that is performed by a set of administrative systems in the network. We will consider the architecture of some of the largest wide-area packet switching networks (the networks that have been most intensively developed in recent years).

TABLE 8.1.

Name of network	Organization and country
ARPA	Universities and research organizations in the USA, as well as Norway, England, and Hawaiian Islands
NPL	National Physics Laboratory in England
SITA	Airline companies worldwide
CYCLADES	Universities and research organizations in France
EURONET	Common Market countries
PSS	Post Office Corporation (England)
JAPNET (DDX)	Ministry of Telephone and Telegraph in Japan
TELENET	Communications Corporation, USA
DATAPAC	Trans-Canada Telephone Company
TRANSPAC	Ministry of Communications, France
INFO-SWITCH	Canadian Ministry of Communications
RPCNET	Italian National Research Council

8.1.
ARPANET

ARPANET, created by the Advanced Research Projects Agency of the United States [2, 79, 164—169], began operation in 1969. The network is intended primarily for uniting the computing resources of American universities working on common scientific problems. At the same time, a number of user systems of different corporations are involved in the network.

The communications network employed by ARPA encompasses primarily the territory of the United States (Fig. 8.1), but, by means of satellite channels, it extends into Western Europe and the Hawaiian Islands. The communications network consists of communications and terminal-communications systems and of the physical links between them.

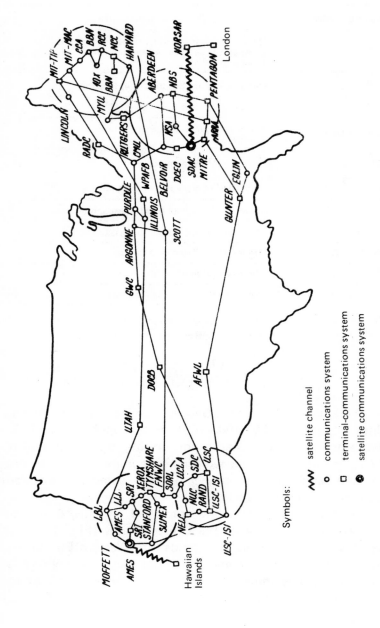

Symbols:

〰〰 satellite channel

○ communications system

☐ terminal-communications system

◉ satellite communications system

Fig. 8.1. Communications network employed in ARPANET.

Communications systems in the network were provided initially by Honeywell DDP—516 minicomputers with a main storage of 24—32 kbytes and a storage cycle of 1 microsecond. Up to four host computer systems may be connected to each such system. The terminal-communications systems were Honeywell H-316 minicomputers with a main storage of up to 64 kbytes. Up to 64 terminals of different types may be connected to them.

Dedicated telephone channels with a capacity of 50 and 56 kbits/sec are employed as physical links in the network. Data is transmitted over these channels in packets of up to 1008 bits. The average packet transmission time over the communications network is 0.2 sec; coast-to-coast packet transmission time amounts to 0.5 sec. The configuration of the communications network is such that information can be transmitted from one point to another via at least two different paths. Each packet is stored in a communications or terminal-communications system until acknowledgement of its receipt by the addressed system is received.

ARPANET successfully utilizes satellite channels. One of them links California to the Hawaiian Islands, transmitting packets at 50,000 bits/sec. The second channel links communications systems in Washington and Europe. The transmission rate of this channel is 9600 bits/sec. As a result of the work that has been done, it has become possible to use satellite communications for user systems within the confines of United States territory. A satellite version of the communications system has been created for this purpose.

The basis of the **satellite communications system** is provided by an ordinary communications system with added hardware and software that supply the following:
- — expanded memory for storing packets awaiting confirmation of successful transmission;
- — linking procedure with the satellite transmitter;
- — time recording for precise timing of the packet transmission process.

Figure 8.2 shows the topology of connection of user systems to the communications network. It is apparent that ARPANET employs an extensive assortment of computers, manufactured by different companies. The administrative system, located in Cambridge, Massachusetts, controls the operation of the entire network and assembles the necessary statistics. A special computer is allocated for this purpose.

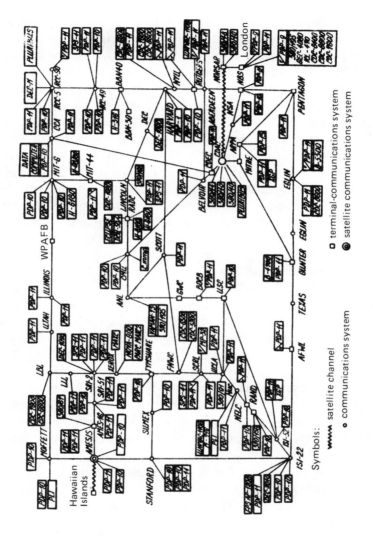

Fig. 8.2. User systems of ARPANET.

ARPANET has three basic groups of protocols which specify the hierarchy of the network software structure (Fig. 8.3). The first, lowest layer is described by the user system/communications system linking protocol. It defines data transmission over physical links, characterizes the routing procedures, and gives the formats of the transmitted units.

The second layer is made up by a host-host protocol that characterizes methods of organizing logical channels linking processes in

290

Layers: User system

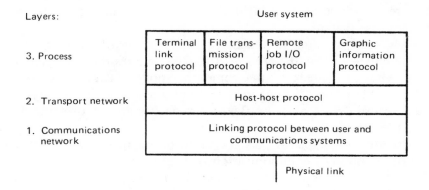

3. Process

2. Transport network

1. Communications
   network

Fig. 8.3. Protocol levels of ARPANET.

different user systems. This protocol also defines rules for controlling data flows via logical channels and for buffering this data.

The third, highest layer contains functionally oriented protocols that support process interaction. The principal ones are shown in Fig. 8.3. The terminal linking protocol converts ordinary terminals with a keyboard and a printer into network terminals. As a result, it becomes possible for the terminal of one user system to interact with user programs in other user systems.

The file transfer protocol defines standards associated with remote reading and writing (via the transport network) and correction (or updating) of files in user systems. The remote job I/O protocol describes a remote method of job execution. The graphics-information protocol describes exchange procedures for graphic information of different users.

Between the second and third layers there are several small protocols that support linking of processes to the transport network. Thus, the connection initialization protocol describes standard modes of simultaneous access of many users via logical channels to processes in one user system.

ARPANET is an experimental field on which various methods of process interaction are developed and tested. Therefore, the network utilizes a considerable number of additional protocols that can interrelate processes in certain (not all) user systems: the protocol for file transmission between PDP-10 computers, the remote

I/O protocol for the UCLA 360/91, and certain other protocols associated with various experiments. The network also implements electronic mail for transmission of data between terminals connected to different user system.

A special terminal intended for packet transmission of speech is being created for ARPANET [170]. The data transmission rate in the backbone channels of the communications network is 50,000 bits/sec. Therefore, efficient loading of physical links becomes possible, because delays of up to 0.5 sec are permissible in speech transmission.

Creation of a special packet speech terminal offers more than multi-party speech communication via a packet switching network. It also opens up extensive possibilities for interactive dialog in which computers speak in human voices. As for human speech perception, only modest results have been obtained along these lines: comprehension of 50—100 words pronounced by the same person.

Research conducted with ARPANET has resolved many theoretical and applied problems that open up possibilities for creating efficient and highly economical packet switching networks. At the same time, a number of complicated problems interfering with network operation have developed [171]. As we know, the operating reliability of a network depends on hardware malfunctions and on the correctness of the proposed operating algorithms. The effect of malfunctions can be eliminated by hardware redundancy. Determination of logical errors in network software, however, is a very severe problem.

Problems of lockouts arising in the network proved to be difficult ones. Three types of such problems should be distinguished. The first is related to **resource lockout** and consists in the following. Assume that processes A and B require resources P and Q. Process A has obtained resource P and is waiting for resource Q to become free. However, process B has been able to obtain resource Q and is waiting for resource P to become free. As a result, execution of both processes is blocked.

The second problem involves **reassembly lockout**; it arose in ARPANET as a result of logical errors in software. It appeared when messages partially assembled from packets occupied storage buffers awaiting delivery of missing packets. At the same time, the communications network attempted to transmit packets pertaining to other messages, while the user system did not accept them because of a lack of free buffers. As a result, the network ceased to operate with this system and therefore could not deliver missing packets of already-received messages.

Finally, there is the problem of **path lockout**, involving the following. Assume that adjacent communications systems C and D are joined by a physical link. The storage buffers in both systems are completely filled. System C attempts to transmit packets to D, while D attempts to transmit to C. But neither system can yield to the other and accept a group of packets from it.

ARPANET is being continuously improved and expanded. The experience gained in its creation and operation is being extensively employed in setting up other networks.

8.2.
CYCLADES

Creation of the CYCLADES network was initiated in 1973 in France under the sponsorship of the Institut de Recherche d'Informatique et d'Automatique (IRIA) [172–176]. This method is intended primarily for linking the computers of scientific organizations and institutes of higher learning. The physical structure of the network is shown in Fig. 8.4 (only user systems connected directly to communications systems are shown). In addition, in the region of Paris another five user systems are connected to the communications network via an interface system. A substantial number of user systems are connected through concentrators (e.g., in Brest, Nancy, Bordeaux, Marseilles, and some other cities). The CYCLADES network is linked to the NPL and ESPO networks via interface systems.

The communications network consists of communications systems joined by physical links. Mitra-15 minicomputers function as communications systems. The data transmission rate over physical links is as high as 48,000 bits/sec. The transport network is a datagram network.

The CYCLADES network furnishes users with capabilities for a number of operations, including the following in particular:
— access to data-bank control systems;
— interaction with information retrieval services;
— remote job I/O;

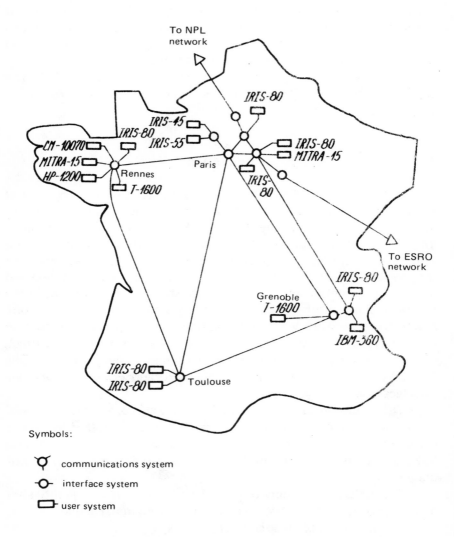

To NPL
network

IRIS-80

IRIS-45
IRIS-80
IRIS-55

CM-10070
MITRA-15
HP-1200
Rennes
T-1600

Paris

IRIS-80
MITRA-15

IRIS-
80

To ESRO
network

IRIS-80

Grenoble
T-1600

IBM-360

IRIS-80
IRIS-80
Toulouse

Symbols:

Ⴘ   communications system

─◯─ interface system

▭ user system

Fig. 8.4. CYCLADES network.

294

— development of user programs.

The following features are provided to users:

— data banks in the field of chemistry and blood diseases;
— simulation systems for electrical circuits, computers, and economic entities;
— programs in the social sciences, linguistics, and programmed instruction.

Considerable effort is being expended to create distributed scientific data banks in the network. Work is also being done to create well-developed access languages for the network.

8.3.
PSS

The PSS network was set up by the Post Office Corporation in England [177]. Studies by this organization showed that in England it would be feasible to replace the existing analog telephone network by an integrated digital network.

In the 1970's, an experimental packet switching network, called EPSS, was set up in England. Three communications systems of this network, in London, Manchester, and Glasgow, began experimental operation in April 1977. Developers and users of computers could evaluate the economic and technical aspects of packet switching using this network. After the experiments were completed, the network was replaced by a new phase, called PSS.

The structure of the PSS network is shown in Fig. 8.5. The network consists of 12 communications systems based on TP-4000 computers developed by the firm of Telenet. Systems are connected by physical links specified by Recommendation X.75. The transmission rate over these links is 48,000 bits/sec. The PSS network furnishes users with channels operating at 2400, 4800, 9600, and 48,000 bits/sec. An interface defined by Recommendation X.25 has been accepted for all these links.

The PSS network is managed by a primary and a back-up administrative system in London. Each system contains a Prime-350 minicomputer with disk memory, tape storage, a display, and a printer. Program loading into all the communications systems of PSS is performed from the administrative system, which constitutes the Network Control Center.

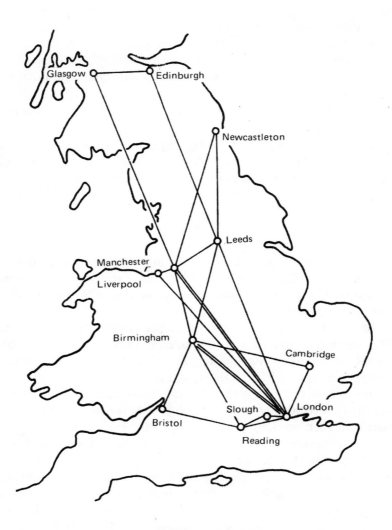

Fig. 8.5. PSS network.

Each communications system has fault self-diagnostics and is capable of informing the Control Center of various hardware malfunctions. All communications systems maintain records on data flows and transmit the resultant statistical data to the Center. The routing arrangements provided by the communications systems depend on the loading of the physical links.

The topology of PSS is such that the average delay in packet transmission does not exceed 0.2 sec. Of course, it depends not only on the topology but also on the operating speed of the communications systems and the rates of the physical links.

The PSS network interacts with packet switching networks in the United States, Canada, and a number of Western European countries via the International Interface System. It is also connected to the EURONET international computer system.

8.4.
EURONET

EURONET was set up by the European Economic Community to meet the needs of this organization [34, 178—182]. Its principal task is to provide user access to banks of scientific and technical documentation in various countries of Western Europe.

The first phase of the communications network, comprising the core of EURONET, is shown in Fig. 8.6. It includes five communications switching nodes, in London, Paris, Frankfurt, Zurich, and Rome. The communications functions are implemented by Mitra-125 minicomputers. These machines are linked together by backbone channels that transmit packets up to 1000 bits in size at a rate of 48,000 bits/sec. Five concentrators, in Dublin, Amsterdam, Brussels, Luxembourg, and Copenhagen, are connected to the communications network by 9600-bit/sec channels. Access to terminals in Spain and Austria is planned. EURONET implements the protocols of Recommendation X.25 of the CCITT.

User systems in EURONET are connected to the network nodes via interface systems, rather than directly. The interface systems perform assembly and disassembly of messages, match network protocols to user systems, and conduct sessions over logical channels via the transport network.

8.5.
DATAPAC

The DATAPAC network began operation in Canada in 1976 [126, 183—188]. The network was created by the Trans-Canada Telephone Company. There are 12 communications systems in the network, four in Toronto, two in Montreal, and one each in Vancouver, Edmonton, Calgary, Winnipeg, Ottawa, and Halifax. Figure 8.7 shows the topology of DATAPAC. To simplify the figure, the

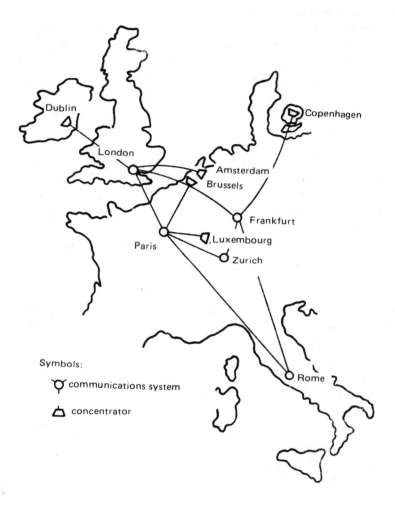

Fig. 8.6. EURONET network.

four systems in Toronto and the two in Montreal are represented by a single point. SL-10 minicomputers manufactured by North-ern Telecon Limited are employed as communications systems in DATAPAC. The communications systems are connected by physical links operating at 56,000 bits/sec. Satellite communications were initiated at the end of 1978.

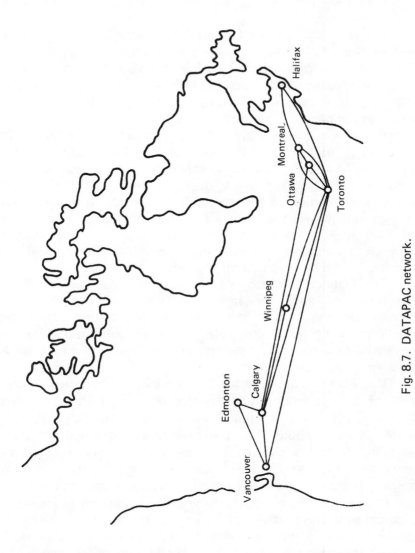

Fig. 8.7. DATAPAC network.

The SL-10 communications system has a modular structure and satisfies the following basic requirements:
— broad range of capabilities, permitting economical use of hardware at network points that differ substantially in terms of capacity and the types of channels employed by system users;
— simplicity of modification of the system configuration;

— ease of introducing new communications-network control functions.

In the first phase, the DATAPAC network included seven user systems (Fig. 8.8). Their number subsequently increased considerably. The administrative system, or Network Control Center, is located in Ottawa and is linked to two communications sytems (for reliability) in Ottawa and Toronto. Communication is by physical links that can handle a rate of 9600 bits/sec.

The center controls the status of the network elements. It is linked to all user systems that operate in the network, receives information from them regarding each request for a session, and assembles statistics on network operation and malfunctions. The center also maintains a continuous link with all interface systems, so that the network operators can have a clear picture of their current state. This promotes rapid fault detection and localization. Data on loading of communications systems and physical links help to plan the development of the network.

The Network Control Center and the communications systems have a multiprocessor structure. This ensures that they remain operational when one of the processors or external devices malfunctions. If a physical link malfunctions, the information flows are rerouted. As a result, accessibility of any user to the network has achieved a figure of 99.963%.

The network provides for the possibility of altering the software of any communications system directly from the Network Control Center. The program is transmitted to the external storage of the communications system and replaces a preceding one upon a command from the center. The tables of configurations of communications systems, lists of physical links, and information routing tables of the communications systems can be similarly updated.

Figure 8.9 shows the structure of the communications system. It contains several modules of backbone channels that interconnect communications computers. In addition, there are modules of terminal channels, each of which can accomodate up to 62 channels that link the system to terminals. Data link control and packet routing are performed by control modules.

In creating the transport network, both the datagram method and the virtual method were thoroughly analyzed. After much discussion and study of the problem, a decision was made to choose a virtual network, so as to minimize the effect of network servicing

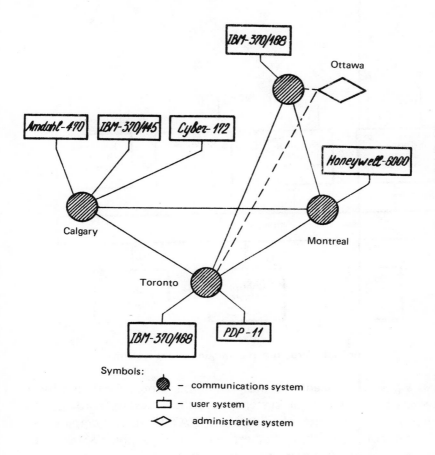

Fig. 8.8. User systems in DATAPAC.

components on user hardware and software. In addition, the developers believed that a virtual network simplifies interaction with asynchronous (start-stop) terminals.

The communications network is specified by Recommendation X.25 of the CCITT and is described by the Standard Network Access Protocol (SNAP). The structure of the standard protocol is shown in Fig. 8.10. This protocol consists of three layers. The first, lowest physical-interface layer specifies the characteristics of physical links made up sequences of four-wire full-duplex synchronous telephone channels. The frame layer describes control of the data link be-

301

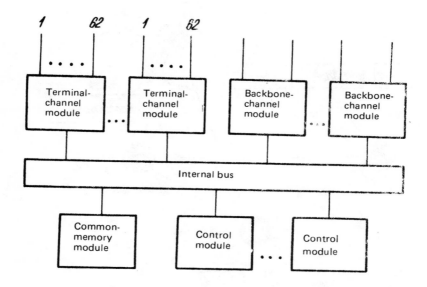

Fig. 8.9. Structure of communications system.

tween a pair of adjacent systems. The basic protocol here is LAP B. However, by no means all systems have the necessary hardware for implementing this protocol. Therefore, DATAPAC also employs the BSC protocol. The third, highest level, namely, the packet layer, supports control of the set of logical channels linking processes in different user systems.

As provided by Recommendation X.25, control packets are transmitted together with information packets in the transport network. In DATAPAC they contain large amounts of information associated with the operation of logical channels. Thus, Table 8.2 shows information transmitted by control packets regarding causes of malfunctions to users in providing communications sessions with the necessary addresses.

Two types of terminals are provided in the network. The first type includes packet (virtual) terminals and terminal systems that implement all network protocols and transmit sequences of standard packets to this network.

User system

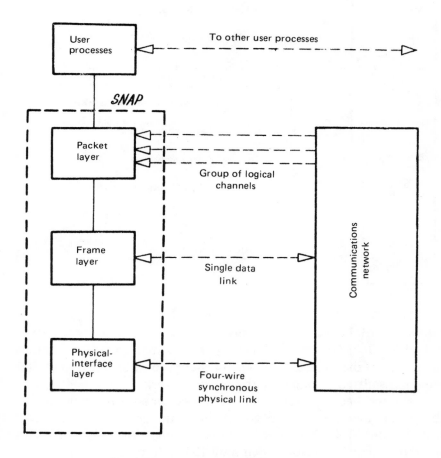

Fig. 8.10. Standard network access protocol.

Packet terminals provide the most efficient interaction with application processes. However, users have large numbers of simple asynchronous (start-stop) terminals that are interacted with by transmitting sequences of symbols. A service called DATAPAC-1000 is provided in order to user them. This is a minicomputer-based interface system, which supports dialog interaction between asynchronous terminals and a packet communications network.

303

TABLE 8.2.

Signal	Information conveyed by signal
Number busy	Called addressee is busy and cannot receive call
Number refuses shared call	Called addressee not designated for shared use
Overflow of network	Temporarily not possible to organize communications session because the communications network has reached its maximum packet capacity
Wrong call	Resources requested are not present in the network
Forbidden access	Requesting user does not have the right to interact with addressee (e.g., data bank)
Error in local procedure	Invalid access procedure by user
Error in remote procedure	Invalid receipt-of-access procedure by user
Not available	Called number unassigned or changed
Malfunction	Addressee malfunctioning because of failures in user system, physical link, or frame transmission module

The DATAPAC protocols support interaction with a large number of IBM-developed systems programs, e.g., HASP, ASP, RES, and JES. Jobs transmitted by these programs are divided into blocks, and the blocks are again assembled into messages after being transmitted through the transport network.

A modified program has been developed that requires 12 kbytes of memory and supports implementation of the SNAP protocol on IBM 3704 and 3705 communications systems. This program makes it possible to employ IBM 360 or 370 computers as user systems in DATAPAC. The program emulates IBM terminals operating in a time-sharing mode. As a result, network users can interact with standard IBM-developed software.

There is also software for the Datanet-355 minicomputer that permits a Honeywell 6078 computer in a time-sharing mode to be connected to DATAPAC. The programs in question occupy 8 kbytes of memory in the Datanet-355 minicomputer.

Extensive development of the DATAPAC network is planned, with the aim of making the network into a nationwide Canadian network.

8.6.
TRANSPAC

The TRANSPAC network was created by the French Ministry of Communications for packet transmission between many computer-owning users [121, 125, 189, 190]. The Société pour l'Etude de Systèmes d'Automatique (SESA) is the developer of the communications network.

TRANSPAC employs 16 communications systems connected by 64,000-bit/sec physical links (Fig. 8.11). Packet transmission time between the most widely spaced pair of communications systems does not exceed 0.2 sec. The size and capacity of the network are such that up to 1500 terminals can be connected to it. The first phase of TRANSPAC became operational in 1978.

Like other computer networks, TRANSPAC employs two types of physical links. Packets of up to 2048 bits (256 bytes) are transmitted over these links. The sizes of these packets are specified by the users by agreement with the network administration. Packets of 128, 256, 512, 1024, or 2048 bits are also authorized. Each physical link is made up of a sequence of telephone channels. Channel errors occur at intervals of not less than 10^{12} bits.

The network also makes extensive use of physical user links operating at rates of from 50 to 64,000 bits/sec. They are intended to provide connection of user systems and terminals to the communications network. A rate of not more than one error per 10^{10} bits is guaranteed for these links.

TRANSPAC has a modular structure consisting of elements that perform routing, transmission, and control. Its overall organization is such that malfunctioning of any individual (hardware or software) component does not spread to the entire network and does not affect the remaining components.

TRANSPAC employs two types of communications systems. Nationwide systems have service personnel who are involved in monitoring and managing the communications systems and user systems and terminals connected to them. Wide-area systems do not have such personnel.

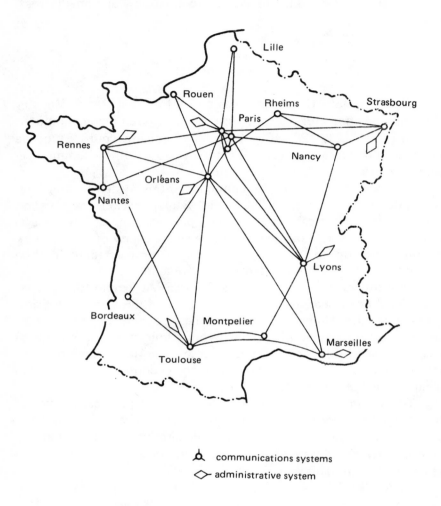

Fig. 8.11. TRANSPAC network.

Communications systems consist of two types of hardware:
— Mitra-125 minicomputers;
— up to 16 communications components, each including an assortment of specialized processors that functions as controllers of synchronous physical links.

The specialized processors are linked to the Mitra-125 processor by means of an information bus. All of them, including the Mitra-

125, are made redundant to ensure reliable operation. Switching from the primary component to the back-up is performed automatically.

Network control is divided into two levels. The upper level contains the administrative system, which constitutes the network control center. It is located in Rennes. The lower level is comprised of local control centers (systems). Each of them has physical and logical resources in the portion of the network allocated to it.

The network control center is based on a Mitra-125 minicomputer with main-memory and disk-storage devices. The center receives signals from the local control centers regarding malfunctions and faults in the portions of the network allocated to them. Therefore, it has information on the state of the entire network. The network control center also monitors the hardware of the entire network. In the event that any local control center malfunctions, the network control center can assume control of the corresponding portion of the network.

Local control centers are also based on Mitra-125 minicomputers, but with smaller amounts of main memory and disk storage (as compared to the network control center). For reliability, local centers are connected to the communications network by a pair of synchronous links operating at 19,200 bits/sec. Local control centers perform a large number of functions, including the following in particular:

— reception of signals regarding malfunctions or failures; informing of the operators of the local and network control centers to this effect;
— initialization (activation) of subordinate hardware;
— monitoring of hardware operation;
— assembly and issuance of local statistics, and delivery of reports to the network control center;
— remote hardware checking.

The protocol hierarchy of TRANSPAC is based on Recommendation X.25 of the CCITT and includes five layers:

— physical link control;
— information channel control (LAP B);
— network control (X.25/3);
— process control (command layer);
— process implementation.

307

Access to the network is possible via the following channels furnished to users:

- leased synchronous full-duplex telephone channels operating at 2400, 4800, 9600, 19,200, and 48,000 bits/sec;
- leased asynchronous half-duplex or full-duplex telephone channels operating at rates between 110 and 1200 bits/sec;
- switched asynchronous telephone channels at rates of from 100 to 300 bits/sec;
- telex (telegraph) channels operating at 50 bits/sec.

Each asynchronous terminal operates in a time-sharing mode with the network.

The TRANSPAC network covers all of France and is highly reliable; delays in data transmission are small. Its creators anticipate, therefore, that it will satisfy most users and will be extensively developed. TRANSPAC is connected to computer networks in other countries.

8.7.
TELENET

Together with DATAPAC and TRANSPAC, the TELENET network is part of the original group of three networks that were based on Recommendation X.25 of the CCITT. It was set up by the GTE-Telenet Communications Corporation and covers the territory of the United States [191]. The central core of TELENET is a communications network that consists of communications systems (Fig. 8.12). The first phase of this network, comprising systems in seven different cities, became operational in 1975. The administrative system or Network Control Center is located in Washington.

The communications systems in the network are provided by specially designed TP-4000 minicomputers, connected in parallel to one another for purposes of reliability (Fig. 8.13). If necessary, yet another minicomputer can be connected into the system. All these computers control the channels linking the communications systems, and also synchronous and asynchronous channels for connecting user systems and terminals to the communications network.

The TP-4000-based communications system of TELENET employs three types of channel processors. The first of them is a low-speed processor, intended for controlling four or eight asynchronous channels operating at up to 9600 bits/sec. The second, medium-speed processor controls four synchronous channels of BSC type, for

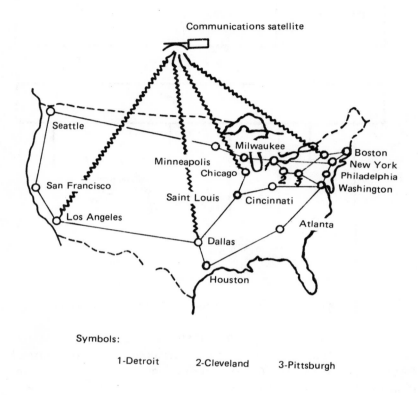

Communications satellite

Seattle

Minneapolis

Milwaukee

Chicago

Boston
New York
Philadelphia
Washington

San Francisco

Saint Louis

Cincinnati

Los Angeles

Atlanta

Dallas

Houston

Symbols:

1-Detroit   2-Cleveland   3-Pittsburgh

Fig. 8.12. TELENET network.

which the transmission rate is 56 kbits/sec. The third type of processor is a high-speed processor for controlling eight channels that transmit data in accordance with Recommendation X.25 or X.75. The
transmission rate is 64 kbits/sec.

The central processor may be backed up by another processor
to enhance reliability. The group of channel processors is also
backed up by an additional processor. Interface processors are
employed to connect nonstandard user systems. Both the central
and the channel processors are based on microprocessors, each
with from 4 to 32 kbytes of main memory and from 0.5 to 1 kbyte
of read-only memory. Memory addressing for the microprocessors
makes it possible to increase this memory to 64 kbytes.

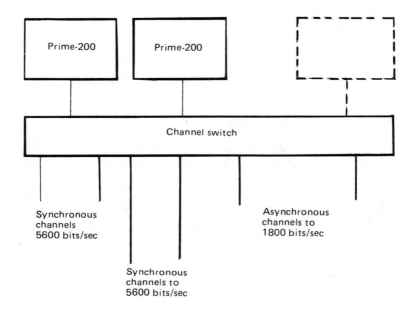

Fig. 8.13. Diagram of machine back-up in communications system.

The TPOS operating system is distributed in the central and interface processors. One of them is designated as the control processor; it controls the entire communications sytem. The remaining processors are controlled. The third layer of Recommendation X.25 is implemented by the central processor, while the first and second layers are implemented by the interface processors. The static topology of the communications network is represented by routing matrices, generated by the administrative system and distributed to all comunications systems. The dynamic topology of the network is governed by the malfunctioning of various systems and of the physical links between them.

TELENET provides more than transmission of X.25 packets; it also offers conversion of the protocols of the three lower levels. These functions are performed for the most widespread types of IBM terminal systems: 2780, 3270, HASP, and so forth.

The administrative system for TELENET is located in Washington and is equipped with two Prime-350 minicomputers with 516-kbyte main memory and 25-Mbyte disk storage.

It is incorporated into the network as a special user system for performing the following functions:
— monitoring of network operation;
— coordination of network hardware;
— checking of new systems connected to the network;
— gathering of traffic data;
— compilation of report documentation;
— control of the loading of new communications-system software;
— monthly billing of network users.

TELENET has generated considerable interest among companies in the United States, since it meets all user requirements involving data transmission between computers and between computers and terminals.

8.8.
ECN

The Experimental Computer Network (ECN) set up by the Academy of Sciences of the Latvian SSR pursues two principal aims:
— research in the field of computer network architecture;
— creation of the basis for an Academy-wide research automation system.

The architecture of the ECN is determined by the following basic requirements:
— there is no main (central) computer in the network; in accordance with the priority assigned to it or to its job, any computer can interrupt the operation of another and give it a new task;
— the network is freely connected, i.e., when the link to the communications network fails, any computer can operate in selfcontained fashion within the limits of its capabilities;
— the computers in the network are structurally and software-specialized for execution of certain groups of functions;
— distributed batch processing, involving various computers and hardware, is employed in the network;
— macro-, mini-, and microcomputers can operate with different operating systems in the network;
— the network has a high degree of survivability, so that it continues to operate when elements malfunction;

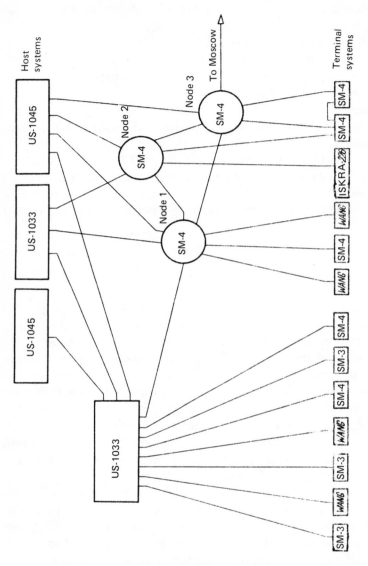

Fig. 8.14. EVC network.

- the network has expansion and development capabilities;
- it is possible for users to employ already available computers and terminal installations and the software for them;
- various process interaction protocols can be employed;
- computers that provide information and computing resources are freed from auxiliary operations to the greatest possible extent.

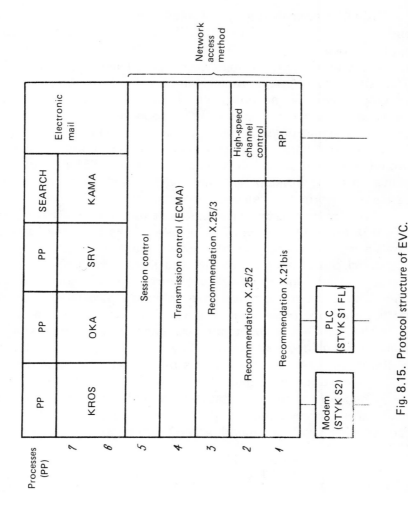

Fig. 8.15. Protocol structure of EVC.

In view of the experimental nature of the ECN, yet another requirement is added: the network should provide for an extensive scope of research on the architecture of multicomputer systems.

An eight-computer experimental network was made available to the personnel of three institutes in August 1977. By the end of 1982, the number of computers at different institutes connected to the network had increased, but the software and services furnished by the network had changed to an even greater extent.

Figure 8.14 shows the structure of the ECN. The network is made up of interacting user (or host) and communications systems.

The **host systems** (Fig. 8.14) determine the principal information and computing resources of ECN. Each of these systems executes applied processes and has for this purpose the OS 6.1 operating system and one of the following systems programs (Fig. 8.15): KROS, TSS, OKA, KAMA, Electronic Mail, and Network Access Method, which implements the protocols of levels 1—5. On the physical level, the network employs analog telephone channels (STYK S2 standard), digital physical lines (STYK S1 FL standard), and parallel RPI (Radial Parallel Interface standard) connections. The KROS programs provide dispatching of computations, TSS provides interactive software development, and KAMA and OKA control data banks and information-retrieval services.

Each of the **communications systems** (units 1—3) consists of 1 + n processors. The central processor of the SM-4 minicomputer implements the procedures of Recommendation X.25/3, while the n channel processors control the data links, (protocols of layers 1 and 2). In addition to data flow control, the communications systems also perform administrative functions associated with diagnostics, statistics, preparation of reports, and electronic mail.

The **terminal minicomputer systems** provide interfacing between users and the network. They provide communication, in a dialog mode, with all user systems of the network, local data processing, and local data banks.

The ECN maintains statistics that define quantitative and qualitative characteristics of the network's operation. An important paramenter is the network accessibility factor:

$$K_{na} = \frac{T}{1440} ,$$

where T is the time over which a user can work with the network (i.e., the network is "healthy"), in min; 1440 is the number of minutes in a day.

In addition, the ECN keeps track of the operating time of each user system. Flows of packets over physical links are also recorded (in each direction separately). Information on operating statistics of the ECN since the beginning of the current 24-hour period are issued upon request at any time they are needed.

8.9.
INTERACTIVE INFORMATION NETWORKS

An **interactive information network** is a particular case of a computer network in which a predominant part is played by processes associated with input, storage, and logical processing of information, and transmission of texts and images. Characteristic features of such networks are as follows:

1) presence of information contained in data banks and of interest to many users;
2) inexpensive terminals operating with information services and accessible to extensive groups of users;
3) simple languages of access to services;
4) dialog modes of interaction;
5) possibility of inputting, editing, and transmitting any correspondence between user terminals.

Interactive information networks intended for many users will gradually replace the telegraph, telex, and mail. In addition, they furnish users with data bases with extensive information-retrieval services. As a result, users obtain a wealth of information, including in particular the following:

— electronic newspapers and magazines;
— electronic mail;
— organization of discussions and debates on an extensive set of topics (politics, urban affairs, trade, etc.);
— urban reference services;
— electronic games;
— information on sports activities and cultural affairs;
— information on domestic services (hours and availability of shops, laundries, dry-cleaning establishments, etc.);
— information of transportation and ticket reservations (for airlines, trains, buses, etc.);
— transfer of wages to current accounts and of money from current accounts in savings banks;
— remote purchases with viewing of merchandise and home delivery;
— household budgeting and finance;
— building security;
— remote monitoring of domestic appliances;

- meter-reading in apartments and commercial premises; billing and payment of rent, electricity, telephone, gas, and so forth;
- medical consultations;
- electronic telephone directories;
- employment advertising;
- useful household advice, . . .

This list alone demonstrates that mass information encompasses an extremely wide set of problems, and that its importance cannot be overestimated.

The effectiveness and timeliness of interacting information networks has been so great that such networks are being developed and created in parallel in many countries. Table 8.3 gives a list of the best-known networks [192—198]. The work under way in different countries differs only in terms of minor features. Therefore, the CCITT has developed an interactive information network architecture [199, 200], called **Teletex,** and has approved Recommendation S.70: "Network-independent basic transport service for Teletex." Thus, the foundation has been created for uniting all development work under way in the field of interactive information networks.

The architecture of Teletex is compatible with the Reference Model of Open Systems Architecture of the International Standards Organization. Therefore, the logical structure of user systems is also represented by seven layers in this case (Fig. 8.16). As usual, the communications system is determined by three layers; the fourth through seventh layers of the system describe only administrative management functions.

The four lower layers (Fig. 8.16) in Teletex are called a **transport station.** The fifth layer is called the **session layer,** while the sixth is called the **document layer.** The seventh layer contains **texts.**

An important feature of the transport layer of Teletex is the fact that this layer is universal and is intended for operation (Fig. 8.17) through three types of communications networks: packet switching, circuit switching, and switched telephone networks.

The customary standard, characterized by Recommendation X.25, is proposed for Teletex in the packet switching network. It includes the following: X.21 or X.21bis physical interface; LAP B channel control protocol; and call and data-transmission procedures. At the same time, in the data link (second) layer the control speci-

TABLE 8.3.

No.	Name of network	Location
1.	ANTIOPE	France
2.	BILDSCHIRMTEXT	West Germany
3.	CAPTAINS	Japan
4.	DATAPOINTS	Sweden
5.	DATAVISION	Sweden
6.	GREEN THUMB	USA
7.	INTELPOST	International
8.	PRESTEL (VIEWDATA)	England, Holland
9.	QUBE	USA
10.	TELETEL	France
11.	TELETEX	International
12.	TELIDON	Canada
13.	TELSET	Finland
14.	TICCIT	USA
15.	VISTA	Canada

fied by Recommendation X.75 can also be used. It expands some-what the procedures described by Recommendation X.25.

In operating via the circuit switching network, virtually the same functions as in the packet switching network are proposed. On the whole, the differences in this case are to be found only in the network layer (Fig. 8.17). This is so because in circuit switching, there is no need to use the data transmission phase stipulated by Recommendation X.25. It is executed in another form only by the transport layer of user systems.

If the user systems interact via a telephone network, then modi-fied versions of X.25 and X.75 are employed to standardize the pro-cedures in this case as well. Only the telephone procedures for the initial part of a call are added to them. On the physical level, standard V.24 is employed, so that ordinary modems (for analog telephone networks) can be used.

317

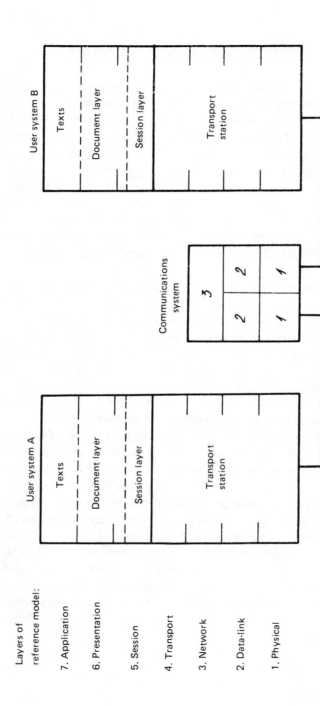

Fig. 8.16. Logical structure of user system.

Layers of
reference model:

7. Application

6. Presentation

5. Session

4. Transport

3. Network

2. Data-link

1. Physical

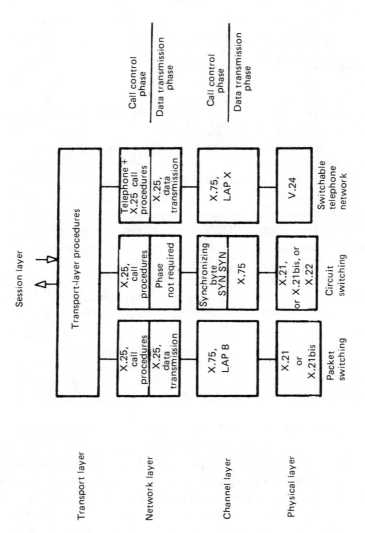

Fig. 8.17. Layer structure of transport network.

The basic network-independent transport service of Teletex as defined by Recommendation S.70 describes information transmission procedures (fourth layer) over any of the three communications networks shown in Fig. 8.17. It includes the following functions:

— establishment of transport connections;
— matching of sizes of transport blocks;
— refusal to receive blocks, with indication of the reasons;

— clearing of transport connections after errors have appeared;
— disconnection of transport connections.

The transport service is furnished to the higher-lying session layer (Fig. 8.16). This layer establishes logical channels between documents (sixth and seventh layers). The primary functions of the session layer are as follows: initialization, transmission, and completion of session. One or more documents may be transmitted during each session. A block created in the session layer (5) consists of a session heading and a body (Fig. 8.18). The latter includes a text and a document heading added to it in the sixth layer (document layer).

Thus, Teletex consists of three basic parts (Fig. 8.19). The first is determined by the communications network (packet switching network, circuit switching network, or switched telephone network). Transport stations (TS) are connected to this network. These stations are connected to processes (PR), defined by layers 5—7.

Figure 8.20 shows an approximate structure of a Teletex terminal system [200]. As can be seen from the figure, the system processes inputted words, and provides text editing and formatting of the entire document. It transmits (or receives) documents via the communications network. Teletex users are provided with printers or displays.

Work is under way at present to develop a general model of a transport service that would include not only Teletex but other forms of text transmission (e.g., Telex and digital fascsimile transmission).

A second widespread form of information network is **interactive Videotex.** The basic difference between this network and Teletex involves the structure of the terminal system; a video screen is a necessary element of this system in Videotex. The screen comes in two forms: display or television. Displays are intended for relatively expensive systems with extensive capabilities. The second case prevails when the terminal system is based on already available domestic equipment such as a color or black-and-white television sets, telephones, and, frequently, household tape recorders (Fig. 8.21). This is done so as to create the cheapest possible user system, employing equipment that the mass user already has. In Videotex, it is sufficient to acquire a simple inexpensive microprocessor with a keyboard for this purpose. As for the modem, it can be constructed in the form of one large-scale integrated circuit.

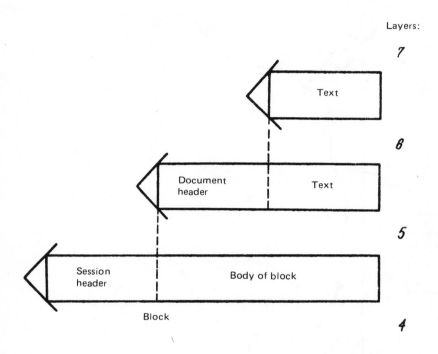

Fig. 8.18. Diagram of block generation.

Thus, the problem essentially becomes one of converting a television set into a multipurpose information and reference service terminal. At the same time, like Teletex, Videotex provides for interaction between a terminal system and other similar terminal systems, as well as with host system that furnish data banks.

In Videotex, the unit of information is the page (frame of a television screen). Some 20—24 lines of 40 symbols (letters, signs) each fit onto this page [198]. Thus, a maximum of 960 symbols can be placed on a page.

Figure 8.22 shows the general structure of interactive Videotex. Here every user with a terminal system can obtain execution of necessary information tasks via the telephone network. In addition,

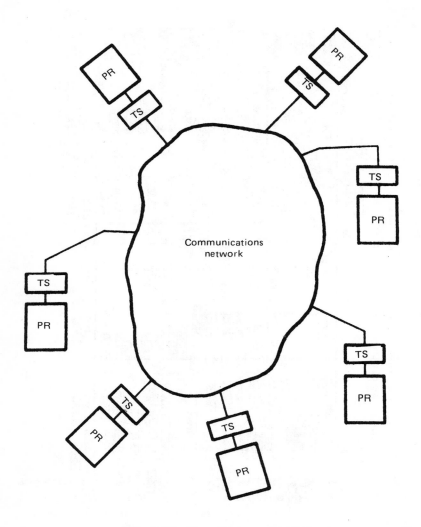

Fig. 8.19. Overall structure of Teletex.

works, e.g., a packet switching network. Then the host systems connected to this network will be accessible to him.

The pioneers in the field of interactive Videotex are England (the Prestel network), France (Antiope), and Canada (Telidon). Subsequently, the Bell System in the United States became involved. At present, the firm of Prestel International has initiated an international Videotex network [201]. In the first phase, user

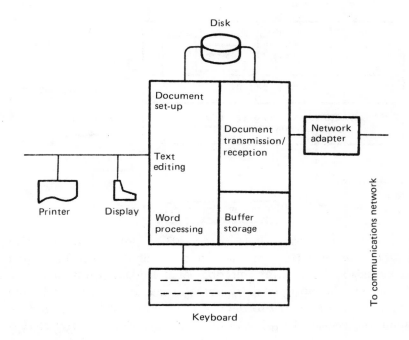

Fig. 8.20. Structure of Teletex terminal system.

systems in England, West Germany, the United States, and Switzerland are connected to the network. In this network, users are able to work with information-retrieval services, play electronic games and enjoy other forms of entertainment, conduct business negotiations, perform commercial operations, use electronic mail, process data, perform operations related to household management, and so forth.

An important form of service furnished by information networks is **electronic mail,** whose structure is shown in Fig. 8.23. Here mail is transmitted electronically via a communications network. Two ways of delivery are possible. If the addressee has an individual terminal (T) of some type, mail is sent to him via a physical link. If he has no such terminal, the traffic is printed out on the printer of a shared terminal (ST) at the destination and is delivered to the addressee via ordinary mail.

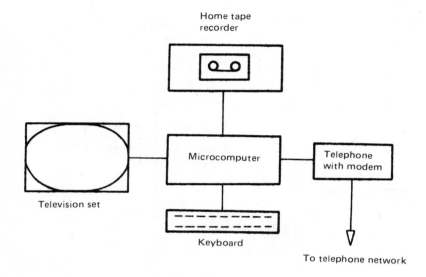

Fig. 8.21. Personal terminal system.

Since the user may not be there when mail is delivered, or his terminal may not be working, a necessary element of electronic mail is at least one host system with a data base that functions as an **electronic mailbox.** This "box" may operate in two modes. In the simplest case, the "box" provides mail only in a "general-delivery" mode (i.e., on demand). At the same time, it can attempt to forward mail to an addressed terminal at a particular time of day that has been specified.

In addition to delivering mail to specified addresses, electronic mail can also disseminate more general information, e.g., advertisements or messages of interest to large numbers of users.

An example of electronic mail is provided by the service that has been set up by the United States Post Office [202]. In the first phase, it covered 12 cities, but telexes in major governmental institutions were subsequently incorporated. The electronic mail service contains the following:

— traffic I/O hardware;
— communications systems;
— facilities for forwarding traffic to the mail.

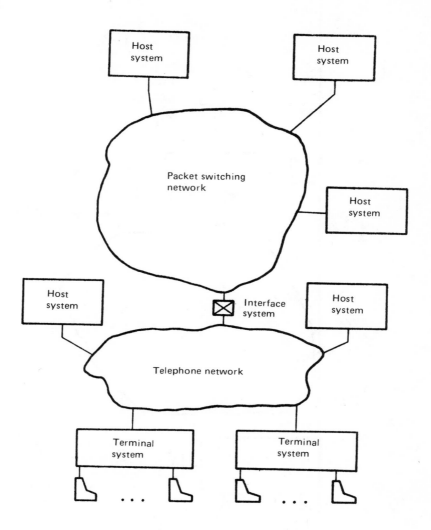

Fig. 8.22. Overall structure of interactive Videotex.

Messages to be transmitted by electronic mail are delivered to user terminals (including telexes) or to post offices equipped with terminals, where they are placed in envelopes and delivered by letter-carrier.

The first large-scale interactive information network of Videotex type was set up in England by the Post Office Corporation [196, 198, 203, 204]. Although it is called Viewdata, it is regis-

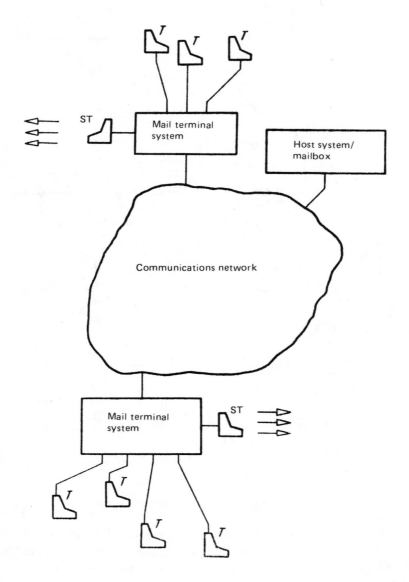

Fig. 8.23. Structure of electronic mail

tered under the trade name Prestel. This network is essentially a distributed information service that uses a large number of different host and terminal systems.

The information unit in this case is a page, i.e., an image supplied to a television or display screen. A page contains 960 symbols (24 rows of 40 symbols each) or a simple figure (78 x 72 elements). Each row is made up of 10 lines of the light field created on the screen by an electron beam. Of these lines, six to eight are used to generate the symbol elements. Image components (symbols, graphic elements) are provided in six colors: red, blue, green, yellow, light green, and pink. These elements are placed on a background that comprises eight colors, namely, black, white, and the six listed above.

The following functions are performed in order to enhance the diversity of images on the screen and to achieve maximum clarity:
— blinking of symbols;
— provision for letters of double height;
— creation of hidden symbols that appear on the screen to check whether or not the user has responded correctly to a query from the host system (the symbols appear after the user presses the necessary key);
— sixfold division of the screen by color bars.

The Prestel network employs two types of host systems, namely, updating and information-retrieval systems. Both systems are based on GEC 4082 computers. Each computer has a 384-kbyte main memory and 12 disk drives with a capacity of 70 Mbytes each.

The updating host system is intended for acquisition of information that will be subsequently furnished to large numbers of users. The system performs the following functions that are necessary for this purpose:
— input, editing, correction, and erasure of pages in a dialog mode;
— restriction of access to each page to a specified group of users;
— establishment of cost of access to pages;
— obtainment of user responses (e.g., merchandise orders, airline ticket reservations, and so forth);
— data on popularity of pages furnished to users (frequency of access to them).

Information is inputted into the data bases from keyboards or tape. Graphic matter is inputted by a video camera or by scanning by points.

The information in each data base can be updated at any time. In the Prestel network, information is inputted and issued in English. However, it is also possible to work with other languages. For instance, versions of the network software that operate with data in German and Swedish have already been implemented.

The information-retrieval host system obtains data from the updating host systems. Once it has these data, it immediately furnishes them to the terminal systems. For this purpose, the retrieval host system provides the following:

— a guide to available information;
— retrieval of needed information in data bases;
— information for users about the cost of retrieval services;
— transmission of user information in response to pages that have been examined.

In the near future, Prestel users will acquire yet another form of service, namely, **remote program distribution.** This stems from the fact that users at terminal systems are making steadily greater use of microcomputers. Therefore, it is becoming feasible to supply the microcomputers with programs from the data bases, which users can employ on-site, in their own simple terminal systems. It is planned that these programs will be used primarily for instruction and for game-playing in a dialog mode.

In the Prestel network, host systems interact via a communications network that conforms to the requirements of Recommendation X.25. Terminal systems are connected via this same network, and also via a switched telephone network. The rate of data acquisition by a terminal over a two-wire telephone channel is 1200 bits/sec, while the transmission rate is 75 bits/sec.

Administrative management of the Prestel network is performed by the National Operations Center (administrative system) in London. It operates 24 hours a day, seven days a week. In performing its functions, the Center is linked to Regional Centers. Each of the latter is responsible for administrative management of all user systems in a given region, and provides support for all users.

Information of the Prestel network is supplied not only to users in England; it is currently available to users in West Germany, Holland, Sweden, and Switzerland. Users in the United States can gain access to the information via the TPSS international packet switching service.

Although Prestel began operation only in 1979, by 1981 the number of pages stored in its computer memories had passed the million mark. In August 1980, the number of terminals registered onto the Prestel system has passed 5,000 with a growth rate of over 500 new users per month. It is estimated that by 1985, some 20% of all color television sets in England (around 400,000) will be connected to the network.

Prestel furnishes users with extensive information, including the following:
— news, including business news;
— sports information;
— weather summaries;
— train and bus schedules;
— telephone numbers of organizations and individuals;
— cookbook recipes;
— useful advice;
— lists and descriptions of sightseeing routes;
— insurance and tax information;
— classified job advertising;
— advertisements and announcements;
— information for businessmen, etc.

The information files in Prestel have the same structure as books and magazines, i.e., they consist of pages which the user can "turn."

An interactive network of Videotex type, known as Antiope, became operational in France in 1980 [196, 208–211]. The network was set up for domestic French needs, but there are plans to link it to information services outside France.

Figure 8.24 shows the structure of the Antiope network. It has two types of users, namely, those that supply information for the network, and those that consume it. To receive information, a user employs a color graphic display or television set. By means of additional hardware including a microprocessor, the display (television) is connected to a local telephone network. Through a local-access point, this network is connected to a nationwide packet-switching network. As a result, all data bases and information-retrieval services connected to the X.25 network are available to users at color displays or television sets.

Antiope users are linked only to their own local-access points (Fig. 8.24). The rate of user interaction with the information service is basically equal to 2400 bits/sec. At this rate, a page is transmitted

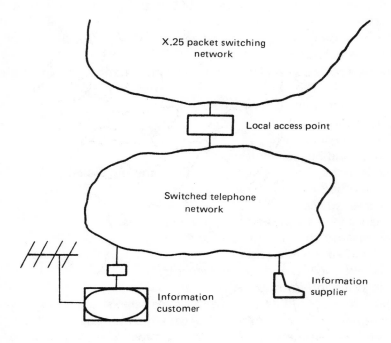

Fig. 8.24. Structure of Videotex network.

in 4 sec. Users can obtain necessary reference information at the network control center regarding the types of available information, data bases, user directory, conditions for obtaining information, state of the information services, and so forth.

A Teletex network for transmitting letters and telegrams is currently being tested in West Germany [205]. Information is sent over the digital channels of the synchronous digital data transmission network of the FRG. The transmission rate is 2400 bits/sec. Since Teletex is compatible with Telex, even in the experimental phase it is possible to interact with any of the 1.2 million telexes world-wide.

Tests are being conducted in a network that is called a nation-wide network. At the same time, all Teletex standards fully conform to Recommendation S.70 of the CCITT. Each terminal system of Teletex has a microprocessor, floppy-disk unit, display, and printer.

According to predictions, there will be 40,000 terminal systems in operation in the FRG in 1985, while by 1990 the number of systems will increase to 130,000. It is estimated that more than half of the 10 billion pieces of mail sent in the FRG will be replaced by the Teletex service.

Preparations are being made [205] for introduction of Teletex into Austria and Sweden in 1982; into England and France in 1983; and into Belgium, Holland, Denmark, Italy, and Norway in 1985. It is anticipated that, by 1987, the Teletex network will transmit up to 4 million messages per day in Western Europe alone.

8.10.
BROADCAST INFORMATION NETWORKS

Attempts toward even greater simplification of the structure of user stations of information networks has resulted in the creation of **broadcast information networks.** An important feature of them is their one-way mode of transmitting information. In this case, therefore, the technology of user operation with the information service is as follows. The service transmits pages of information in an infinitely closed cycle, while the user selects the necessary information and scans it on the screen of his television set.

In all the interactive information networks considered in the preceding section, information is sent via the communications network to one addressee. In broadcast networks, in contrast, information is sent directly to all users; the users, in turn, select what they require from the information flow.

Figure 8.25 shows the structure of a mass information network. The network consists of three basic elements: a television transmitter located at a television station; a single video channel (broadcast channel) that uses an antenna or television cable; and user stations in the form of standard television sets. When necessary, the television sets are supplemented by small special decoders (D) with a memory of one page of text (television frame).

As for the nature of information transmission, two methods are basically employed. The first of these, called **narrow-band,** involves transmission via a standard television installation together with ordinary television programs. For this, information is transmitted in the television channel that is normally employed for beam suppression during back-sweeping across the screen. Naturally, the encoding

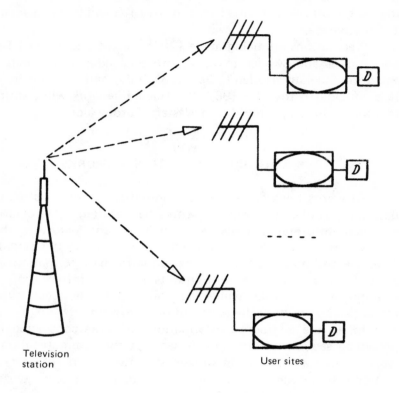

Television
station

User sites

Fig. 8.25. Structure of mass information network.

techniques must be compatible with the method for transmitting ordinary television programs. As a result, the television station transmits standard programs and user information (frames) almost simultaneously.

Mass information is transmitted to users in batches at a rate of around 7 Mbits/sec. Information pages usually contain 24 rows of 40 symbols each. When the method under consideration is employed, up to 300 pages of information (television frames) are transmitted, at a rate of 100 pages per 24 sec. To select needed pages from the flow of transmitted pages, each television set includes a decoder with a keyboard and text memory with a capacity of one page. The decoder selects the necessary page, stores it, and transmits it to the television screen. Once this page is no longer needed, the user presses a button and selects a new page. After the information has been scanned, the user can switch to any of the ordinary television programs available.

The second method, called the **broadband** method, involves the use of a specially dedicated television program (channel) for transmission of mass information. This program operates around the clock or at certain designated times. In the latter case, ordinary television programming is carried at other times. When this method is employed, the entire television channel is occupied constantly or at certain times. Thus, large amounts of information can be transmitted.

Broadcast networks were initially developed in England [195]. At present, work is under way in many countries. Table 8.4 indicates the best-known broadcast networks [195, 198]. Comparison of Tables 8.3 and 8.4 reveals that the names of some networks are the same. This means that some networks (e.g., Videotex in France) are complex, i.e., they transmit in both the broadcast and the interactive modes.

An example of a broadcast information network can be provided by the Teletex network set up by the BBC and IBA in 1976 [207]. In this network, text and simple graphics are transmitted in digital form as part of an ordinary television signal. The pages of the Teletex "telejournal" provide mass information and are frequently updated. The telejournal contains the following sections:
— foreign and domestic news;
— sports news;
— financial information;
— weather summaries;
— trip routes;
— puzzles and question-and-answer games.

All Teletex materials can be received by an ordinary television set to which a decoder with memory has been added. The cost of the latter is around 10% of the cost of the television set. It is included in the television set free of charge for anyone who wants it, however, since it is paid for by the advertisement that is carried. The decoder memory capacity is 7 kbits, adequate for storing one television frame.

Around 100 pages (frames) are transmitted in the telejournal. To scan it, it is first necessary to check the table of contents (al-

TABLE 8.4.

No.	Name of network	Country	Mode of transmission
1.	BILDSCHIRMZEITUNG	West Germany	Narrow-band
2.	BIBLOS	Belgium	_"_
3.	CEEFAX	England	_"_
4.	ORACLE	England	_"_
5.	TELETEX	England, Denmark, Holland	_"_
6.	TELIDON	Canada	_"_
7.	TEXT-TV	Sweden	_"_
8.	VIDEOTEX	France, West Germany	_"_
9.	QUBE	USA	Broad-band

phabetical index of the material, with page numbers). The table of contents is placed on one page. Then, by punching in the appropriate number, the page appears on the screen. Information is transmitted during the otherwise-unused intervals of suppression of the television back-scan. The data transmission rate during these periods is 6.93 Mbits/sec.

Information in the Teletex network is displayed in 6 colors; text is presented against one of six color backgrounds. Effects involving blinking of symbols or words are also used. In instruction situations, answers to questions remain invisible until the "show" button is pressed. Texts with letters of different sizes are extensively employed. It is also possible to superimpose text on an ordinary television image.

Recently, tests have been conducted of a combined Teletex network intended for reception of both broadcast and interactive information. A microprocessor with a keyboard is added to the television set for this purpose. The result is a terminal information system (Fig. 8.21). Four types of activity can be performed with this system:

— calculation of monthly credit payments;
— information on insurance problems;
— instruction programs;
— games.

CHAPTER 9

LOCAL COMPUTER NETWORKS

Local networks have been created twice. At the outset, the first computer networks were local. They grew rapidly, however, and soon became large wide-area networks. At the same time, it became clear that together with wide-area networks there is also a need for extensive use of local networks. Thus, they reappeared, but in a different capacity, based on advanced architecture principles and extensive use of microprocessor technology.

Today the term **local** applies to those computer networks whose user systems are at short distances from one another (usually within one to three adjacent buildings). Local networks have not only been independently developed; in most cases they have become the primary elements in wide-area networks.

9.1.
PURPOSE OF LOCAL NETWORKS

Decentralization of data processing is gaining more and more ground every year. If we allow for the fact that information flows circulate primarily within enterprises, companies, or organizations, the reason for the appearance and rapid development of local computer networks becomes apparent.

Analysis of local networks revealed that they provide greater reliability of data processing than do large wide-area networks. In local networks, it is much easier to optimize data processing; better conditions are established for integrating the processing of various kinds of information (administrative management, control of technological processes, business document processing, and so forth).

Because of the small distances between user systems, in local networks there is frequently no need to use telephone channels, and the transmission rate of data units can be increased in fairly simple fashion. Since transmission errors are reduced in the process, the detection and correction algorithms for these errors become simpler.

In terms of their functional purpose, local networks can be divided into two groups. The first group includes general-purpose networks that provide all sorts of data processing in institutions, corporations, or scientific centers. The second group is made up of local specialized networks. These include, for example, networks for design studies in design offices, networks for financial operations in national banks, and so forth.

Local networks can be set up on the spot, thus providing an enterprise or organization with the necessary data-processing base. Frequently, however, local networks develop gradually, with constant expansion of their information capabilities. Such networks may include computers manufactured by different organizations and companies. It is more efficient, however, to employ computers and other hardware that have been specially created for local networks.

Local information and computing networks, like wide-area ones, can perform a wide range of tasks. At the same time, local networks can much more efficiently implement a number of important functions for enterprises or organizations:

a) Planning of operations:
— matching and compilation of plans and graphs;
— compilation of plans for meetings that are convenient for the participants:
— compilation of daily, weekly, or monthly electronic worker schedules;
— reminders regarding approaching deadlines, conferences, or meetings.

b) Primary production:
— technological process control;
— design;
— development of new technology;
— set-up of production.

c) Business and accounting:
— personnel records;
— compilation and editing of documents;
— storage, retrieval, and forwarding of correspondence and reports;
— monitoring of the execution of decisions and instructions;
— dissemination of general memoranda.

d) Text control:
-- compilation and editing of texts (reports, papers, plans, correspondence);
— preparation of drawings and figures;

— text storage and retrieval.

e) Current operations:

— planning, reports, and legal documentation;

— remote conferences;

— control of the course of operations and projects;

— dynamic correction of plans.

It should be borne in mind that the people at the terminal consoles of local networks are the ordinary personnel of enterprises and organizations, i.e., administrative staff, engineers, skilled workmen, accounting personnel, and so forth. In addition to the customary requirements for computer networks, local networks should meet certain other requirements:

— work sites should be equipped with simple and convenient terminals;

— users should not be required to have special skills in computer mathematics and techniques;

— data processing should be provided in user-convenient form;

— a set of simple and convenient access procedures to the network should be developed;

— it should be taken into account that, for some time to come, enterprises and organizations will use mixed information services in which some documents are in paper form while others are stored in electronic user-system memories.

As for information-retrieval services, these services should also incorporate programs that make it possible to filter and concentrate the initial information, and to extrapolate data and to determine the necessary statistical interrelationships in them. The result is information of a new type, e.g., predictive information that helps a staff member discover new aspects of the state of the controlled entity. Local networks make it possible to feed information to computer storage once and then to repeatedly process and utilize it, as necessary, to solve a variety of problems.

9.2.
STAR NETWORKS

As a rule, it is overly extravagant to set up large numbers of normal communications systems in a local network. In view of the extensive use of microprocessors and the flexibility of the architecture, therefore, single-unit **local star networks** are attracting more and more interest. They have two important advantages:

1. The fact that there is only one element makes it possible to connect the communications and administrative systems together.

2. Local (institutional) telephone stations can be replaced by a communications-administrative system that utilizes all existing telephone distribution frames and cables.

A single-element network is simple to implement, diagnose, and manage. It also exhibits good modularity. Addition of a user system to the network, or elimination of a system from the network, does not alter the nature of operation of the rest of the network.

Figure 9.1 shows an example of the structure of a single-element local computer network. This network includes seven user systems and one communications-administrative system. The latter provides routing of the information transmitted throughout the local network.

Single-element local networks for transmission of both data and speech have been becoming more popular in recent years. They can be created either from scratch or on the basis of an existing local automatic telephone exchange (ATE). In the latter case, the ATE is replaced by a packet switching system, and A/D and D/A converters are added to the telephone instruments. In addition, various data-processing systems are incorporated into the network. As a result, while maintaining already existing cables, it is possible to convert an analog telephone network into a single-element local computer network.

An example of a communications system for such a network is provided by the IBX/S 40 system developed by the InteCom Corporation [212, 213]. On the basis of this system, a local network is established; its overall structure is shown in Fig. 9.2. As shown in this figure, computers, terminals, disk equipment, copying devices, and facsimile and telephone equipment can be connected to the network through interface converters or adapters. In short, virtually everything that might be needed for data processing in an institution, organization, or institute can be provided.

The IBX/S 40 system, whose structure is shown in Fig. 9.3, switches packets containing data or digitized speech. Data is transmitted at a rate of 56 kbits/sec. Packet switching is performed by 32-bit processors of the main control device. The latter is connected to 16 switching units. A switching unit, in turn, has 16 microprocessor sections that service up to 256 users with a capacity of 128 kbits/sec. Since there are 16 units in all, it is possible to connect 4096 data- and speech-transmitting users to the communications system.

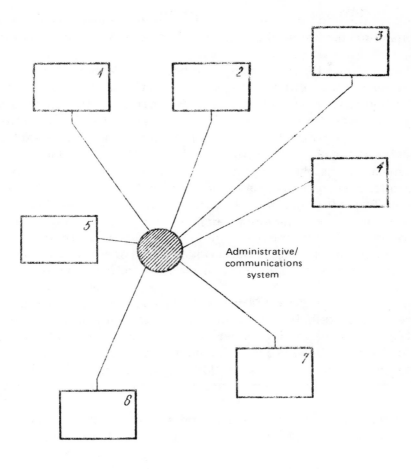

Administrative/
communications
system

Fig. 9.1. Local star network.

The GTE Telenet Company has developed something similar [214]. It has developed a communications system and interface converters that support connection to a local computer network of ordinary analog telephone instruments, text processors, facsimiles, computers, and other information sources and consumers. Digital data are transmitted in the network at rates of up to 56 kbits/sec in synchronous modes or up to 19.2 kbits/sec in asynchronous modes. The interface converter for telephone equipment is in the form of of a small attachment. As in the preceding example, both speech and data are transmitted over the network.

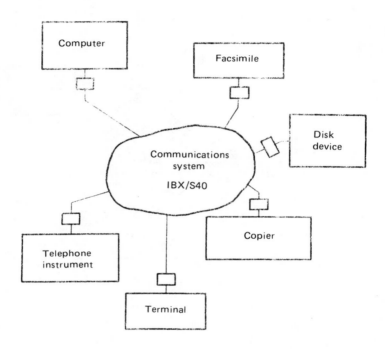

Fig. 9.2. Local network based on IBX/S 40 system.

The network in question can operate in a self-contained mode or can be connected to the large TELENET communications network (§8.7). In this case, a large number of low-speed terminals (100 or more) connected to a local network can not only interact with the network resources but also form part of the TELENET network via one common physical link.

The International Telephone and Telegraph Corporation has developed a similar communications system, called ARC (Advanced Communications System) for local networks. This system is intended for supporting packet switching and speech transmission in organizations. The system embodies the protocols specified by Recommendation X.25 of the CCITT.

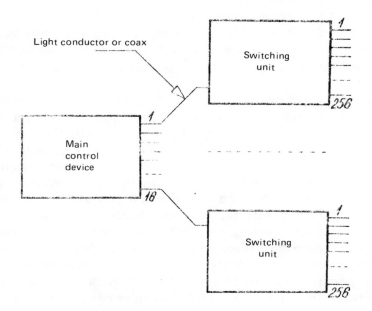

Fig. 9.3. Structure of IBX/S 40 system.

9.3.
RING NETWORKS

Ring networks have a simple architecture, one that has attracted many development engineers. These networks employ degenerate communications systems, each with only three inputs. Two of these inputs are connected into a ring, while the third is connected to "its own" user system. In the ring, outside the system, there are virtually no repeaters to introduce additional noise and distortion. As a result, the physical medium of a ring network can be entirely passive, and therefore highly reliable. The use of light conductors is also simpler in rings, because there is no need for light mixers. The structure of the communications system is also greatly simplified; it may even lack such "classical" functions as routing.

At the same time, ring networks have shortcomings, which have led to development of alternative topologies. A major shortcoming of ring networks is the functional "brittleness" of a chain of 100 or more communications systems. Malfunctioning of one of them causes the entire ring to malfunction. Considerable effort may be required to locate the damage.

A second shortcoming of ring networks is their relatively low data transmission rate. This stems from the fact that each packet transmitted between user systems must pass through large numbers of communications systems, and be subject to logical processing in each of them.

To enhance network reliability, supporters of ring networks propose various schemes that make it possible to disconnect malfunctioning communications systems (together with the user systems connected to them) from the system. For example, it has been suggested [216] that the data links between communications systems in the ring be run in such a way that they pass through a common central point. This point would contain the necessary switching apparatus for disconnecting damaged portions of the network, and for creating the necessary detours. This arrangement can enhance the reliability of data transmission. In terms of topology, however, it converts a ring into a complex double star.

An example of a ring local computer network is the **Cambridge Ring** network (Fig. 9.4). This is an inexpensive network in which the physical links together with degenerate communications systems are in the shape of a ring [111, 217–219]. The systems in question have specific functions and are called stations. The number of stations is equal to the number of user systems (including the administrative system). Two ring circuits and one user circuit, connected to the user system, run to each station.

The Cambridge Ring employs an original method of packet transmission between user systems. This method is based on the fact that each user system has its own station, and the station address corresponds to the user-system address. This makes possible continuous transmission around the ring of empty frames that constitute packet containers.

Data is transmitted in Cambridge Ring as follows. When a user system needs to transmit a packet, it forwards it to the station, which inserts it in an empty frame. Each station connected to the ring examines the addresses of frames passing through it and makes a copy of each packet addressed to it. It then forwards this packet to "its own" user system. The addressee station places a marker in the frame containing the packet of which a copy was made (i.e., it

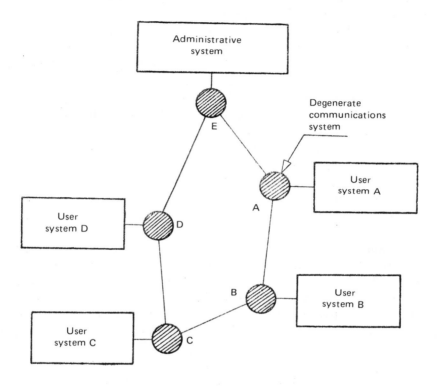

Fig. 9.4. Structure of local ring network.

alters the status of the frame). In this manner the station indicates that the packet has been received. As it moves around the ring, the frame again arrives at the sending station. This station checks to see if there are errors in the frame; if there are not, it deletes the packet (the frame again becomes empty). If there are errors in the frame, the sending station again transmits it around the ring (after error correction).

When one of the elements malfunctions, the ring ceases to operate. In addition to the primary ring, therefore, a spare should be available. The maximum distance between stations connected by physical links is 200 meters. Each physical link employs twisted-pair conductors. The ring operates in a full-duplex mode at rates of 100—300 kbits/sec. Stations used in the Cambridge Ring are based on Intel 8080 microprocessors, with 64-kbyte memories.

A station consists of a repeater and of channel link controllers. The Cambridge Ring also has systems that provide user service and that execute administrative functions.

Certain malfunctions (e.g., symbol inversion in one particular bit) can give rise to endless circulation of frames in the network. Such situations are eliminated by a special control station that removes such frames from the network.

The Cambridge Ring employs Recommendation X.25, but with some modifications. The second protocol layer in the network performs data link control functions:

- synchronization of data transmission;
- frame generation;
- information flow control;
- addressing;
- error detection;
- errror messages.

Data are checked by the sending station upon return of a frame after it has traversed the entire ring. Therefore, there is no check-symbol field in the frame. The network control mechanism is also simple — acknowledgement of receipt of a frame by the next station. The network layer in the Cambridge Ring provides simplified routing multiplexing, and establishment of virtual channels (layer 3 of X.25).

9.4.
BROADCAST-CHANNEL NETWORKS

The development and initial sucesses of broadcast channels led to rapid development and deployment of **broadcast-channel local networks.** Figure 9.5 shows the structure of such a network. It consists of a broadcast channel and of a group of user systems. Each of the latter is subdivided into a station and a user. The **station** is the device that interfaces the user to the broadcast channel. In different networks, this device executes the protocols of the two of four lowest layers. The remaining protocols are implemented by the user. Stations are designed in the form of one or more microprocessor subassemblies. A **user** is a computer, terminal, disk, copier, printer, or any other information equipment.

Broadcast-channel networks can be subdivided into several groups, in relation to their size. **Small broadcast-channel networks** include those that incorporate microcomputers and the hardware

344

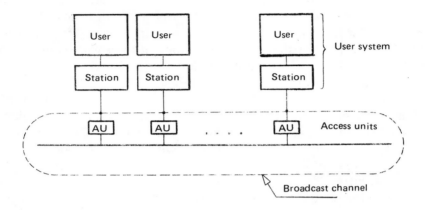

Fig. 9.5. Structure of broadcast-channel local network.

that interacts with them (small disk drives, printers, displays, main-storage devices, and so forth). These networks are of modest size, use simple physical media, and have a simplified architecture. As compared to other broadcast-channel networks, their capabilities are limited. However, they are inexpensive and simple to operate, and their resources can fully meet the needs of a small institution or enterprise. Examples of such networks are DDB, Omninet, and Z-net.

The **DDB (Domestic Digital Bus) network** was set up by Phillips [220] and is intended to provide information exchange between household electronic equipment. This equipment includes, in particular, a television set, video recorder, and network control console. Although this equipment is of analog type, the home backbone line that connects them provides transmission of data in digital form. It will subsequently be possible to connect home terminals (including displays) and printers to the network.

The broadcast channel of the DDB network is based on a two-wire backbone line, whose maximum length is 150 m. Up to 50 different devices can be connected to this line. Each of these devices can assume control and can communicate with other equipment of the network. Access to the backbone line is in a time-sharing mode. Devices may have differing transmission priorities.

Control commands for the equipment (activation, deactivation, change of mode) are transmitted over the broadcast channel. Information is exchanged in the form of packets, whose size varies from 138 to 8290 bits/sec, depending on which of the three modes of operation is employed. Each packet includes a starting bit, and also the following fields: mode field, fields of addresses of destination and sender, and data transmission control field. Microprocessor LSI circuitry is installed in the equipment to provide connection to the network. This circuitry decodes the commands and performs the necessary component control functions.

The **Omninet network,** developed and offered to clients by Corvus Systems [221], is one of the simplest. The physical medium in the broadcast channel (Fig. 9.6) is provided by a cable with a single twisted pair. The length of the twisted pair does not exceed 600 m without repeaters, or 1200 m with them. The transmission rate is 1 Mbit/sec.

The simple structure of the broadcast channel and the relatively modest transmission rate make it possible to set up an inexpensive local network that can be readily installed and is not complicated to operate. It can include up to 64 microcomputers or disk drives. In the second phase, hardware will be developed for connecting printers (Fig. 9.6) and for interaction (via a telephone network) with various kinds of other equipment or computer networks.

Omninet employs a seven-layer protocol hierarchy (Fig. 9.7), based on the Reference Model of Open Systems Architecture. The four lowest layers are implemented in adapters called transport processors (TP; Fig. 9.6). All transport processors in the network are identical, except for a small part of the circuitry that is intended for interfacing with particular network users. Each transport processor has a 2-kbyte ROM and 128-kbyte main memory.

The network employs multiple access with carrier sensing prior to sending of a frame. To simplify the transport processors, during transmission there is no monitoring of possible collisions of frames sent by two user systems.

For simplicity, so-called **microvirtual channels,** rather than ordinary virtual channels, are employed in Omninet. These logical entities provide execution of virtual-channel functions in the network, but only over a few microseconds. Microvirtual channels guarantee that, if a packet is not delivered error-free to the addressee, the sender will be informed to this effect. Moreover, erroneous duplication of packets is prevented, and the addressee receives the packets in the same order in which they were sent.

346

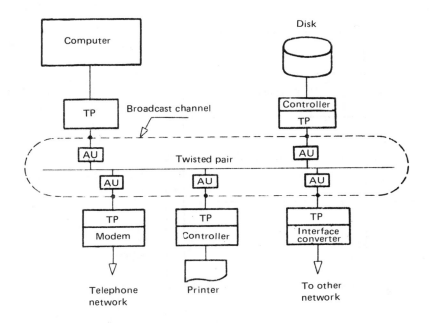

Fig. 9.6. Omninet network.

The **Z-net network**, created by the Zilog Corporation [112, 113, 222], is intended to support interaction of a large number of microprocessors. The structure of this network is shown in Fig. 9.8. A coaxial-cable broadcast channel links up to 256 user systems, including microcomputers, external storage devices, displays, printers, and so forth. Information is transmitted in packets, the body length being 512 bytes. The transmission rate over the coaxial cable is 0.8 Mbits/sec; the cable may be up to 2 km long.

Three types of stations, based on Z80A microcomputers, are employed to connect the various users. Each of these stations operates with one parallel and five serial user circuits, that connect the user systems to the broadcast channel. Computers, terminals, and peripherals are connected to them. Only Zilog microcomputers, however, can be connected to Z-net. When necessary, an entire Z-net can function in a wide-area network as a multiconsole terminal of some type, e.g., an IBM 2780 or 3780.

347

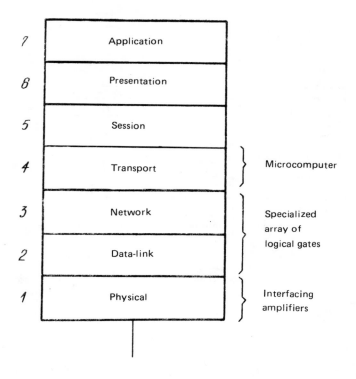

Fig. 9.7. Protocol hierarchy of Omninet.

Medium-size broadcast-channel networks are oriented primarily toward minicomputers. At the same time, these networks can include an extensive assortment of microcomputers. The assortment of devices and equipment associated with text processing is expanded in this case. Medium-size networks are intended for large institutions or enterprises. Examples of such networks are provided by Ethernet, ARC, and Net-One.

Ethernet, which was created by the Xerox Corporation [108, 109, 111, 113, 218, 223–229], is intended for combining mini- and microcomputer user systems, disk drives, printers, and copiers. At the outset only Xerox was involved in the creation of Ethernet, but in 1980 it joined forces with the firms of DEC and Intel.

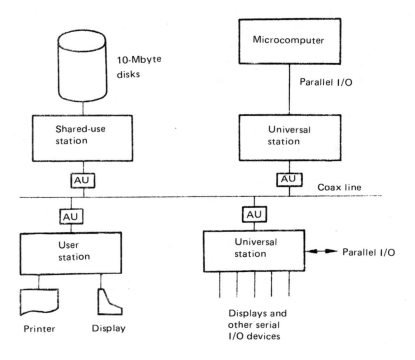

Fig. 9.8. Structure of Z-net.

The broadcast channel in Ethernet is based on a highly reliable passive element, namely, a coaxial cable consisting of one or more segments up to 500 m long. Up to 100 user systems can be connected to each segment. If there are several segments in a cable, they are connected by repeaters (amplifiers). User systems in the same building or in adjacent buildings are connected to the channel via adapter stations.

In 1980, the Xerox Corporation began to produce equipment designated as System 8000. This equipment includes the following: a system with a data base containing up to 10,000 pages of text, a laser printer, and adapters for connecting various computers and hardware. Equipment manufactured by other companies can also be connected to the network. If necessary, several local networks can be combined into a common system.

The structure of a single-segment local Ethernet network is shown in Fig. 9.9. Here the broadcast channel consists of a coaxial cable with access units (AU) installed directly on it. Terminators (TR) are placed at the ends of the cable. The transmission rate over the channel is 10 Mbits/sec. The user circuit connecting the access unit to the user system (via its adapter A) can be up to 50 m long.

The length of each broadcast-channel segment does not exceed 500 m. Therefore, larger Ethernet configurations are obtained by connecting 2—5 segments through the user of repeaters. Figure 9.10 shows a three-segment local network. It unites nine user systems (1—9).

It should be borne in mind that, in the logical sense, Ethernet defines only the two lowest layers of a computer network (data link). In accordance with the general concept accepted by DEC,

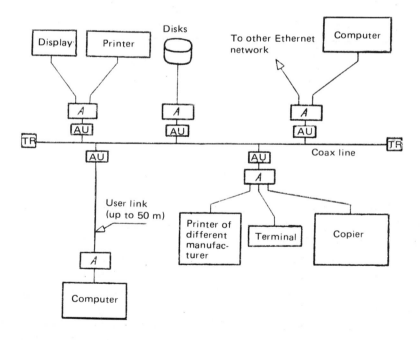

Fig. 9.9. Structure of Ethernet.

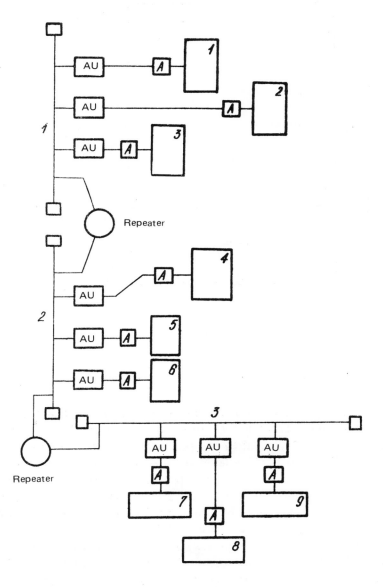

Fig. 9.10. Three-segment network.

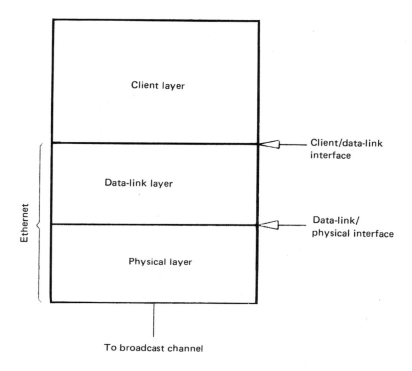

Fig. 9.11. Hierarchy of layers of Ethernet.

Xerox, and Intel, the data-link and physical layers, characterizing transmission via a broadcast channel, are described (Fig. 9.11). As for the remaining layers, they are represented by one complex layer called the **client** layer. This layer is independent of the characteristics of the broadcast channel, and in general, therefore, it can have an arbitrary structure and can incorporate the necessary number of different functional layers. For example, in the Intel Local Network Architecture (ILNA), shown in Fig. 9.12, the complex client layer is represented by three functional layers: application, session, and transport [230]. The architecture of Unet, developed by the 3COM Corporation [230], provides a five-layer representation of the complex client layer (Fig. 9.13). The upper layers are controlled in the computer by the UNIX operating system, while the middle layers are implemented by a preprocessor.

352

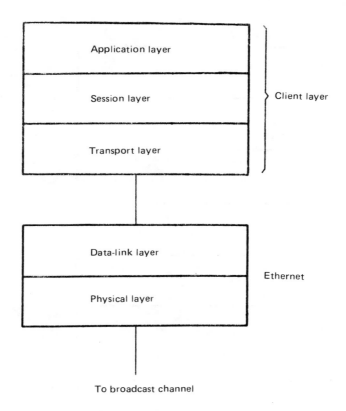

Fig. 9.12. Protocols of ILNA network.

Functions to be performed by the adapter stations that form part of the user systems are described in accordance with the logical structure of Ethernet. These functions are shown in Fig. 9.14. As the figure indicates, adapters implement tasks specified by the data-link and physical layers, and also interface with the clients (remaining part of the systems). Adapters are also connected to access units which provide physical interfacing to the coaxial cable.

Ethernet users can interact with data banks, perform distributed data processing, transfer files between systems, and execute a number of other functions. One of the data bases can be used as a "mailbox" for electronic mail. Correspondence is forwarded via this mailbox to one user or to a list of users. Each user either stores traffic addressed to him in this mailbox, or cancels this traffic.

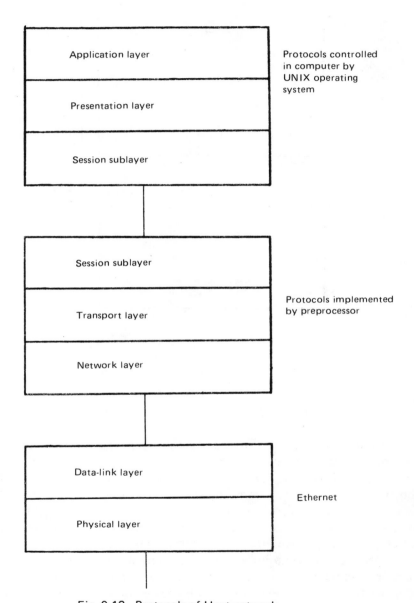

Fig. 9.13. Protocols of Unet network.

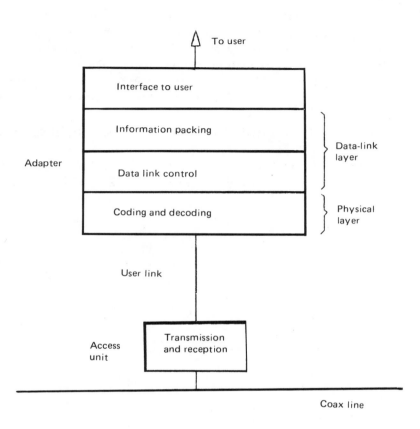

To user

Interface to user

Information packing

Data link control

Coding and decoding

Adapter

Data-link layer

Physical layer

User link

Access unit

Transmission and reception

Coax line

Fig. 9.14. Structure of adapter station.

In 1981, a multifunctional information system (type 860) was created for Ethernet. This system processes texts, business documents, and data. The system has a full-page display and a printer.

A number of organizations and corporations have begun to develop user systems that are specially intended to be connected to Ethernet. For example, Stanford University has created a text- and graphic-processing terminal system [231]. The core of this system is a central microprocessor (Motorola MC 68 000) with a 250-kbyte main memory, a graphic microporcessor, and an adapter. These components interact with one another via a common bus (Multibus). A graphic display, keyboard, and graphic manipulator arm are connected to the core. The display screen is mounted in such a way that its large dimension is vertical.

The broadcast channel of Ethernet employs multiple access with carrier sensing and collision detection. Upon detection of collisions of frames sent by several user systems, transmission of data units is repeated. The waiting time of user systems before repeat transmission increases in relation to the number of the repetition (first, second, third, . . .). This is done to eliminate peak loading of the channel.

Data are transmitted in sequences of packets or in single datagram packets. Packets are packed into frames, each of which begins with the 6-byte address of the recipient (Fig. 9.15). The length of this field makes it possible to have up to 2^{48} addresses, one of

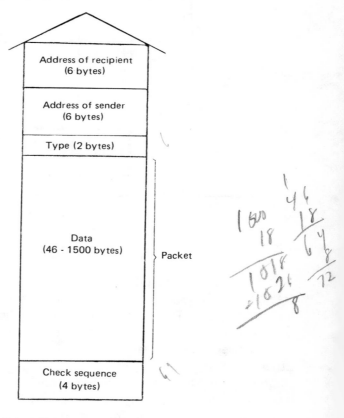

Fig. 9.15. Structure of Ethernet frame.

which is common. Frames with this address are received by all user systems. As a result, broadcast transmission of information becomes possible. The address of the frame sender is placed in the 6-byte field that follows.

A two-byte field that specifies the type of frame is employed by the upper protocol levels for sending control information and for data transmission. The data field contains a packet whose size varies from 46 to 1500 bytes. The information contained may be arbitrarily encoded and may be in any format. Frames terminate with a 4-byte check-sequence field. A field this large ensures a high degree of error detection. Errors may be corrected by data-link-protocol procedures.

Around 100 Ethernet networks are already in operation in various countries. The operating statistics for one such network are as follows. The network includes 120 user systems. Around 300 Mbytes of information are transmitted per day. Only 4% of the theoretical broadcast-channel capacity is employed during the peak hour, however, while for the peak minute the figure is 17%. Some 99% of all frames are sent without repeat transmission. Only 0.03% of the frames collide in the channel. Errors occur (on average) once every 6000 transmitted frames. A number of companies, including ADM, Mostec, and Zilog [232], have begun to manufacture VLSI circuitry that provides connection of user systems to Ethernet.

Ethernet is a simple and inexpensive local computer network. However, in the opinion of the experts of an IEEE working group [223], the network has a number of shortcomings, including the following in particular:

— the network employs its own protocol rather than the HDLC standard data-link control protocol;
— most error correction is performed by user programs, a feature that can lead to incompatibility of these programs;
— there are no adapter stations for access to wide-area computer networks through modems.

The **Attached Resource Computer System (ARC) network** was created by the Datapoint Corporation [224, 233–236]. The Radio Shack division of Tandy Corporation joined the project in September 1981. The network is intended primarily for distributed data processing. The broadcast channel of the network is based on coaxial cable (Fig. 9.16) that links all user systems spread throughout an organization or enterprise. These systems may include computers, speech-

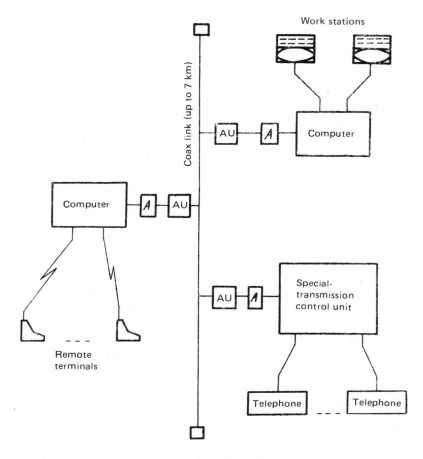

Fig. 9.16. Structure of ARC.

transmission control equipment, printers, and external storage devices. The transmission rate over the channel is 2.5 Mbits/sec. According to Tandy, the adapter station used to connect user systems to the channel in ARC is 3—5 times cheaper than in Ethernet, because of its simplicity.

The ARC network performs data storage and retrieval, computation, and text processing. Data, speech, and documents can be transmitted over the broadcast channel. Four priorities are established

358

for electronic mail: night-letter, regular, urgent, and instant. As soon as a document is delivered, a message indicating the time of delivery is displayed on the sender's screen.

Datapoint has also created the Lightlink broadcast channel that employs modulated noncoherent infrared signals and is intended for servicing a group of buildings within a circle 3–4 km in diameter. As in the case of a coaxial link, data are transmitted in digital form.

The **Net/One network** of the Ungemann-Bass Corporation was created [110, 113, 237, 238] to link computers made by different manufacturers, primarily systems intended for networks: Ethernet of Xerox, ARC of Datapoint, and Z-net of Zilog. In this case the broadcast channel is a coaxial cable up to 1200 m long. Repeaters (amplifiers) are employed when greater lengths are required. The data rate over the channel is up to 10 Mbits/sec. Up to 200 user systems can be connected to the channel, with a minimum spacing between them of 2.5 m. In principle, the coaxial cable can be replaced by another type of physical medium, e.g., a light conductor.

The company manufactures two types of adapter stations for Net/One, consisting of identical units. Figure 9.17 shows the structure of the model-1 adapter. As the figure indicates, the adapter consists of two parts: a network microprocessor and a part called a receiver/transmitter interface. These two parts interact via a common bus that transmits data at 8 Mbits/sec. The adapter has two buffers: a 2-kbyte buffer for transmitted frames and a 4-kbyte one for received frames. Frames move through the buffers on a first-in first-out basis.

The network processor supports interfacing with serial (up to four inputs) and parallel (up to two inputs) user circuits. The base of the network processor is provided by a Z80A microprocessor with a 64-kbyte main memory and a 4–16 kbyte serial-parallel memory. Frames are sent and received by facilities for direct access to memory. In the user circuits that connect user systems to the broadcast channel, the transmission rate may be as high as 19,200 bits/sec.

The receiver/transmitter interface supports interaction with the broadcast channel. Connection to this channel is effected by nondisruptive tapping. The receiver and transmitter which constitute the access unit are mounted directly on the coaxial cable and are connected to the adapter by a nine-wire cable not more than 24 m long.

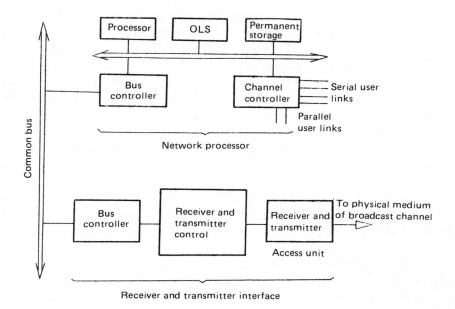

Fig. 9.17. Structure of Model 1 adapter.

The Model 2 adapter performs the same functions as the Model 1. In the Model 2, however, there may be up to three more application microprocessors on the common bus (Fig. 9.18). As a result, the number of serial and parallel user circuits that can be controlled by one adapter is substantially increased.

In the Model 2 adapter, the network processor becomes a central processor, coordinating all the operations of the entire multiprocessor device. It controls the frame traffic through the adapter. The application processor performs virtually the same functions as the network processor in Model 1. Each adapter gathers statistics on its operation and performs a number of diagnostic functions.

For local network control, a microprocessor-based administrative system has been created whose functions include the following:

— monitoring of any data transmission;
— diagnostics and analysis of network operation;

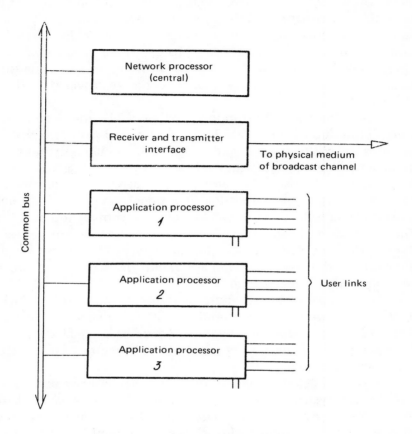

Fig. 9.18. Structure of Model 2 adapter.

— statistics of packets in the broadcast channel;
— determination of adapter malfunctions;
— alteration of the configuration and addresses in the network.

Net/One employs the seven-layer hierarchy of protocols of the network model. It is possible to implement a virtual full-duplex channel mode and an individual datagram mode. The second mode is convenient when it is necessary to disseminate information to all local network users at once. Linkage to user systems is effected by means of a modified Recommendation X.25. The broadcast channel is transparent for any types of codes.

361

Large broadcast-channel networks are primarily intended for linking together large computers and powerful peripheral equipment: disks, tapes, high-speed wide-format printers, and so forth. At the same time, necessary minicomputers can also be connected. Large networks are characterized by complex protocols, a diversity of information resources, and high data-processing and data-transmission rates. They are intended for large scientific centers and industrial complexes. Examples of large local networks are provided by Hyperchannel and LCN.

The **Hyperchannel network** was developed by the Network Systems Corporation [108, 239–244]. An unusual feature is that the aim was to create a large multimachine computer installation by using network-architecture methods and to provide high-speed communication with users. Therefore, the Hyperchannel network is a data processing center consisting of a small number of large computers at relatively short distances from one another (up to 1 km). They interact with one another at the standard operating rates of their block-multiplex channels (50 Mbits/sec). In addition to computers, large direct-access external devices (disks or tapes) can also be connected to Hyperchannel.

An example of the structure of Hyperchannel is shown in Fig. 9.19. Here three IBM 327X terminal systems interact with two IBM 370 computers. Topologically, the broadcast channel consists of three parts, two of which form self-contained circuits, while the third links them together.

Hyperchannel can have up to four coaxial backbone cables that link the user systems of the local network. Therefore, each adapter station is connected simultaneoulsy to 1–4 coaxial cables. Each adapter has a 4–8-kbyte buffer storage for transmitted and received frames.

Information in Hyperchannel is transmitted in frames that contain the addresses of the sender and recipient, as well as a control sum for checking purposes. Data link control (protocol level 2) is effected by a version of the HDLC protocol.

The data transmission procedure in Hyperchannel is fairly complex, involving multiple access both with time sharing (window period) and without it (random engagement of the channel in competition period). The essential features of the procedure are as follows:

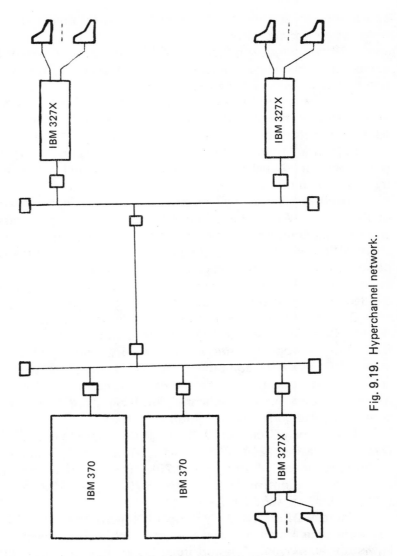

Fig. 9.19. Hyperchannel network.

1. When the broadcast channel is engaged, all user systems are blocked and cannot initiate transmission.

2. When the channel is freed up, a time interval τ_1 is established during which only an addressee user system that has received a frame can send an acknowledgement of its receipt and of the fact that there are no errors therein.

3. After τ_1, there is a window period in which user systems are alloted a time during which they can transmit. Priorities for window

allocation are established in accordance with predictions of the needs of the various users.

4. If the window period has ended and no user system has occupied the channel, a competition period occurs during which all user systems have equal chances of engaging it.

5. Frame collisions are detected on the basis of a control sum at the end of frames. If a frame contains an error, no acknowledgement of its receipt is sent.

6. If after an interval τ_2, the coaxial line is not engaged, there is a repetition of period τ_1 during which channel use is governed by user system priority.

Priorities are specified by counters located in the adapters of user systems. When the channel is engaged with transmission of any sort, all counters are reset to zero. They are activated when the channel becomes freed up. They also determine τ_2 and the window period. In more recent versions, a decision was made to avoid user-system priorities and to change over to task priorities, tasks being divided into urgent and normal tasks.

One of the first Hyperchannel network was established by Boeing Computer Services, this being a local network known as BSC. The network has three data processing centers, which include large CDC and IBM computers. A Cray-1 computer will soon be added to the network. By the end of 1981, more than 100 different networks based on Hyperchannel, utilizing 25 different types of computers, had gone into operation.

The **Loosely Coupled Network (LCN)** was created by Control Data Corporation [244–248]; it is intended for linking computers of different manufacturer (Fig. 9.20). The manufacturers include, in particular, Control Data (Cyber 170, Cyber 200, etc.), IBM (360, 370, 303X), and DEC (PDP-11).

Figure 9.21 shows the protocol hierarchy used in LCN. As in the Reference Model of Open Systems Architecture, seven protocol layers are employed. The top three layers, however, have different names. The bottom four (transport part) are implemented by adapter stations (A). The upper layers (5–7) of LCN are set up in conformity with the requirements of the Reference Model. They provide file- and job-transmission capabilities for user systems, as well as interaction of application processes.

Computers are linked to the broadcast channel by means of an adapter station (Fig. 9.20). This is a small computer with its own

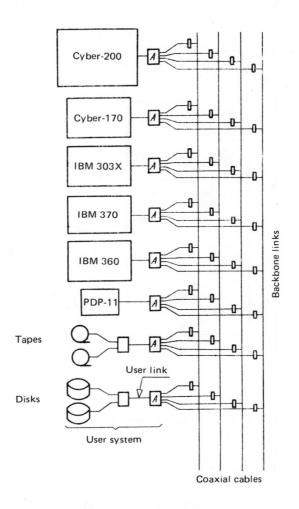

Fig. 9.20. LCN network.

internal bus, which accomodates a processor, 64-kbyte main memory, and controllers that provide interaction with the network user (computer or external device), operator, and user circuit of the broadcast channel. The latter is a coaxial cable with a transmission rate of 50 Mbits/sec. The length of the circuit is 15 m.

The broadcast channel contains several backbone channels (up to four), each operating at 50 Mbits/sec. The maximum length of the backbone is 915 m. The number of adapters connected to the

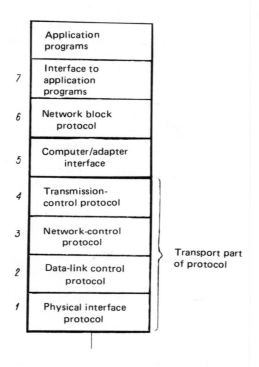

Fig. 9.21. Protocol hierarchy of LCN.

backbone depends on its length. At the maximum length (915 m), only four adapters can be connected; if the length does not exceed 76 m, then up to 28 can be accomodated.

User systems are connected to the broadcast channel by one or more adapters. The use of more than one adapter increases the reliability and speed of transmission. Each adapter interacts with 1—4 backbones of the broadcast channel.

Packets from 513 to 4096 bytes in size are transmitted between user systems. Interaction with the broadcast channel is effected using a round-robin priority allocation (multiple access with time-sharing). Two modes of operation are employed. In the single-packet mode, upon receiving acknowledgement that a frame has been delivered to the addressee system, the sender system disconnects from the channel, leaving it to other systems. In the packet-sequence mode, the channel is maintained by the sender until all necessary packets are transmitted.

The last group of local networks includes **ultralarge broadcast-channel networks,** having large information resources distributed over an extensive area. These networks are intended for very large enterprises and science centers, and for medium-size cities. Examples can be provided by Mitrenet and Localnet.

The **Mitrenet network,** a creation of the Mitre Corporation [108, 218, 249, 250], is based on cable-television equipment already produced commercially by this company. The network is capable of simultaneously transmitting video information, ordinary television, radio programs, speech, and digital data over a broadcast channel. In addition, it provides for creation of paging systems for service personnel, building security, heating and ventilation control, and so forth.

To provide transmission of this diverse information, the broadcast channel is divided into the necessary number of subchannels by means of frequency multiplexing. Within each subchannel there is multiple access with time-sharing, or random access of user systems.

Mitrenet is a large local network that requires installation of large numbers of one-way repeaters (amplifiers) in coaxial cables. Therefore, the broadcast channel consists of two trees, connected at the base, which differ only in terms of the direction of the repeaters they employ (Fig. 9.22). The channel employs all the standard techniques of ordinary cable television: coaxial cables, splitters, taps, repeaters, connecting sleeves, and so forth.

It should be pointed out that local Mitrenet networks can also be constructed around a single tree of coaxial cables with two-way amplifiers. In this case, however, the broadcast channel should be divided into two subchannels (two frequency bands), one providing transmission in one direction, the other in the other direction. To utilize the entire frequency band, therefore, the authors of the local network prefer to use two trees as shown in Fig. 9.22.

The company was one of the first to set up local networks. Therefore, it has developed a number of different methods of multiple access to broadcast channels. These include:

— synchronous time-sharing;
— asynchronous time-sharing;
— random access with timing;
— access with carrier sensing;
— access with collision detection.

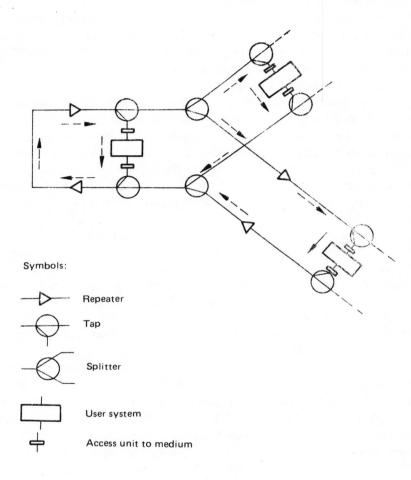

Symbols:

▷ Repeater

⊖ Tap

⊘ Splitter

▭ User system

⟊ Access unit to medium

Fig. 9.22. Structure of Mitrenet.

The essential features of channel operation with time-sharing are shown in Fig. 9.23. In a synchronous mode the transmission cycle is divided into n time ranges, where n is the number of user systems connected to the channel. Here the i-th system, $n \geqslant i \geqslant 1$, is allotted the i-th range, during which it can transmit one frame (if necessary). In the asynchronous mode, user systems employ transmissions of varying length. This makes it possible to send one or more than one frames in a session.

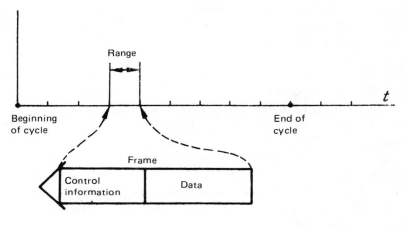

a. Synchronous mode

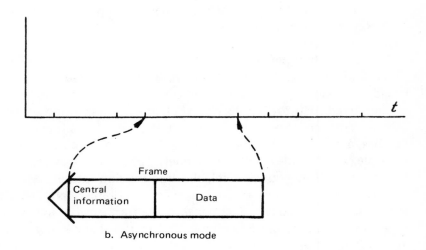

b. Asynchronous mode

Fig. 9.23. Broadcast-channel time sharing.

Random access with timing is implemented in the Dual-Mode System network. The transmission rate in this network is 7.4 Mbits/ sec. In the Mitre-CSMA network, the random-access method is improved by replacing timing with the requirement that every user system monitor the broadcast channel and begin operation only when the channel is free.

The Mitre-LWT network implements random access with collision detection during transmission. Two types of microprocessor-base adapters for user systems, operating at 0.3 and 1.2 Mbits/sec, respectively, were developed for this local network.

The local network has an administrative system based on a PDP-11 minicomputer. Its functions include checking the operation of the channel and modification of the channel configuration and of user-system addresses. To support administrative-system operation, each user system provides appropriate information, including the following: results of checks in the system; state of the system; statistics on transmitted and repeated frames; number of collisions in the channel, and so forth.

The use of cable-television equipment in local networks has a number of advantages, including the following in particular:
— high rate of data transmission;
— low susceptibility to noise;
— use of reliable standard commercially-produced equipment.

However, a negative feature of the approach is the very high cost of broadcast channels.

The **Localnet network** was developed by the Syntek Corporation [118, 233, 251, 252]. In this network, users interact via a coaxial broadcast channel. However, a radio or microwave channel can also be employed. Up to 24,000 virtual channels, connecting up to 256 user systems, are run in the broadcast channel. The broadcast channel has a tree configuration, up to 40 km in extent. Frequency multiplexing provides 120 subchannels. Each user can transmit information over any subchannel; the transmission rate is 2 Mbits/sec.

Localnet employs a seven-layer protocol hierarchy. Multiple access to the broadcast channel with carrier sensing and collision detection is employed. For connection to the channel, user systems incorporate a System 40 adapter station, with a capacity of 2 Mbits/sec. The System 20 adapter is employed for small user systems.

A list of manufacturers of hardware and software for broadcast-channel information and computing networks is given in Tables. 9.1 and 9.2 [238, 244]. The following abbreviations of multiple access methods have been employed: TS, time-sharing; TP, token-passing; CS, carrier sensing; and CS-CD, carrier sensing and collision detection.

Table 9.1 gives information on nine networks with deterministic multiple access. Three of them (Cablenet, DEC Dataway, and Video-

TABLE 9.1.

No.	Company	Name of network	Maximum size (km)	Physical medium	Access method	Transmission rate (Mbits/sec)	Maximum number of user systems	Applications
1.	Amdax	Cablenet	140	Coax line	TS	7 or 14	16,000	General-purpose
2.	Apollo Computer	Domain	1	Coax line	TA	10	100	Science and education
3.	Control Data	LCN	0.9	Coax line	TA	50 (per subchannel)	28	Data processing
4.	Datapoint	ARC	7.5	Coax line	TA	2.5	255	General-purpose
5.	DEC	DECdataway	4.7	Twisted-pair	TS	0.056	31	Commercial
6.	Gould	Midway	4.5	Coax line	TA	1.5	250	Industrial
7.	Interactive System	Videodata	75	Coax line	TS	0.1 (per subchannel)	248 (per subchannel)	General-purpose
8.	Prime Computer	Primenet	0.2 (between systems)	Coax line	TA	8	200	General-purpose
9.	Stratus Computer	Stratalink	0.2 ÷ 0.4	Coax line	TA	2.8	32 (Stratus computers)	Commercial, hospital, airline companies

TABLE 9.2.

No.	Company	Name of network	Maximum size (km)	Physical medium	Access method	Transmission rate (Mbits/sec)	Maximum number of user systems	Applications
1.	Corvus Systems	Omninet	1.2	Twisted-pair	CS	1	64 (microcomputers)	Office automation and instruction
2.	Digital Communications	Infobus	140	Coax line	CS-CD	1 (per subchannel)	256	Hospitals, large institutions
3.	IBM	Series/1 Ring	1.5 (between computers)	Coax line	CS-CD	2	16 (Series/1 computers)	Data processing
4.	Logica	Polinet	–	Coax line	CS	10	–	Data processing
5.	Nestar Systems	Cluster/One	0.3	16-pair line	CS-CD	0.24	65 (Apple computers)	Small organizations
6.	Network Systems	Hyper-channel	1	Coax line	CS	6.3 or 50	256	Organizations and data processing
7.	Syntek	Localnet	10-40	Coax line	CS-CD	0.128 - 2	256	General-purpose

data) employ time-sharing (TS) methods. The remaining six employ new access methods involving transfer of authorization (TA) for channel use. It should be pointed out that the high operating speed and large number of user systems in Cablenet is provided by the fact that several subchannels with different transmission frequency bands are set up in the broadcast channel. The networks under consideration are from 0.2 to 140 km in extent, thus making it possible to set up both small networks and networks that encompass a considerable territory. In most cases, the physical medium of the broadcast channel is coaxial cable. Networks differ considerably in terms of the number of user systems involved: from 32 microcomputers to 16,000 diverse user systems.

The group of information and computing networks with random multiple access (TD-CM) shown in Table 9.2 is more numerous. Most of these networks use the method with carrier sensing and collision detection. At the same time, however, collision detection (CD) is omitted in a number of cases in order to simplify the software. These networks include from 16 to 256 user systems. They differ considerably in terms of transmission rate: from 0.025 to 50 Mbits/sec.

CONCLUDING REMARKS

Operation of packet-switching networks has revealed that they are highly efficient and can furnish users with many diverse resources and methods of interacting with them, including dialog modes involving large numbers of computers. Computer networks have become so important that the significance of their development is frequently compared to that of the development of computers themselves.

Computer networks can combine into a single process a wide variety of data-processing operations: control of technological conditions; scientific, planning, and financial calculations; document storage; and data retrieval. As a result, it has become possible to effect a wholesale conversion of operations associated with acquisition, storage, transmission, retrieval, and delivery of information into a self-contained industry. A new and extremely important sector of the economy has appeared.

The efficiency of a computer network is directly related to the size of the network. Therefore, the creation of large numbers of extensive networks belonging to different government departments and agencies places limitations on the positive benefits of networks. On the other hand, creation of very large computer networks entails unnecessary investments of capital, as well as cumbersome and unreliable operation. An alternative is a multilevel hierarchy of compatible wide-area and local computer networks. In this hierarchy, computers and data links are divided into several categories in terms of their importance, and accordingly placed on different levels. The lower the network level, the smaller its optimum size should be.

Standardization of the parameters and characteristics of networks becomes particularly important. There is a great danger that manufacturers and users will spend many millions on setting up good networks that will prove to be very similar to one another but incompatible.

It should be pointed out that the concept of a hierarchy of networks makes it possible to set up local unrelated networks in the first stage (the necessary standards being observed). It is by no means obligatory that they be large. To create a local network, it is sufficient to have 5—7 minicomputers that are specialized for certain functions.

Computer networks can employ (and still do employ) ordinary telephone channels. The economic and technical parameters of networks improve considerably, however, upon conversion to digital methods. A particularly important problem, therefore, involves the creation and setting up of communications networks based on high-speed (>1 Mbyte/sec) digital channels and microcomputer communication control techniques.

Computer networks are becoming more and more widely used for acquisition, storage, and transmission of mass information. In the near future, they will encompass digital television, "electronic newspapers", and electronic mail. With each passing year, therefore, computer networks will play a more important social role, providing information exchange among millions of users.

REFERENCES

1. V. Lazarev and G. Savvin, Communications Networks, Control, and Switching [in Russian], Svyaz, Moscow, 1973, 264 pp.
2. D. Davis and D. Barber, Communications Networks for Computers, John Wiley and Sons, London, 1973, 575 pp.
3. Franklin F. Kuo. Computer-Communication Network, Prentice-Hall, Inc., Englewood Cliffs, N.J., 1973, 525 pp.
4. S. Samoilenko, Data Processing Systems [in Russian], Nauka, Moscow, 1975, 252 pp.
5. Ya. Vystavkin, Networks for Data Exchange Between Computers [in Russian], Nauka, Moscow, 1975, 216 pp.
6. P. Bratukhin, V. Kvasnitskii, V. Lisitsyn, et al., Design Fundamentals for Large Information and Computing Networks [in Russian], Statistika, Moscow [n.d.], 296 pp.
7. V. Glushkov et al., Computer Networks [in Russian], Svyaz, Moscow, 1977, 280 pp.
8. R. Cypser, Communication Architecture for Distributed Systems. Addison-Wesley Publishing Company, London, 1978, 711 pp.
9. D. Doll, Data Communication, Wiley-Interscience, New York, 1978, 493 pp.
10. A. Butrimenko, Development and Operation of Computer Networks [in Russian], Finansy i statistika, Moscow, 1981, 156 pp.
11. Provisional Reference Model of Open Systems Architecture (Revision I). ISO/TC97/SC 16, 1978, 97 pp.
12. Comments on Provisional Reference Model of Open Systems Architecture (Revision I). IFIP WG 6.1 General Note 175, 1978, 27 pp.
13. Proposed Open Systems Architecture. American Telephone and Telegraph Company. CCITT COM XVII-no. 125-E, 1978, 23 pp.
14. Reference Model of Open Systems Architecture (Version 3), ISO/TC 97/SC 16, 1978, 84 pp.
15. The Use of a Variety of Transmission Media in an Open Systems Architecture. ECMA TC23/78/49, 1978, 4 pp.
16. Data Processing - Open Systems Interconnection - Basic Reference Model. ISO/DP 7498, 3 December 1980, 98 pp.

17. Data Processing - Open Systems Interconnection - Basic Reference Model. Draft proposal ISO/DP 7998. 6 August 1981.

18. W. Hughes, C. Lemmond, H. Parks, G. Ellis, E. Poussin, and R. Wilson, "A semiconductor nonvolatile electron beam accessed mass memory", Proc. IEEE, no. 8, 1230—1240, 1975.

19. "IBM transistorless memory units," Elektronika, no. 2, 5—6, 1976.

20. L. Altman and Ch. Cohen, "The gathering wave of Japanese technology", Electronics, no. 12, 99—105, 1977.

21. Advertisement: "The Intel 8748 — first single-crystal microcomputer with resident electrically programmable ROM," Elektronika, no. 13, 95—96, 1977.

22. H. Blume, D. Budde, H. Raphael, and D. Stamm, "Single-chip 8-bit microcomputer fills gap between calculator types and powerful multichip processors", Electronics, no. 24, 99-105, 1976.

23. "Single-crystal emulator of central processor of Nova 1200 minicomputer," Elektronika, no. 25, 6—7, 1976.

24. D. Wilnai and P. Verhofstadt "One-chip CPU packs power of general-purpose minicomputers", Electronics, no. 13, 113—117, 1977.

25. L. Altman, "Five technologies squeezing more performance from LSI chips", Electronics, no. 17, 91—93, 1977.

26. "Intel microcomputer peripherals," Elektronika, no. 4, 95—96, 1978.

27. J. De Weese and T. Ligon "An NMOS process for high-performance LSI circuits", Hewlett-Packard Journal, 26—31, November 1977.

28. Advertisement: "Logic arrays that can be programmed in operation," Elektronika, no. 6, 89—90, 1975.

29. P. May and F. Schiereck, "High-speed static programmable logic array in LOCMOS," IEEE J. Solid-State Circuits, no. 3, 365—369, 1976.

30. F. Withington, "Beyond 1984: a technology forecast," Datamation, no. 1, 54—57, 1975.

31. L. Curran, "A 12-bit hybrid data-acquisition system," Elektronika, no. 18, 67—68, 1977.

32. A. Erikson, "Digital TV: when, not if," — Electronics, no. 13, 94—95, 1977.

33. "Videotape recording system for TV broadcasting," Elektronika, no. 13, 15, 1977.
34. The Financial Times, 11—12, 21 February 1977.
35. M. Alexander, "Computers cannot solve everything," Fortune, 23—28, May 1969.
36. Computer Engineering Survey: Electronics in 1975 [in Russian], Nauchno-issledovatel'skii institut ekonomiki i informatsii po radioelektronike, Moscow, 1976, 62 pp.
37. "IBM expands output of small computers," Elektronika, no. 4, 7—8, 1978.
38. Computer-Communication Networks, ed. by N. Abramson and F. Kuo. Prentice-Hall, Inc., Englewood Cliffs, New Jersey, 1973, 526 pp.
39. S. Sczupski, "Survey of computer engineering," Elektronika, no. 21, 24—37, 1975.
40. S. Sczupski, "Coming cheap, powerful computers," Electronics, no. 25, 67—68, 1975.
41. "Survey of computer engineering," Elektronika, no. 21, 24—30, 1975.
42. "1-Mbyte semiconductor memory using IC up to 16 kbits," Elektronika, no. 15, 8—9, 1977.
43. "Inexpensive portable computer," Elektronika, no. 19, 17—18, 1975.
44. "IBM enters the minicomputer market," Elektronika, no. 24, 3—4, 1976.
45. Advertisement: Computer Design, 28, March 1977.
46. "LSI-11 microcomputer by DEC," Elektronika, no. 11, 90, 1975.
47. R. Capece, "Microcomputer families expand, part 2: the new boards", Electronics, no. 26, 65—72, 1977.
48. The Financial Times, 5, 3 May 1977.
49. "Personal computers," Elektronika, no. 4, 12, 1977.
50. "Home information and computing system," Elektronika, no. 10, 8—9, 1977.
51. IBM Personal Computer. Hardware. IBM, 1981, 4 pp.
52. IBM Personal Computer. Software. IBM, 1981, 4 pp.
53. W. Fraser, "Potential technology implications for computers and telecommunications in the 1980's," IBM Syst. J., no. 2, 333—347, 1979.

54. E. Joseph, "Forecasts and trends pointing to future computer systems," Technol. Trends: Commun. Comput. Elec. Energy Elec. Compon. Instrumen., 18–27, New York, 1975.
55. "Survey of MSD integrated semiconductor memories," Zarubezhnaya elektronika, no. 2, 64–92, 1975.
56. The Financial Times, 3, 17 June 1975.
57. D. Chen and J. Zook, "An overview of optical data storage technology," Proc. IEEE, no. 8, 207–230, 1975.
58. J. Harris, R. Rohde, and N. Arter, "The IBM 3850 mass storage system: design aspect," Proc. IEEE, no. 8, 1171–76, 1975.
59. Advertisement: Electronic Design, no. 29, 34–78, 1975.
60. "Terminal with plasma indicator and microprocessor control," Elektronika, no. 20, 73–74, 1975.
61. I. Wieselman, "Hard copy computer output and its future," AFIPS Conf. Proc., 363–370, 1977.
62. H. Ritea, "Automatic speech understanding system", Compcon. Fall 75, Washington, 1975, How Make Comput. Easier Use, New York, 319–322, 1975.
63. E. Vodovoz, "The digital 'talkies' are coming. A new class of readouts," EDN, no. 1, 12–13, 1975.
64. J. Kutsch, "A talking computer terminal," AFIPS Conf. Proc., 357–362, 1977.
65. J. Smith, "Europe inches toward commonality," Electronics, no. 15, 76, 1975.
66. "Erste digitale Ubertragungsstrecke fur das Integrierte Fernschreib und Datennetz des DPB," Nachr. Elektron., no. 3, 71–72, 1977.
67. A. Butrimenko, "Technical and economic base of computer networks in Western Europe and North America," Problemy sozdaniya i razvitiya MSETI, no. 3, 49–67, 1976.
68. Report of a Delphy Study: Data Communications in Europe through 1985. IBM World Trade Corporation, December 1975, 36 pp.
69. L. Curran, 'Earth station market widens," Electronics, no. 13, 91–92, 1977.
70. "Survey of electronic engineering: SBS chooses Hughes satellite," Elektronika, no. 21, 4–5, 1977.

71. Metaconta IOC. Toll Switching System. System Description. Bell Telephone Mfg. Co. Belgium, Antwerp, ED I 7703, 1977, 55 pp.

72. Data Transmission Systems [in Russian], Svyaz, Moscow, 1976, 520 pp.

73. M. Ohtsuki, L. Fudemoto, and I. Yoshibayashi, "A new high-speed PCM repeater utilizing hybrid integrated circuit technology," Fujitsu Scientific and Technical J., no. 4, 109—126, 1974.

74. N. Inoue, N. Sakurai, T. Miki, and H. Kasai, "PCM-400 M digital repeated line," IEEE Int. Conf. Commun. San Francisco, vol. 2, 24/11—24/15, 1975.

75. J. Sipress, "T4M: new superhighway for metropolitan communications," Bell Laboratories Record, vol. 53, no. 9, 352—359, 1975.

76. "Canada high capacity digital system goes on line," Telephony, no. 11, 116—126, 1975.

77. "Signal transmission at 800 Mbits/sec over single-code fiber-optic cables," Elektronika, no. 13, 17, 1977.

78. D. Forrester, and T. Fellows, "DUV in Canadian data network," Nat. Telecommun. Conf. New Orleans, vol. 1, 7/7—7/11, New York, 1975.

79. L. Roberts, "Packet network design — the third generation," Information Processing, North-Holland Publishing Company, 541—546, 1977.

80. R. Gundlach, "Digital take-over is under way," Electronics, no. 21, 82—86, 1975.

81. "Demonstration of Comsat digital TV line," Elektronika, no. 16, 9—10, 1977.

82. "Digital switching device for 500-line WATS," Elektronika, no. 16, 6—8, 1977.

83. J. Martin, Systems Analysis for Data Transmission [Russian translation], Mir, Moscow, 1975: vol. 1, 256 pp.; vol. 2, 432 pp.

84. M. Schwartz, R. Burstein, and R. Pickholtz, "Terminal-oriented computer networks," in: Data Transmission Systems and Computer Networks [Russian translation], Mir, Moscow, 177—197, 1974.

85. H. Frank and W. Chow, "Topological optimization of computer networks," in: Data Transmission Systems and

Computer Networks [Russian translation], Mir, Moscow, 147—162, 1974.

86. H. Frank, "The analysis of network performance," Network Systems and Software. Infotech State of the Art Report 24, Publ. Infotech Information Ltd., Nicholson House, Maidenhead, Berkshire, England, 203—234, 1975.

87. Pool Ithiel de Sola, "International aspects of computer communications," Telecommun. Policy, no. 1, 33—51, 1976.

88. R. Wickham, "The impact of SDLC on the data communications hardware market", Wescon Profess. Program, San Francisco, vol. 19, 18.5/1—18.5/3, 1975.

89. A. Kryukov, Yu. Martynov, and V. Razgon, Data-Transmission Software [in Russian], Svyaz, Moscow, 1978.

90. T. Johnson, Packet Switching Services and the Data Communications User, London, Ovum, 1976, 241 pp.

91. J. Forgie, "Speed transmission in packet-switched store-and-forward network," AFIPS Conf. Proc. Anaheim, Cal., 1975, Montvale, N.J., AFIPS Press, vol. 44, 137—141, 1975.

92. "Tests of subscriber information service," Elektronika, no. 20, 99, 1975.

93. W. Arnold, "Britain to get wired city — via telephone," Electronics, no. 5, 76, 1976.

94. Data Transmission: Balanced Class of HDLC Procedures, ISO 6256, ISO/TK 97, 1980, 20 pp.

95. CCITT Sixth Plenary Assembly, Geneva, 27 September-8 October 1976. Orange Book, vol. VIII, 2. Public Data Networks, Geneva, 1977, 217 pp.

96. CCITT Sixth Plenary Assembly, Geneva, 27 September-8 October 1976. Orange Book, vol. VIII, 1. Data Transmission over the Telephone Network. Published by the International Telecommunications Union. Geneva, 1977, 225 pp.

97. P. Bilanski and D. Ingram, "Present systems and future developments," Digit. Transmiss. Syst., Stevenge, 329—339, 1976.

98. RPI Interface for Radial Connection of Devices with Parallel Data Transmission, Intergovernmental Commission for Collaboration of Socialist Countries in the Field of Computer Engineering, December, 1976, 12 pp.

99. Draft Standard ISO/TC 97/SC 6. Geneva 3 731, February 1973, 25 pp.

100. N. Teichholtz, "Digital network architecture," Communications Networks. Online, 13—24, 1975.

101. C. Ruger, "Eight factors aid network design and user interface," reprinted from Data Communications, August 1977, 6 pp.

102. A. Durniak, "New networks tie down distributed processing concepts", Electronics, no. 25, 107—122, 1978.

103. Synchronous Data Link Control. General Information. IBM, 1975, 48 pp.

104. High-level Data Link Control Procedures. Proposed Draft International Standard on Elements of Procedures (Independent Numbering). ISO/TC 97/SC 6. (Tokyo — 17), Editorial revis. May 1975, 51 pp.

105. R. Sander and V. Cerf, "Compatibility or chaos in communications," Datamation, 50—55, March 1976.

106. W. Riley, "LAN standards controversy looms: Ethernet versus IEEE-802," Electronic Design, SS-25/SS-29, September 1981.

107. V. Hamacher and G. Schedler, "Collision-free local area bus network performance analysis," IBM J. Res. Development, no. 6, 904—914, November 1981.

108. I. Cotton, "Technologies for local area computer networks," Computer Networks, no. 4, 197—208, 1980.

109. R. Metcalf and D. Boggs, "Ethernet," Communications of the ACM, no. 7, 395—404, 1976.

110. C. Bass, J. Kennedy, and J. Davidson, "Local network gives new flexibility to distributed processing," Electronics, no. 21, 114—122, 1980.

111. "In your future: local computer networks," EDP Analyzer, no. 6, 1—13, 1980.

112. M. Marshall, "Z—Net simplifies the development of computer networks," Elektronika, no. 11, 6, 1980.

113. A. Durniak, "Local communications networks," Elektronika, no. 13, 77—79, 1980.

114. H. Matsunaga, C. Matsuda, M. Kajiwara, T. Shikama, and H. Takahashi, "The performance of protocol in the satellite channel," ICCC-80, Atlanta, 445—450, 1980.

115. H. Takahashi, K. Uchida, K. Matsumoto, and H. Inuki, "Experimental system for satellite computer network via CS," ICCC-80, Atlanta, 451—456, 1980.

116. Overview of IEEE Local Network Standards Activity in the USA. ISO/TC 97/50. no. 2118, 1—15 September, 121—126, April 1981.

117. M. Schindler, "Networks may look alike, but software makes the difference," Electronic Design, 121—126, April 1981.

118. R. Allan, "Local-net architecture, protocol issues heating up," Electronic Design, 91—102, April 1981.

119. IEEE Computer Society, Project 802. Local Area Network Standards Committee. Version 5.2. ISO/TC 97/SC 6, no. 2188, June 1981, 280 pp.

120. IEEE Project 802, a status report: Local Network Standards Committee. Draft B. IEEE Computer Society. Draft. 19 October 1981, 408 pp.

121. A. Danet, R. Despres, B. Jamet, G. Pichon, and P. Schwartz, "Packet switching in a public data transmission service: the TRANSPAC network," Communs. Networks. Eur. Comput. Conf. London 1975, 331—347, Uxbridge, 1975.

122. Advanced Function for Communications System. Summary. IBM, 1974, 25 pp.

123. V. Cerf. A. McKenzie, R. Scantlebury, and H. Zimmerman, "A proposal for an internetwork end-to-end protocol," INWG Geneva; Note no. 96, London, 29 July 1975, 29 pp.

124. P. Kirstein, "Management questions in relationship to the University College London Node of the ARPA Computer network," Proc. of the Third Intern. Conf. on Comput. Commun., Toronto, 279—285, 3—6 August 1976.

125. A. Danet, R. Despres, A. Rest, and G. Pichon, "The French public packet switching service: the TRANSPAC network," Proc. of the Third Intern. Conf. on Comput. Commun., Toronto, 251—260, 3—6 August 1976.

126. D. Twyver and A. Rybczynsky, "DATAPAC subscriber interfaces," Proc. of the Third Intern. Conf. on Comput. Commun., Toronto, Trans-Canada Telephone System, 143—149, 3—6 August 1976.

127. Project 15. International Organization for Standardization, ISO/TC 97/SC 6, no. 1403, February 1977, 8 pp.

128. G. Bochmann, "Standards issues in data communications," Telecommunications Policy, 381–388, December 1977.

129. F. Hertweck, E. Raubold and F. Vogt, "X.25-based process/process communication," Computer Network Protocols, Liege, 1978.

130. D. Barber, T. Kalin, and C. Solomonides, "An implementation of the X.25 interface in a datagram network," Computer Network Protocols, Universite de Liege, E6/1-E6/5, 1978.

131. Revised Recommendation X-25 Preface and Level 3. Study Group VII – Contribution no. 384. CCITT, August 1979.

132. A. Rybczynski, B. Wessler, R. Despres, and J. Vedlake, "A new communication protocol for accessing data networks," Conf. Rec. Int. Conf. Commun. Philadelphia 1976, 20/7–20/11, N.Y. 1976.

133. G. Davis, "Exploring 1977's data communications technology explosion," Data Communication, 75–83, December 1977.

134. D. Weir, J. Holmblad, and A. Rothberg, "An X-75-based network architecture," ICCC-80, Atlanta, 741–750, 1980.

135. Public Data Networks. Eurodata Foundation, Lutyens House. Finsbury Circus, London EC2M 71.Y. 1979, 233 pp.

136. E. Morris, "European users start to reap benefits of packet switching," Comm. News, no. 11, 32–36, 1979.

137. D. Medcraft, "Data network plans for the UK," ICCC-80, Atlanta, 30–34, 1980.

138. Public Data Networks. Plans of the European Telecommunications Administrations. Eurodata Foundation, London, 1981, 141 pp.

139. Recommendation X-75. Terminal and transit call control procedures and data transfer system on international circuits between packet-switched networks. VIIth Plenary Assembly. Document no. 10, 1980, 84 pp.

140. R. Kahn, University College, London, ARPANET project. Dept. of Statistics and Computer Science. University College, London, February 1976, 108 pp.

141. J. Huber, "EDX – A uniform system architecture for circuit, packet and message switching," ICCC-80, Atlanta, 195–201, 1980.

142. DPS-25. Packet switching system. SESA, 1980, 23 pp.

143. J. Guyon, "A multi-microprocessor-based internetwork: Hermes," Network 80, London, 119—128, June 1980.

144. "X-25 switching unit for 1500 virtual networks," Elektronika, no. 24, 98, 1980.

145. "Processor for X-25," Datamation, 285, December 1980.

146. Transport protocol. Standard ECMA. 3rd draft. ECMA/TC 24/SO/16. February 1980.

147. "Sanders' use of IBM Systems Network Architecture," Elektronika, no. 14, 11—12, 1976.

148. J. Gray and C. Blair, "IBM's Systems Network Architecture," Datamation, 51—56, April 1975.

149. P. Cullum, "The transmission subsystem in Systems Network Architecture," IBM Systems J., no. 1, 24—38, 1976.

150. J. McFadyen, "Systems Network Architecture: an overview," IBM Syst. J., no. 1, 3—23, 1976.

151. J. Gray, "Network services in Systems Network Architecture," IEEE Transactions on Communications, 104—116, January 1977.

152. P. Moulton and R. Sander, "Another look at SNA," Datamation, 74—80. March 1977.

153. R. Berglund, "Comparing network architectures," Datamation, 79—85, February 1978.

154. "IBM boosts for X-25 standard," Computer Weekly, 1—14, 10 February 1977.

155. P. Hirsch, "Should packet networks offer datagram services?" Datamation, 154—157, October 1977.

156. E. Sussenguth, "Systems Network Architecture: a perspective," Proc. of the Fourth International Conf. on Computer Communication, Kyoto, 353—358, 26—29 September 1978.

157. F. Canecci, E. Ferro, L. Lazzeri, et al., "RPCNET: architecture and service," Avtomatika i vychislitel'naya tekhnika, no. 6, 1978.

158. P. Franchi and G. Sommi, "RPCNET features and components," Communications Networks, Online, 81—93, 1975.

159. L. Lencini and G. Sommi, "Architecture and implementation of RPCNET," Proc. of the Third Intern. Conf. on Comput. Commun., Toronto, 605—611, August 1976.

160. G. Cori and M. Maier, "Design and implementation of software for a distributed control computer network," Proc. of the Intern. Symposium on Technology for Selective Dissemination of Information, Republica di S. Marino, 89–93, September 1976.
161. D. Eade, P. Homan, and J. Jones, "CICS/VS and its role in Systems Network Architecture," IBM Syst. J., no. 3, 258–286, 1977.
162. E. N. Belov, "Development tendencies of record-performance computers," Zarubezhnaya radioelektronika, no. 8, 15–31, 1977.
163. V. Burstsev, "Computers: the generational race," Pravda, 4 April 1978.
164. D. Wood, "A survey of the capabilities of 8 packet switching networks," Proc. Symp. Comput. Networks: Trends and Appl., Gaithersburg 1975, 1–7, New York, 1975.
165. S. Butterfield, R. Rettberg, and D. Walden, "The satellite IMP for the ARPA network," Proc. Seventh Inter. Conf. Syst. Scie. Comput. Nets., 70–73, 1974.
166. D. Walden, Computer Systems Division. Bolt, Beranek and Newman, Incorporated. Infotech State of the Art Report 24. Publ. Infotech Information Ltd., Nicholson House, Maidenhead, Berkshire, England, 287–316, 1975.
167. K. Fuchel and S. Heller, "Two dissimilar networks: is marriage possible?" Proc. Symp. Comput. Networks: Trends and Appl., 19–24. Gaithersburg, 1975, New York, 1975.
168. A. Stokes and P. Higginson, "The problems of connecting hosts into ARPANET," Communs. Networks. Eur. Comput. Conf., London 1975, 25–33, Uxbridge 1975.
169. M. Gerla and L. Kleinrock, "On the topological design of distributed computer networks," IEEE Trans. Communs., no. 1, 48–60, 1977.
170. B. Gold, "Digital methods of speech transmission," Proc. IEEE, no. 12, 5–33, 1977.
171. L. Kleinrock, "ARPANET lessons," Conf. Rec. Int. Conf. Commun., Philadelphia 1976, vol. 1–3, 20/1–20/6, New York, 1976.
172. M. Irland, "Simulation of CIGALE 1974," Fourth Data Commun. Symp. Network Struct. Evol. Oper. Environ. Quebec City 1975, 5/13–5/19, New York 1975.

173. H. Zimmermann, "The CYCLADES end-to-end protocol," IEEE 1975, Data Communs. Symposium, 37—43.

174. L. Pouzin, "The CYCLADES network. Present state and development trends," Proc. Symp. Comput. Networks: Trends and Appl., Gaithersburg 1975, 8—13, New York, 1975.

175. M. Robin, "Le congress IFIP 1977," Bulletin de Liaison de la Recherche en Informatique et Automatique, no. 39, 19—22, October-November 1977.

176. M. Gien, J. Grange, "Performance evaluation in CYCLA-DES," Proc. of the Fourth International Conf. on Computer Communication, Kyoto, 23—32, 26—29 September 1978.

177. D. Medcraft, "Data network plans for the UK," Proc. of the Fifth Internat. Conf. on Comp. Comm., Atlanta, 29—34, 27—30 October 1980.

178. H. Zimmermann, "Terminal access protocols on EURONET," Second European Users Workshop on End-to-End Protocols, NPL, Teddington, England, 1976, 6 pp.

179. D. Barber, A European Informatics Network: Achievement and Prospects. INWG, General Note no. 117, 1976, 7 pp.

180. F. Arciprete, A. Repichini, "Packet switching technique for public and dedicated data communications networks," European Conference on Electrotechnics 77, Venice - Italy, EUREL IEEE, 3.1 1.1—3.1 1.10, 3—7 May 1977.

181. G. Davies, J. Gresser, P. Kelly, and J. Thomas, "The EURONET telecommunications and information network," Proc. of the Fourth International Conf. on Computer Communication, Kyoto, 189—194, 26—29 September 1978.

182. P. Kelly, "EURONET DIANE — A European harmonization project," Proc. of the Fifth Internat. Conf. on Comp. Comm., Atlanta, 659—663, 27—30 October 1980.

183. P. Cashin, "DATAPAC network protocols," Proc. of the Third Int. Conf. on Comput. Commun., Toronto, 150—155, August 1976.

184. W. Clipsham and F. Glave, "DATAPAC network overview," Proc. of the Third Int. Conf. on Comput. Comm., Toronto, 132—136, August 1976.

185. C. McGibbon and H. Gibbs, "DATAPAC — A phased approach to the introduction of a public packet-switched

network," Information Processing, North-Holland Publishing Company, 509—513, 1977.

186. C. McGibbon, H. Gibbs, and S. Young, "DATAPAC — Initial experiences with a commercial packet network," Proc. of the Fourth International Conf. on Computer Communication, Kyoto, 103—108, 26—29 September 1978.

187. Dixon R. Doll, Data Communication, Wiley-Interscience, New York, 1978, 493 pp.

188. D. Sproule and M. Unsoy, "Transit delay objectives for the Datapac network," Proc. of the Fifth Internat. Conf. on Comp. Comm., Atlanta, 685—692, 27—30 October 1980.

189. F. Lamond, "European data communications prepares for the electronic eighties," Datamation, 190F-190Z, December 1977.

190. R. Despres and G. Pichon, "The TRANSPAC network: status report and perspectives," Network 80 Conference, 209—232, 1980.

191. L. Roberts, "TELENET: principles and practice", Communs. Networks. Eur. Comput. Conf., London 1975, 315—329, Uxbridge 1975.

192. D. Forrester, "DUV in Canadian digital data network", Nat. Telecommun. Conf., New Orleans, 7/7—7/11, 1975.

193. "Viewdata in Nederland," Kabelvisie, no. 5, 151,153, 1978.

194. J. Soulsby, "Electronic mail," Computer Communications, 12—13, February 1979.

195. R. Clark, "Videotex — an overview of electronic information services," Computer Communications, 51—55, April 1979.

196. "Bell and Knight-Ridder test the Viewdata system," Elektronika, no. 17, 8—11, 1980.

197. "Survey of video data services with information displayed on a home television set," Radioelektronika za rubezhom, no. 19, 1—30, 1980.

198. J. Madden, "Videotex in Canada," Computer Communications, 58—64. April 1980.

199. W. Staudinger, "Protocol architecture and its applications for CCITT standardized services," IFIP Symp. in Canada, 1981, 11 pp.

200. G. Routhorn and P. Carruthers, "Teletex and its protocols," IFIP Symp. in Canada, 1981, 17 pp.

201. H. Hindin, "Videotex direction still unclear," Electronics, no. 10, 101–102, 1981.

202. G. Puccioni, "Towards the electronic message service," Telecom. J., no. 8, 477–486, 1979.

203. M. While, "Viewdata — a review," Inform. Sci (Gr. Brit.), no. 4, 145–153, 1978.

204. Prestel: The Technology. Post Office Telecommunication, London, 1981, 22 pp.

205. J. Gosh, "Europeans test fast data link," Electronics, no. 7, 101–102, 1981.

206. The Financial Times, no. 28165, 11–15, 1980.

207. P. Mothersole, "Teletex and Viewdata," Proc. Inst. Elec. Eng., no. 12, 1350–1354, 1979.

208. "CBS opts for French version of teletext system," Elektronika, no. 18, 8–9, 1977.

209. B. Marti, "Videotex developments in France," Computer Communications, no. 2, 60–64, 1979.

210. "Teleprocessing and new services: the present and the future," Telecommun. J., VII, 415–423, 1979.

211. "Videotex developments in France," Computer Communications, no. 2, 60–64, 1979.

212. H. Hindin, "Controlling the electronic office: PBXs make their move," Electronics, no. 7, 139–148, 1981.

213. E. Morris, "Digital services and electronic mail pace network advances," Communications News, 66–72, May 1981.

214. H. Hindin, "WATS for digital-exchange switching," Elektronika, no. 15, 91–93, 1977.

215. J. Saltzer, D. Clark, and K. Pogran, "Why a ring," Proceedings Seventh Data Comm. Symp., Vol. II, IEEE, Mexico, 211–217, October 1981.

216. H. Hindin, "Communications," Electronics, no. 21, 216–220, 1981.

217. S. Wilbur, "Low level protocol in the Cambridge Ring," Networks 80, London, 265–276, June 1980.

218. H. Cravis, "Local networks prove practical for datacom systems in close proximity," Datamation, 98–104, March 1981.

219. P. Coen and M. Cole, "Plugging in local area networks," Datamation, 216/17–216/18, March 1981.

220. "Two backbone lines for controlling domestic electronic equipment," Elektronika, no. 19, 19–20, 1981.

221. M. Hahn and P. Belanger, "Network minimizes overhead of small computers," Electronics, no. 17, 125–128. 1981.

222. J. Estrin and B. Carrino, "Local network enlists Z 80s for distributed processing," Electronics, no. 3, 149–153, 1981.

223. H. Hindin, "Shortcomings of the Ethernet system," Elektronika, no. 15, 13–14, 1980.

224. M. Edwards, "Office automation developments show communications' key role," Communications News, 42–46, July 1980.

225. The Ethernet — A Local Area Network. Data Link Layer and Physical Layer. Specifications. Digital Computer Corporation; Intel Corporation; Xerox Corporation. Version 1.0, September 1980, 82 pp.

226. "Telephone-ordered stock transfers," Elektronika, no. 2, 11–21, 1981.

227. "Xerox entering networking field with two new service offerings," Communications News, 44–45. February 1981.

228. "New integrated office network uses Ethernet," Communications News, 2, January 1981.

229. R. Ryan, "Local network architecture proposed for work stations," Electronics, no. 17, 120–124, 1981.

230. G. Sideris, "Software helps networks grow with compatibility," Electronic Design, SS-39/SS-43. September 1981.

231. M. Marshall, "Work station of Stanford University becomes comercially operational," Elektronika, no. 21, 12–13, 1981.

232. "Sources for local-net products," Data Communications. 69–70, December 1981.

233. B. Musgrave, "Coaxing on Co-ax," Datamation, special edition, 40–44, 1980.

234. Attached Resource Computer. ARC. Datapoint. 1981, 12 pp.

235. "The future works now: Datapoint," Datamation, 214–215, March 1981.

236. "Old local network better than the new one," Elektronika, no. 19, 5–6, 1981.

237. "Network for data exchange between organizations with incompatible hardware," Elektronika, no. 11, 6–8, 1980.

238. "Stepped-up pace products race," Data Communications, 117–133, December 1981.
239. J. Thornton, "New approach to network storage management," Computer Design, 81–85, November 1975.
240. "Network systems," Datamation, special edition, 43, 1980.
241. I. Chlamtac and W. Franta, "Message-based priority access to local networks," Computer Communications, no. 2, 77–84, 1980.
242. "Local access from remote locations," Datamation, 120, June 1981.
243. IEEE Project 802 "Working Document" on Local Area Network Standardization. ISO/TC 97/SC 6, no. 2188, June 1981.
244. W. Iversen, "Consolidation of large computers into a high-speed computer network," Elektronika, no. 13, 9–11, 1981.
245. Loosely Coupled Network. The Total System Approach to Your Local Networking Requirements. CDC, 1981, 6 pp.
246. Network Access Device (Loosely Coupled Network), Control Data Corp., 1981, 2 pp.
247. Trunk Interface Option for Network Access Devices (Loosely Coupled Network), Control Data Corp., 1981, 2 pp.
248. Network Access Device (Loosely Coupled Network), Control Data Corp., 1980, 2 pp.
249. N. Meisner, "Time division digital bus techniques implemented on coaxial cable," Proc. of Comp. Netw. Symposium, NBS, 112–117, December 1977.
250. G. Hopkins, "Multimode communication on the MITRE-NET," Computer Networks, no. 4, 229–233, 1980.
251. "Local-net architecture protocol issues heating up," Electronic Design, 91–102, April 1981.
252. L. Yencharis, "Local-net communications improves at both ends," Electronic Design, 111–116, April 1981.

DICTIONARY OF TERMINOLOGY*

ACCESS METHOD — Procedure for gaining access to a shared resource, e.g., a **broadcast channel**

ACCESS UNIT — Hardware and software intended for interfacing **user system** or **physical link** and **physical medium** of **broadcast channel**

ADAPTER — Device for interfacing **computer** and **physical link**

ADMINISTRATION — Application process that provides administrative management of resources of **systems** and capable of restarting these systems

ADMINISTRATIVE SYSTEM — System that describes administrative management procedures for **computer networks** or parts of them, e.g., **communications networks**

ALGORITHMIC LANGUAGE — A formalized language used for writing algorithms

ANALOG CHANNEL — Telephone channel used for data transmission between **systems**

ANALOG COMPUTER — A piece of **hardware** used for modelling processes that involve the variation of analog (continuous) processes

APPLICATION LAYER — **Layer** that supports control of **application processes**

APPLICATION PROCESS — **User program** or human operator; source or consumer of information in a **computer network**

APPLICATION-PROCESS CONTROL — An element of the **software structure** of a **computer network** that is directly concerned with **application processes**

ARCHITECTURE — A concept of the interrelationship between elements in a complex system (**computer network, computer,** semiconductor chip, etc.)

ASYNCHRONOUS TERMINAL — Terminal in which the transmission of every information character, containing 5—9 bits, must be accompanied by control characters

AUDIO INFORMATION — Information that can be perceived by the human auditory system

BACKBONE LINE — A **physical link** that connects two adjacent **communications systems**

---

*Words in **boldface** are defined in the Dictionary.

BASIC CONTROL — Control of data streams in a **computer network,** involving interaction of **application processes** of **user systems**

BIT — Unit of information having the two values 0 and 1

BIT-STUFFING — Procedure for adding to a **frame,** prior to delivering it to a **physical link** (and similarly, for removing from the frame after transmission), a bit so as to ensure **transparency** of the **data link**

BLOCK — A data unit that contains data to be received or issued by a **process**

BROADCAST CHANNEL — **Physical medium,** hardware, and (possibly) software which provide data transmission directly from a sender **user system** to all the remaining user systems in a **computer network**

BROADCAST INFORMATION — Information intended for all **users,** or for large numbers of them

BROADCAST TRANSMISSION — **Data** transmission that is effected immediately by all **user systems**

BUFFER — Part of memory used for temporary storage of incoming information

BYTE — Group of eight **bits** in succession, taken as a single information character

BYTE-STUFFING — Procedure for adding to a **frame,** prior to delivering it to a **physical link** (and similarly, for removing from the frame after transmission), the requisite number of special characters so as to ensure **transparency** of the **data link**

CHARACTER — A letter, number, or auxiliary symbol (parenthesis, comma, period, arithmetic symbol, etc.)

CLOSED SYSTEM — A system that does not conform to the standards of **Open Systems Interconnection**

COMMUNICATION LINK — A **physical medium, hardware,** and (possibly) **programs** that effect transmission of information from one communications switching node to another or to a subscriber

COMMUNCIATIONS NETWORK — Data transmission network made up of a **broadcast channel,** loop, or set of interconnected **communications systems**

COMMUNICATIONS SERVICE — **Service** that provides data transmission between transport levels of **user systems** via a **data transmission network** or **broadcast channel**

COMMUNICATION SYSTEM — A **system** specialized for execution of information routing functions in a **communications network**

COMPUTER — An aggregate of programs and hardware intended for information processing and containing one or more universal **processors** that interact with a common **main storage**

COMPUTER INSTALLATION — Set of software- and structurally specialized **computers** that jointly execute an information and computing process

COMPUTER NETWORK — A multicomputer system that incorporates, as a minimum, **user systems, communications** systems, and **data links**

COMPUTER NETWORK CONTROL — An element of the **software structure** of a **computer network** that provides administrative management of the network

COMPUTER PROGRAM — A program written in **computer** language

CONCENTRATOR — A device for connecting several low-speed **physical links** to one high-speed one

CONNECTION — Logical association established to link two or more **entities,** supported by functions of **layer** below them

CONTROL FRAME — A **frame** used to transmit information needed to control a **data link**

CONTROL INFORMATION — Information transmitted between **entities** to provide interaction procedures for them

CONTROL PACKET — A **packet** used to transmit information needed to control a **transport network**

DATA — 1. Information about processes or entities. 2. Information for whose transmission a particular **layer** of a **computer network** is created

DATA BANK — A set of software, language, organizational, and hardware facilities that enable **users** to input and store data to receive information against their queries

DATA BASE — A set of **user data** that is important for some area of human activity

DATA CIRCUIT-TERMINATING EQUIPMENT — Hardware used for supporting interaction between channels of **computers** and **communications channels**

DATAGRAM — A self-contained **packet** which, from the standpoint of a **communications network,** is unrelated to other packets to be transmitted via this network

DATAGRAM TRANSPORT NETWORK — A **transport network** that provides transmission of individual mutually independent **packets (datagrams)**

DATA LINK (or CHANNEL) — A logical system consisting of two **physical-link** or **broadcast-channel** control programs, connected by **physical link**

DATA LINK CONTROL — An element of the **software structure** of a **computer network** that provides access to **data links**

DATA-LINK LAYER — Layer that supports transmission of **data units** over **data links**

DATA TERMINAL EQUIPMENT (DTE) — A data source or consumer; in a **computer network**, a **user system**

DATA UNIT — A generalized term that specifies the "piece" of data to be transmitted: **block, fragment, packet, datagram, frame** or **message**

DATA UNIT IDENTIFIER — A code that identifies a given **data unit** in the stream of other units

DEVICE PROGRAM — A **program** implemented by **hardware**

DIALOG — Mode of interaction between a **user** and a **computer** in which the questions (or queries) of one of the "interlocutors," and the rapid responses of the other, repeat dynamically

DIGITAL CHANNEL — A **communications channel** created specially for transmission of digital data

DIGITAL COMPUTER — See **computer**

DISPLAY — A **terminal** with a keyboard and a screen, used to depict alphanumeric and, possibly, graphic information

DISTRIBUTED DATA PROCESSING — Data processing performed by several **user systems**

ELECTRONIC MAIL — A service that provides transmission and storage of any kind of text

EMULATION — Process of utilizing **hardware** or **software** such that one **computer** or **terminal** can function as another computer or terminal

END-TO-END TRANSMISSION — Data transmission between **processes**, effected via a **communications network**

ENTITY — Active element on one of the **layers** of a **system**

FIELD — Region of a **frame**, packet, or memory used for recording certain information

FILE — A data set that is organized in some way (employee records, information on a certain piece of equipment, experimental data, etc.), and located in a given **system**

FILE CONTROL — A method that provides remote access to **files**, as well as file processing and transfer to their destination

FLAG — A control symbol that separates **frames** from one another in a **data link**

FRAGMENT — Data array produced by **transmission control** program

FRAME — A continuous sequence of bits that is transmitted to the **physical layer** or received from the physical layer as a single whole

FRAME COLLISION — A situation in which **frames** of several **user systems** are transmitted simultaneously over a **broadcast channel**

FRAME FORMAT — Structure of a **frame** that determines the information it contains and methods of encoding it

FULL-DUPLEX CHANNEL — A physical link over which data is transmitted in both directions simultaneously

GATEWAY — A system that provides an **interface** between computer networks or **user systems**

GLOBAL COMPUTER NETWORK — A **computer network** whose **systems** extend over a very large territory (different countries, continents, etc.)

HALF-DUPLEX CHANNEL — A **physical link** over which data is transmitted in one or the other direction

HARDWARE — A set of technical devices (**computers, processors,** memory units, I/O devices, **modems, adapters, terminals,** converters, amplifiers, etc.)

HOST SYSTEM — **System** that provides basic information resources

INFORMATION FRAME — A **frame** containing an **information packet**

INFORMATION NETWORK — A particular case of a **computer network** that performs primarily logical data-processing tasks

INFORMATION PACKET — A **packet** containing a **fragment**

INFORMATION RETRIEVAL SERVICE — A **service** intended for providing **users** with information of interest to them

INITIALIZATION — Execution of procedures that ensure that the **hardware** of **data links,** physical links, or **logical channels** is set to a state such that they can perform their functions

INSTRUCTION — An indication that a particular operation is to be executed (e.g., TRANSMIT DATA)

INTEGRATED CIRCUIT — An electronic circuit containing transistors, diodes, resistors, capacitors, or other elements, and constructed on the surface of or inside a semiconductor chip

INTEGRATED NETWORK — A **communications network** that provides both **packet** and circuit switching using the same hardware

INTELLIGENT TERMINAL — A **terminal** containing one or more **microcomputers,** and thus able to execute service processes (job setup and editing, message checking and forwarding to physical link, etc.)

INTERACTION — A procedure for transmitting, during a **session,** a group of **service data units** as a single entity

INTERACTION CONTROL — A method which provides dynamic interaction between **users** or user **programs**

INTERFACE — Hardware or program that joins two **computer networks, computers,** external devices, or programs; also interaction rules for **entities** on adjacent **layers** of a **computer network**

INTERFACE DATA UNIT — A data unit transmitted via an **interface** between adjacent **layers**

JOB CONTROL — A method which provides control of setup, remote input, and execution of jobs, as well as transmission of the output results

LAYER — Level of a **computer network** that executes one of its principal tasks

LAYER INTERFACE — Rules for interaction of **entities** on adjacent **layers** of a **system**

LAYER SERVICE — The functions of a **layer** that are provided to entities of the next higher layer

LEASED TELEPHONE LINE — Sequence of telephone and non-switched connections at telephone exchanges that provides permanent connection between two **computers** or **terminals**

LOCAL-AREA NETWORK — A computer network whose **user systems** are not widely separated from one another

LOGIC MODULE — Group of interrelated programs that execute a particular function of a **computer network**

LOGICAL CHANNEL — An abstract line connecting two interacting **entities** in a **computer network**

LOGICAL STRUCTURE OF COMPUTER NETWORK — Representation of a **computer network** in the form of interconnected logical components

LOGICAL UNIT OF COMPUTER NETWORK — An element of the **logical structure of a computer network**

MACROINSTRUCTION (or MACRO) — A sequence of interrelated **instructions** that execute a particular function

MAIN STORAGE — Memory device in which information is written and read at high speed

MANCHESTER ENCODING — A means for combining **data** and synchronization signals into a single sequential signal stream

MESSAGE — Data unit containing **user** task or response of **computer** to this task; of arbitrary size

MICROCOMPUTER — Ultrasmall **computer** consisting of one or more large-scale integrated circuits

MINICOMPUTER — Small **computer** that operates with 12—16-bit words and intended for handling a modest number of programs (generally in real time)

MODEM — Device for connecting a **computer** to an **analog channel**

MONITORING — Higher element of **administrative management**

MONOLOG — Mode of interaction between **user** and **computer** in which one party transmits data that does not require an immediate answer

MULTIPLEXER — Device that provides data transmission from several sources over the same **physical link**

NETWORK ACCESS METHOD — Group of interrelated functions of the **session, transport, network, data-link,** and **physical** layers

NETWORK ADDRESS — Address of a **port** in a **computer network**

NETWORK CONTROL — An element of the **software structure** of a **computer network** that performs procedures of information **routing** in the network

NETWORK CONTROL CENTER — See **administrative system**

NETWORK CONTROL LANGUAGE — Set of instructions employed by **transmission control** program

NETWORK LAYER — Layer which provides facilities for establishment and maintenance of interaction between **user systems, routing,** switching of data units, etc.

NETWORK TERMINAL — A **virtual terminal** that interacts with a **communications network**

OPEN SYSTEM — A **system** that meets the standards of **Open Systems Interconnection**

OPEN SYSTEMS INTERCONNECTION (OSI) — Concept of interaction of **systems** in a **computer network,** developed by the International Standards Organization (ISO)

OPERATING SYSTEM — Set of interrelated **programs** that support managament of the operation of a **computer**

OPERATOR — Person who interacts with **computer** or **terminal;** also, a symbol of **algorithmic language** that calls for execution of a particular data-processing or -transmission operation [also rendered as "statement" in English]

PACKET — A **data unit,** without disassembly into parts, that is transmitted via a **communications network**

PACKET FORMAT — Structure of a **packet** that determines the information it contains and methods of encoding it

PACKET SWITCHING NODE — A set of hardware and software facilities that support switching of **packets**

PACKET TERMINAL — A **terminal** which can be connected to a **computer network** with the status of a **user system**

PERMANENT VIRTUAL CIRCUIT — A permanent connection of two remote **processes** by a **logical channel**

PERSONAL SYSTEM — **User system** intended for simultaneous operation with one **user**

PHASE — One of the stages of operation of a **system** or its elements (establishment, maintenance, or termination of communication, data transmission, etc.)

PHONEME — A unit (or element) of the speech system of a language

PHYSICAL CONNECTION — A **connection** of **physical layer entities** that is created in the **physical layer**

PHYSICAL INTERCONNECTION FACILITIES — Set of hardware and software facilities, and also a **physical medium,** that provides transmission of information between **systems**

PHYSICAL LAYER — Level that supports control of physical links or **broadcast channels**

PHYSICAL LINK — A physical medium, hardware, and (possibly) software for transmission of information between two or more **systems**

PHYSICAL LINK CONTROL — A program that provides interfacing of a **system** and a **physical link**

PHYSICAL MEDIUM — Space or material whose physical properties support signal transmission: twisted-pair conductors, coaxial cable, waveguides, the "ether," light conductors, etc.

PHYSICAL STRUCTURE OF COMPUTER NETWORK — Representation of a **computer network** in the form of interconnected **hardware**

PHYSICAL UNIT OF COMPUTER NETWORK — An element of the **physical structure** of a **computer network**

PORT — End of a **logical channel**

PRESENTATION CONTROL — An element of the **software structure** of a **computer network** that ensures the description of the meaning of the transmitted information

PRESENTATION LAYER — Layer that supports interpretation of the meaning of the transmitted data

PRESENTATION LAYER — Layer that supports interpretation of the meaning of the transmitted data

PROCESS — Information and computing resource of a **computer network** that includes **session control, presentation control,** and **application-process control**

PROCESSOR — **Hardware** consisting of a processing device (arithmetic and logic unit) and control device, and intended for execution of a sequence of **instructions** and a number of other auxiliary functions

PROGRAM — A complete and exact description, in some formal language, of a data-processing process that yields a solution of the problem under consideration; an element in the **software structure** of a **computer network**

PROTOCOL — Summary of rules and formats that specify interaction between entities of similar **layers** of **systems**

PROTOCOL DATA UNIT — Data unit used in accordance with a **protocol** to connect two or more **entities** of the same **layer**; it contains **control information** and (possibly) **user data**

PURGE — Mechanism for removing all **data blocks** from a **connection**

RANDOM ACCESS — Access procedure that allows a **user system** to transfer **data** to a **broadcast channel** without explicit coordination with other user systems

READ-ONLY MEMORY (ROM) — Storage device in which data is entered upon manufacture (nonprogrammable device) or over a prolonged period of time (reprogrammable device); reading of data is performed at high speed

REFERENCE MODEL OF OPEN SYSTEMS ARCHITECTURE - Model of interaction of **application processes** in an **information and computing network,** developed by the International Standards Organization

REMOTE-PROCESSING INSTALLATION — Remote-processing **hardware (multiplexers, modems,** etc.) and software that support interaction between **terminals** and a **computer**

RESET — A function intended for restoring interaction of **entities** after the appearance of errors or hardware malfunctions

RESOURCE — Set of **application processes** executed in a **user system**

RESOURCE LOCKOUT — Situation in which two users attempt to access the same resource and render its use mutually impossible

ROUTING — Process of selecting routes for **packets** in **computer networks**

ROUTING TABLE — Table stored in a **communications system,** which specifies the **physical connections** via which **packets** are to be sent in accordance with the destination addresses they contain

SATELLITE CHANNEL — **Backbone line** connecting terrestrial **communications system** to communications satellite

SERVICE — A group of functions distributed over a **computer network** and intended for executing a particular general network task

SERVICE ACCESS POINT — Point of connection of two **entities** on adjacent **layers**

SERVICE DATA UNIT — Data unit used for providing **service**

SESSION — Interrelationship between two **entities** of the **application layer** that specifies transmission of **data** between them

SESSION CONTROL — An element of the **software structure** of a **computer network** that characterizes the procedures for transmitting **data units** through the **transport network**

SESSION LAYER — Layer that supports interaction **sessions** between **application processes**

SIGNAL MODULATION — Variation of the parameters (amplitude, frequency, or phase) of a sinusoidal curve in relation to the values of a discrete signal

SIMPLEX CHANNEL — **Physical link** over which data is transmitted in one direction only

SOFTWARE — Operating system; or diagnostic, systems, service, or other **program**

SOFTWARE STRUCTURE OF COMPUTER NETWORK — Representation of a **computer network** in the form of interrelated **programs**

START-STOP TERMINAL — See **asynchronous terminal**

STATEMENT — See **operator**

STATUS — Characteristic of **computer, physical link, logical channel,** or **program** that defines a specific aspect of their operation (feature: primary or secondary computer; state: waiting for answer, etc.)

SUBSCRIBER CIRCUIT — Short **connection** between **user system** and nearby **broadcast channel**

SUBSCRIBER LINK — **Data link** that connects **user system** to **communications system**

SWITCHED CIRCUIT — A sequence of **communication links** and switched connections that form a temporary connection (over the time of a **session**) between **computers** or terminals

SYNCHRONOUS TERMINAL — A terminal capable of immediate transmission of a multibyte data unit (framed by control characters)

SYNCHRONOUS TRANSMISSION — A mode of data transmission in which the instants of appearance of a character or group of characters depend on the method of synchronization of the data-exchange process

SYSTEM — A self-contained association capable of processing data and of executing functions described by **protocols**; includes one or more computers and their software, peripherals, **terminals,** data-transmission facilities, and human **operators**

SYSTEMS PROGRAM — **Program** that organizes connection between **terminals** and **user programs** (e.g., the SRV program, which enables a subscriber to conduct a dialog with a computer)

TRANSPARENCY — Property of a **logical channel, physical connection, protocol,** or **program,** or being able to transmit data encoded in arbitrary fashion

TERMINAL — A set of **hardware** facilities and (possibly) **programs,** employed by **users** for data I/O to a **computer** or **network**

TERMINAL-COMMUNICATIONS SYSTEM — A **system** that executes functions of information **routing** in a **computer network,** and interaction between **terminals** and the network

TERMINAL SYSTEM — A **system** that supports interaction between **terminals** and a **computer network**

TOKEN ACCESS — An access procedure that allows a **user system** to transmit **data** to a **broadcast channel** after receiving the necessary authorization (enablement signal) from it

TRANSMISSION CONTROL — An element of the **software structure** of a **computer network** that provides transmission of information from one **process** to another

TRANSPORT LAYER — **Layer** which effects transmission of information between **user systems**

TRANSPORT NETWORK — A logical system that provides transmission of information from a **process** in one **user system** to a process in another

TRANSPORT SERVICE — **Service** which executes the functions of the **transport** and **network layers**

UNBALANCED PROTOCOL — **Protocol** specifying interaction between requesting (initiating) and answering parties

UNIT — See **block**

USER — Person who interacts with a **computer network** or **computer** to perform necessary information and computing tasks

USER PROGRAM — An element in the **software structure** of a **computer network** that performs information and computing tasks for a **user** (computation, data bank, information and reference or retrieval services, etc.)

USER SERVICE — **Service** that supports forms of data representation and control of data processing

USER STATION — See **terminal**

USER SYSTEM — A system that furnishes or consumes **computer network** resources

VERSION — Variant of a continually updated **program,** operating system, or **computer network protocol**

VIDEO INFORMATION — Information that can be perceived by the human visual system

VIDEOTEX — An **information network** in which information, supplied to a large number of **users,** is displayed on television sets or inexpensive **terminals**

VIRTUAL — Logical description of a process, form of data representation, channel, piece of hardware, etc., including its parameters and functions to be executed by it

VIRTUAL CALL — Temporary connection between two remote **processes** by a **logical channel**

VIRTUAL CIRCUIT — Form of interaction of **entities** of two **systems** via a **logical channel** that connects them

VIRTUAL DATAGRAM TRANSPORT NETWORK — A combined **transport network** that provides transmission of both sequences of interrelated **packets** and individual mutually independent packets **(datagrams)**

VIRTUAL FILE — Description of logical functions that characterize the standard form of representantion of a **file**

VIRTUAL JOB — Description of logical functions characterizing the standard form of a job

VIRTUAL TERMINAL — An abstract terminal consisting of a real **terminal** with a **processor** (or emulator of a processor) added to it

VIRTUAL TRANSPORT NETWORK — A transport network that provides transmission of sequences of interrelated **packets**

WIDE-AREA NETWORK — **Computer network** whose user systems are separated considerably from one another (over a region or country)

LIST OF ABBREVIATIONS

BTAM	Basic Telecommunications Access Method (method employed in Soviet Unified System computers)
US Computers	Computers of the Unified System (Soviet Union and Comecon countries)
RPI	Radial Parallel Interface (employed in Soviet SM computers)
KAMA	Systems program of US computers that controls data banks
KROS	Systems program of US computers that controls execution of user jobs
CCITT	International Consultative Committee on Telegraphy and Telephony
ISO	International Standards Organization
DTM	Data Transmission Multiplexer
GTAM	General Telecommunications Access Method (method employed in US computers)
RDP	Remote Data Processor in US computers
SM Computers	System of small computers adopted by the Soviet Union and Comecom countries
TSS	Time-Sharing System (systems program of US computers that supports dialog modes of operation)
Comecon	East-bloc countries linked by economic, commercial, and other agreements
ECN	Experimental Computer Network created for the Academy of Sciences of the Lithuanian SSR

SUBJECT INDEX*

---

*Terms in the Index are given in **boldface** in the text.